Edited by
GINA M. NÚÑEZ • AZURI L. GONZALEZ

COMMUNITY ENGAGEMENT AND
HIGH IMPACT PRACTICES
IN HIGHER EDUCATION

Kendall Hunt
publishing company

D0222905

Kendall Hunt
publishing company

www.kendallhunt.com
Send all inquiries to:
4050 Westmark Drive
Dubuque, IA 52004-1840

Published in the United States of America

Contents

Anthropology

Communications

Education

Engineering

English

Health Science

Nonprofit and Border Studies

Philosophy

Political Science

Environmental Science

Social Work

Women's Studies

Acknowledgments

I want to thank a few people for making this book possible. When I was first hired to teach at University of Texas at El Paso (UTEP), all I knew was that I wanted to get my students involved in the community. I did not know much about service-learning and high-impact practices. I would like to thank all of my peers, colleagues, and students who have been open and willing to support community engagement, bridge building, and social justice efforts that benefit from community–university partnerships. I want to thank Dr. Kathy Staudt and dedicate this book to her to honor her vision and commitment to the Center for Civic Engagement and the Kellogg Foundation for supporting the institutionalization of the Center at our university. To my co-editor Azuri Gonzalez and colleague Jenna Lujan, thank you for your professionalism, dedication, and commitment to service-learning over the years. To my engaged faculty colleagues, I welcome you and encourage you to integrate your research, teaching, and service efforts with your students and your community in mind. I am particularly grateful to David Josue Lopez and his staff, who have consistently shown up to monthly meetings, conferences, and events beyond the call of duty. You knocked on the university's doors, and I am glad we could open them to build bridges that connect students and senior adults for generations to come. Finally, I cannot do the engaged work I do without the support and understanding of my son Adam and husband Ali, who often wonder where I go on Saturday mornings in the spring semesters and why I participate in so many other evening and weekend events as part of my community partnerships.

Gina Nunez, PhD
Director of Women and Gender Studies and Associate Professor of Anthropology
The University of Texas at El Paso

The UTEP is a unique institution where a sense of place is embedded in all the work we do with our students, programs, courses, and community partners. I have been fortunate to experience community engagement as a student, lecturer, community partner, community engagement professional, and also now as a graduate student pursing my doctorate in education, focusing my research on the institutionalization of community engagement. I want to thank this institution for supporting our work and for staying true to our public mission. I want to also sincerely thank each of our contributors in this book who are exemplar scholars and continue to break barriers in their disciplines and in higher education; I consider them mentors, champions, and ultimate leaders in community engagement. I especially hold in high regard my mentor, and founding director of the Center for Civic Engagement, Kathy Staudt, and my co-editor Gina Núñez, who besides being a great scholar, is the epitome of commitment to community. Also, my two faculty-fellows in-residence, who have guided me in scholarly endeavors and who also contributed to this book, Mark Lusk and Amy Wagler. I also sincerely thank my team at the Center for Civic Engagement for their support, especially Assistant Director Jennifer Lujan and graduate student Varinia Felix-Parra; without their assistance, this book would not have been possible. Last, I thank my two children Cosette and Antonio for their patience and the motivation they inspired in me. I am proud to say they are both children already committed to their community through Girl Scouts and Cub Scouts, respectively.

Azuri L. Gonzalez, MA
Director of the Center for Civic Engagement
The University of Texas at El Paso

A special note to community partners:

To our community partners and future collaborators, we welcome this opportunity to discuss partnerships that honor and recognize the critical roles that organizations have in the co-construction of knowledge for university students. Without their support and collaboration, our students would have a much harder time finding spaces to grow through active learning and practice with your professional guidance and support. We hope to engage you within reciprocal relationships that seek to challenge the ways communities have at times been ignored and unfairly used in academic endeavors; your willingness to reach out and make universities accountable to the needs of community have allowed us to reach out to our faculty, students, and academic leadership to solidify and institutionalize civic engagement within the university. We do not take these opportunities for mutual growth for granted, and recognize there is still much work to be done to prepare future professionals in the most holistic ways possible as human beings that care, think, and act to build a more equitable and just world.

About the Authors

Dr. Guillermina G. Núñez-Mchiri is associate professor of anthropology and director of women and gender studies at UTEP. She teaches courses in Ethnographic Research Methods; Death, Dying, and Bereavement; Anthropology of Food, Culture, and Society; Interdisciplinary feminist theory and methods; and Death, Dying, and Bereavement. Her classes incorporate high-impact practices involving service-learning, undergraduate research, internships, and engagement opportunities through community partnerships. Dr. Núñez received her Ph.D. in Cultural Anthropology from the University of California Riverside in 2006, her MA in Latin American studies in 1998, and her BA in International Business with a specialty in Spanish and Portuguese in 1994 from San Diego State University. She has a partnership with the City of El Paso's Park and Recreation Department working with older adult athletes who are challenging the social stigmas of aging through active living and competitive athletics. Dr. Núñez is an applied anthropologist with specialization in ethnography and the U.S.–Mexico border region. She has published on a number of topics related to *colonias,* immigration and human rights, housing and social justice, Latina identity, Latinas in STEM fields, immigrant youth and education, and the applications of Ethnography and Service-learning in higher education. In 2012, she received the 2012 University of Texas Regents Outstanding Teaching Award for her contributions to transforming higher education at the state level.

Azuri Gonzalez served The University of Texas at El Paso and the Center for Civic Engagement (CCE) for 15 years and as director for the past 9 years. Through her work at the CCE, she has been instrumental in the institutionalization of community engagement at UTEP and led the institution's first Carnegie's Community Engagement Classification (2010). She has taught first-year entering student program university courses, focusing on student engagement and service-learning, as well as co-taught a Women's Studies course on nonprofits, social entrepreneurship, and volunteerism and an educational leadership course on community advocacy. She has also served on a number of boards including the YWCA USA, the YWCA El Paso del Norte Region, the Women's Fund of El Paso, and the Nonprofit Enterprise Center. She has presented her work at various venues including Campus Compact 30th Anniversary Conference, the Engaged Scholarship Consortium, American Association of College's and University Conference, and served as a panelist for the Texas One Light Conference. She appreciates her academic roots in political science at UTEP, where she earned both her bachelor's and master's degrees. She is currently pursing her education doctorate, with a research focus on community engagement in higher education.

Relevant publication:

Staudt, K., & Gonzalez, A. (2011). Sustaining a university engagement center at borders: Taking risks in a risk-avoidant atmosphere. *Metropolitan Universities, 22*(2), 65–78.

Introduction and Use for Book

By: Azuri L. Gonzalez and Gina Núñez

Welcome to a rich collection of cases about engaged and active teaching and learning strategies in a multi-lingual, multi-cultural region. *COMMUNITY ENGAGEMENT AND HIGH-IMPACT PRACTICES IN HIGHER EDUCATION* addresses how faculty, students and community partners have organized themselves around community needs and issues of mutual interest. By collaboratively working together, in each scenario, faculty members, students and community partners discuss their strategies, successes, and challenges of working to address specific social needs identified in their community. Through the diversity of chapters included in this book, we seek to marry the service-learning, community engagement practices literature with the high-impact practices literature while centering on meeting the needs of community alongside student learning.

We also seek to challenge students, faculty, and community partners to explore the many ways in which high-impact practices can lend themselves to serve the needs of community, when these are shaped and organized around such needs. More simply put, community needs are complex and require a creative use of methods of engagement to appropriately engage, learn, and serve in a manner that is meaningful and impactful. We are confident such case is made in each of the examples presented within.

Why Community Engagement and High-Impact Practices?

The research and practice around community engagement in higher education has grown, moving from the margins of higher education into a more central role of the institution. A prime example can be found through initiatives like that of the Carnegie Foundation: the Community Engaged Institution Elective Classification. Hundreds of higher education institutions have sought and achieved such designation (Driscoll, 2008). While community engagement has been part of higher education for over a century, terms like service-learning, community-engaged scholarship, and community-based research have become more widely recognizable, studied, understood, and practiced in the last three to four decades (Bringle & Hatcher, 2000; Butin, 2010; Zlotkowski, 2015).

Similarly, George Kuh (2008b) brought to the forefront high-impact student engagement, as widely embraced and promoted by the American Association for Colleges and Universities (AAC&U). Student engagement practices such as internships, capstone courses, diversity and global learning experiences, among others, have been identified as activities that yield positive outcomes for students in higher education, especially when students experience two or more experiences within their college career (Kuh, 2008a).

Community engagement and *service-learning* can be found among the ten recognized high-impact practices by AAC&U. With this book, however, we wish to share the many ways in which these high-impact practices may be combined to better serve community purposes and needs in addition to serving as impactful learning practices for students.

We are essentially utilizing Andrew Furco's benefit diagram (Figure 1), where service-learning is positioned in the middle, indicating that it should meet both the student and community needs equally. We set a similar expectation as an outcome of utilizing the other high-impact practices (capstone courses, internships, global learning, etc.) in community settings. In the same manner that service-learning should meet actual community needs and simultaneously yield positive learning outcomes for students, all other high-impact practices, when organized around community needs, could also have the same outcome.

Thus, each chapter in this book offers such scenarios, cases, and situations where community partnerships required the engagement of students to address specific needs. In many cases, more than one high-impact practice was implemented, and in each case, there were successes and challenges that accompanied such

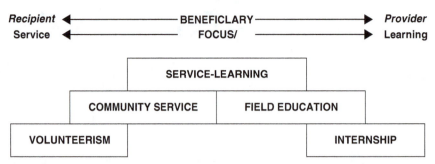

From Service-Learning: A Balanced Approach to Experiential Education by Andrew Furco. *Expanding Boundries: Serving and Learning.* Washington, DC: Corporation for National Service, pp. 2-6. Copyright © 1996 by Andrew Furco. Reprinted by permission.

models. In each case, academic learning took place, course or academic credit was earned, and a community need was met (or continues to be met). Community partners are highlighted and identified as key to the formation of such partnerships and, in many of the chapters, are also co-contributors.

Book Contributions, Inspirations, and Goals

When we began conceptualizing the need for this book, we knew that we wanted to develop a resource and tool for faculty, students, and community to collaboratively partner to address community issues, who hadn't already done so and had an interest in doing so. We recognized that many resources existed through sources like Campus Compact, but we also knew that not all faculty from various disciplines would embrace service-learning as the method of choice. Butin and other scholars (2005) explain, for example, that some faculty may find it academically dangerous to integrate service-learning into their courses, if this is not something recognized or rewarded within their disciplines, or departments and institutions through the tenure and promotion process. Concerns of legitimacy and academic rigor are often questioned and may serve as deterrents for engaging in this type of enterprise (Calleson, Jordan, & Seifer, 2005). We have thought about these debates and critiques and are mindful about the dynamics and internal politics involved in stepping out of traditional academic roles.

Yet, after searching for best practices within our institution to help others identify possible engagement models, we recognized that a wide variety of high-impact practices were effectively being utilized to serve both community needs and to support student academic learning outcomes, they were just not labeled service-learning or community engagement.

We further confirmed this as we drew from our experience inventorying community engagement hours within our institution to effectively complete the Corporation for National and Community Service's President's Higher Education Honor Roll. We learned through the process that soliciting and receiving data reports was one challenge, but that the greatest challenge was having faculty, staff, and students realize that their academic community engagement was in fact service-learning and vice-versa. People held strict definitions of what service-learning was (i.e., associated it with undergraduates or K-12, community service project-based within a course) and didn't associate their community engagement work with the institution's overall collective engagement.

With the need to identify examples, models and to continue to promote a public purpose and high-impact teaching and learning practices, it became evident that we needed to marry the two concepts generally, and offer an array of examples from faculty who have dealt with the successes and challenges of engaging their students in truly meaningful community engagement endeavors.

In all, the purpose and contents of this book is to build on the accumulated knowledge and experiences about the effectiveness of high-impact practices on student learning (Kuh, 2001; Kuh, Kinzie, Shuh, & Whitt,

2011; Kuh, Palmer, & Kish 2003; Quaye & Harper, 2015) as well as the years of knowledge gained from the evolution of service-learning (Bringle & Hatcher, 2000; Butin, 2010; Jacoby, 2009; Stanton, Giles, & Cruz, 1999; Zlotkowski, 2015).

We have learned from great giants who have pushed the boundaries of higher education to ensure that a greater response to our communities is continuously pursued (Boyer, 1996; Driscoll, 2009; Furco, 1996; Harkavy, 2006; Holland, 1997; Zlotkowski, 1998). Today, there is also wide support from entities and programs such as the Engaged Scholarship Consortium, Campus Compact, International Association for Research on Service-Learning & Community Engagement, the Corporation for National and Community Service and its Higher Education Honor Roll, Carnegie's Community Engagement Classification, C. Peter Magrath Community Engagement Award, American Association of Public and Land Grant Universities, Community Campus Partnerships for Health, and countless other efforts to raise the profile of the invaluable role community engagement work plays in higher education.

We subscribe to the powerfully drafted commitments by the major national community engagement organization, Campus Compact, as part of a 2016 initiative to reinvigorate higher education institutions in civic engagement purposeful action:

> **"We empower** our students, faculty, staff, and community partners to co-create mutually respectful partnerships in pursuit of a just, equitable, and sustainable future for communities beyond the campus—nearby and around the world.
>
> **We prepare** our students for lives of engaged citizenship, with the motivation and capacity to deliberate, act, and lead in pursuit of the public good.
>
> **We embrace** our responsibilities as place-based institutions, contributing to the health and strength of our communities—economically, socially, environmentally, educationally, and politically.
>
> **We harness** the capacity of our institutions—through research, teaching, partnerships, and institutional practice—to challenge the prevailing social and economic inequalities that threaten our democratic future.
>
> **We foster** an environment that consistently affirms the centrality of the public purposes of higher education by setting high expectations for members of the campus community to contribute to their achievement."

Source: Creating a Great Campus Civic Action Plan (Campus Compact, 2016)

We also recognize there is a broader audience engaged in a debate about social justice, equity and reciprocity as part of a broader debate on the functions, values, and future of higher education (Hess, Lanig, & Vaughan, 2017; Quaye & Harper, 2015) which should continue. However, we believe this volume will highlight key examples about the engagement in underserved communities with vulnerable populations, but also in conjunction with a population of students who serve in their own *backyard* (Sobel, 2004).

This brings us to the goals of this book. Through this book our goals are to:

1. Highlight the variety of ways in which high-impact practices may be combined to address community needs within an academic setting and partnership models that extend beyond service-learning.
2. Share some of the nuances that go into forming partnerships around a particular community issue or need.
3. Give voice to faculty leaders who have integrated various forms of high-impact practices into their courses or projects and can share from years of experience what has ultimately worked and continues to be a challenge.
4. Raise awareness about a number of complex and challenging issues affecting communities.
5. Widen the range of disciplines, practices, and interventions that could be utilized to address those issues.

6. Inspire additional creativity from academics, communities, and students who can identify additional ways to utilize the many tools shared in this book to address other challenges.
7. Offer tools and resources for students, community partners, and faculty to take charge of learning in various spaces, using a wide variety of methods.

We consequently offer this book as a testament to the value that the application of such philosophical and theoretical principles have added to the classroom learning experience, to students, and to the impact they can have in the community.

About the Chapters and Contributors

What we offer is a compilation of elaborate examples of community engagement by faculty, students, community members, and professionals that have integrated various methods in their courses to achieve higher levels of impact. They have all methodically engaged students to acquire complex theory and knowledge while serving concrete social and environmental needs.

The diverse faculty members represented in this book illustrate the intricacies involved in applying distinct disciplines in society, all while intentionally and mindfully responding to specific student contextual needs. Contributions to this book were made from a place-based educational context where participating students come from the very community they serve and the faculty who support them have a keen understanding of the regional community (McInerney, Smyth, & Down, 2011). The represented engaged institution and faculty members have long-standing relationships with community partners and entities, and together co-teach and learn with students.

Audience

We invited faculty to share their experiences by keeping three major audiences in mind, faculty, students, and community partners. Each of these groups has a role to play while forming and strengthening the knowledge creation and sharing that takes place in community settings. We acknowledge that the faculty member is usually the person in charge of structuring the learning experience in the classroom and the one likely to integrate community engagement as part of that learning. However, we do not concede that faculty members are the only ones capable of designing such experiences, especially when these structured learning experiences are meant to respond to community needs. Moreover, there is a broader range of readers and actors within communities and higher education institutions who can benefit from this collective knowledge.

Faculty, Instructors, Teachers

Faculty members, entrusted with the design and structure of the learning experience for the student, may choose to incorporate high-impact practices in their teaching and invite community partners as co-teachers. Faculty may come from very distinct disciplines, yet we believe that a variety of models and examples shared within this book can open up new and innovative opportunities for adaptation, adoption or implementation. We were purposeful about including sections on challenges so that readers know may have learned from the experiences of faculty members who experienced them and how they went about addressing them. We hope that faculty also make use of the digital component of this book that contains additional teaching and partnership-building tools.

Students

Students are absolutely capable of leading their learning experience. Students can be invited to review the various case studies and community–university partnerships to develop their own academic journeys via community engagement. We anticipate students may find special interest in the chapters that address community issues of most relevance to them, but we recommend that all chapters are studied carefully to develop additional critical perspectives about the issues presented.

Throughout our experience, we have found that oftentimes students begin with a major, and then navigate their ways around various courses until they find the fields that they are most passionate. We believe the volume of chapters and issues included in this book will offer a similar wide range of perspectives that can further inform the student's major selection and focus.

We invite students to make this book as useful as possible by taking inventory of their skills, interests, passions, work experiences, and leadership efforts. This is a book for students to engage in throughout your undergraduate, graduate, and post-graduate education. We are all lifelong learners and the possibility to engage in high-impact practices is an ongoing invitation.

Community Partners

We have been fortunate to work with diligent and strong community partners who have worked with us and regularly hold us accountable to our responsiveness to community. With that in mind, while this book is set-up within the institutional framework of a university or higher education institution, we wanted to ensure that tools, resources and recommendations were also made for community partners. Community sections in each chapter are in many cases informed by the very community partners who participated in the project, as mentioned previously, some are co-contributors for the respective chapters.

We have much respect and admiration for the community partner agencies that choose to work with higher education institutions, despite our differing institutional cultures. Nonetheless, we are excited to invite community partners to utilize resources within this book both in the context of their own partnerships with higher education institutions, or within their own programming and organizational efforts. Several of the critical tools and sample programs described in this book do not rely on the existence of a higher education partner. We certainly encourage and advocate for such partnerships, but the wealth of knowledge in this book was attained and collected in partnership with community, in the mutual exchange of knowledge and resources, that we happily make it available for wider usage and application wherever a community need may be served.

Other Readers

If you are holding this book and reading this portion, readers are part of the audience. We assume that community engagement, high-impact practices or higher education are familiar realms and connected to interests and leadership. If not, readers are still holding or reading a book that has so much wealth of knowledge from so many individuals who have carefully crafted and employed thoughtful methods to impact student and community learning.

This discussion of audiences is not meant to be a general statement but rather an invitation of inclusivity. We acknowledge that the faculty member is usually the person in charge of structuring the learning experience in the classroom and the one likely to integrate community engagement as part of that learning. However, we do not concede that faculty members are the only one capable of designing such experiences, especially when these structured learning experiences are meant to respond to community needs.

Readers of all types will notice that each chapter offers recommendations for faculty, students and community with respect to the covered program, project or case study. Each contributor makes a case for the importance of the issue presented and provides unique methods by which the issue was and can be explored, whether it is about health disparities, democracy, the environment, air quality or even the commitment to more socially responsive students. Students' potential professional formations are considered as engineers, pharmacists, policy analysts, physical therapists or air quality professionals, for example, and in various cases key to the focus of the activity in relation to the community need (be it at the micro or macro level).

The beauty of each chapter is it builds on the layers upon layers of learning opportunities presented to the reader. The thought-provoking methods may be critically analyzed for their application beyond the classroom or setting.

Organization of Each Chapter

Chapters in this book follow a similar format and offer the following

1. **Introduction** – each chapter offers an insight into the topic, as well as the type of high-impact practice integrated with community engagement. In some cases, contributors invite the reader to also learn a bit more about the contributor(s) or the setting for the project.
2. **Case study** – the majority of the chapter offer the reader the example around which the experience is framed and learned from. It is in these case studies that the reader may learn more about the origin of the partnership or project as well as how it was utilized in the context of the classroom.
3. **Successes** – contributors share their experiences with the practice and what they identified to have contributed to the successful use of the practice.
4. **Challenges** – contributors are candid about what were some of the greatest challenges experienced through their specific case.
5. **Specific tips and recommendations** – each one of the chapters offers readers information about how to go about implementing the practice, program or project. They also make specific recommendations for Faculty, Students, and Community Partners, and are labeled as such.
6. **Resources, tools and further reading** – some projects and programs have a wealth of tools and additional resources that have been made available for readers via links, images, or through the digital component of this book. These resources may be handouts that may be easily replicated or utilized within the book.
7. **Conclusion** – each contributor chose to end the chapter with their final thoughts on their project or with final overall reflections on the experience.

Special Features and Icons

Academic Discipline

Each of the chapters is labeled and color-coded to indicate the primary discipline that was utilized in the described program, course, or project. We say "primary" because community projects, by their very nature, cannot be addressed through a single disciplinary lens. Nonetheless, we thought it to be helpful to identify the primary academic discipline in which these kinds of projects and efforts could effectively be integrated into, and offering a visual of the number of various disciplines represented in this book.

High-Impact Practice Icons

Each chapter is also accompanied by one or more high-impact practices icon. It is truly remarkable to see how many of these high-impact practices can be effectively intertwined to engage students in the most productive and significant ways that will also work for the community partnership. For consistency purposes, we utilized AAC&U's high-impact practice terms (see the definitions section for these) where in some cases high-impact practice terms are grouped (i.e., Diversity/Global Learning). However, refer to how each of the chapters describes the use of the practices, and in many cases, how they were differently employed, combined, and utilized.

SERVICE LEARNING,
COMMUNITY-BASED LEARNING

COMMON INTELLECTUAL
EXPERIENCES

COLLABORATIVE
ASSIGNMENTS AND PROJECTS

INTERNSHIPS

FIRST-YEAR SEMINARS AND EXPERIENCES

DIVERSITY/GLOBAL LEARNING

WRITING-INTENSIVE COURSES

UNDERGRADUATE RESEARCH

CAPSTONE COURSES AND PROJECTS

LEARNING COMMUNITIES

Pre-Reflection Questions

Given the diversity of topics, practices, and approaches to community engagement, we wanted to invite the reader to take a moment to reflect on relevant concepts to prepare them for digesting the chapter. We hope that as this book is read and utilized by different people, these questions are also modified and expanded to fit the learning needs of the target audience. For those not familiar with the use of reflection questions, these offer a pause for the reader to stop and think about times when certain dynamics were at play and to examine attitudes, thoughts, behaviors, and actions that existed at the moment. By doing so, one prepares the mind to absorb the new information from that particular lens and may also offer the opportunity to ask additional critical questions of the material.

Definitions

For the purposes of this book, the following definitions will be useful to learn and understand. In many chapters, each contributor addresses the way they approach community engagement and what combination of high-impact practices they integrated into their community partnership. Each contributor has a different approach to the way that they engage their students with community organizations, but that in each case, there is a clear intent as to what issues and societal needs they are contributing towards addressing.

While the community engagement definitions below are not comprehensive or absolute; they are helpful in drawing a distinction between models and the way they might look and operate. Nonetheless, our institution has adopted the Carnegie's Community Engagement definition as follows:

> *Collaboration between institutions of higher education and their larger communities (local, regional/state, national, global) for the mutually beneficial exchange of knowledge and resources in context of partnership and reciprocity.*

While we acknowledge that community can vary geographically, for the purposes of this book, our "community" refers primarily to community partners serving specific community needs and working with specific community stakeholders. At the same time, given our place-based approach to learning, in most of the cases, our community refers to the region surrounding the institution. We use this definition for our contributions, but the applications of the work included here transcend boundaries, regions and distinct communities. We invite others to identify what community means to them, and how it can best be collaborated with and in.

Ways of Engaging With the Community

Community Engagement – Work or participation that is done in the community. May take the form of any of the engagement models (partnership, collaborative or student focus)

Civic Engagement – Engagement in the community for the purpose of building knowledge, motivation, and participatory behavior in democratic society.

Community Service – Community engagement done for the purpose of serving the community. Community is the primary beneficiary.

Service-Learning – Teaching method where there is service to the community attached to academic learning objectives.

Community-Based Internship – Extended, structured, experience organized in the community where the primary beneficiary is the student, but may serve a community purpose. Professional development and preparation are key desired outcomes.

Clinical/Field Experience – Field and professional development that may be performed in the community where the student is the primary beneficiary, and where the community is either the laboratory and/or the community partner is a collaborating teacher. These types of experiences may be regulated and defined by accrediting bodies in certain disciplines like nursing and pharmacy. Community may benefit.

Community Outreach – Activity performed solicit community participation in a desired activity, event, or program or to disseminate information to the community. Community may benefit.

Community-Based Research – Research conducted in the community that may have community implications or benefits.

Community-Based Participatory Research – Research conducted in and with the community where the community has input and decision-making authority on the focus, purpose and methods of the research project.

Community Partnership – A collaboration where desired outcomes and expectations from participating partners are understood and agreed upon. The community partnership may be short term or long-term and may involve a singular activity with a start and end date, or may include a variety of activities, and engagement models and may the partnership into an ongoing relationship. Ultimately, it should be reciprocal and mutually beneficial.

Community Collaborative – Community interaction for a specific purpose, typically for a short term desired outcome. May evolve into a community partnership.

High-Impact Practices

High-Impact practices are organized and structured forms of engaged learning typically, for undergraduate students, which have been carefully studied and assessed for a number of years. Primarily defined by Kuh (2008b) and tracked by the National Survey of Student Engagement, students who engage in quality high-impact practices will yield positive learning outcomes and specific skills applicable to the "real world", and desired by likely employers

There are several key educational practices that are commonly and effectively incorporated into high-impact practices, and several of these can be identified within the contributed case studies in this book. Such practices have evolved but generally revolve around the following:

- student-faculty contact
- cooperation among students

- active learning
- prompt feedback to students
- time on task
- high expectations
- respect for diverse students and diverse ways of knowing
- quality of teaching received
- influential interactions with other
- students in non-course–related activities
- a supportive campus environment

(Astin, 1993; Pascarella, Edison, Nora, Hagedorn, & Terezini, 1996; Miller, Rycek, & Fritson, 2011; Quaye & Harper, 2015)

Taking these key practices into account, and categorically thinking about how they engage student in the community, contributors of this book also use the high-impact practice definitions provided by AAC&U to identify their community engagement programs, projects, classes, and models. Each also emphasizes the manner in which some of these high-impact practices were combined and utilized simultaneously in order to properly address community needs.

High-Impact Educational Practices

First-Year Seminars and Experiences

Many schools now build into the curriculum first-year seminars or other programs that bring small groups of students together with faculty or staff on a regular basis. The highest- quality first-year experiences place a strong emphasis on critical inquiry, frequent writing, information literacy, collaborative learning, and other skills that develop students' intellectual and practical competencies. First-year seminars can also involve students with cutting-edge questions in scholarship and with faculty members' own research.

Common Intellectual Experiences

The older idea of a "core" curriculum has evolved into a variety of modern forms, such as a set of required common courses or a vertically organized general education program that includes advanced integrative studies and/or required participation in a learning community (see below). These programs often combine broad themes—e.g., technology and society, global interdependence—with a variety of curricular and cocurricular options for students.

Learning Communities

The key goals for learning communities are to encourage integration of learning across courses and to involve students with "big questions" that matter beyond the classroom. Students take two or more linked courses as a group and work closely with one another and with their professors. Many learning communities explore a common topic and/ or common readings through the lenses of different disciplines. Some deliberately link "liberal arts" and "professional courses"; others feature service learning.

Writing-Intensive Courses

These courses emphasize writing at all levels of instruction and across the curriculum, including final-year projects. Students are encouraged to produce and revise various forms of writing for different audiences in different disciplines. The effectiveness of this repeated practice "across the curriculum" has led to parallel efforts in such areas as quantitative reasoning, oral communication, information literacy, and, on some campuses, ethical inquiry.

Collaborative Assignments and Projects

Collaborative learning combines two key goals: learning to work and solve problems in the company of others, and sharpening one's own understanding by listening seriously to the insights of others, especially those with different backgrounds and life experiences. Approaches range from study groups within a course, to team-based assignments and writing, to cooperative projects and research.

Undergraduate Research

Many colleges and universities are now providing research experiences for students in all disciplines. Undergraduate research, however, has been most prominently used in science disciplines. With strong support from the National Science Foundation and the research community, scientists are reshaping their courses to connect key concepts and questions with students' early and active involvement in systematic investigation and research. The goal is to involve students with actively contested questions, empirical observation, cutting-edge technologies, and the sense of excitement that comes from working to answer important questions.

Diversity/Global Learning

Many colleges and universities now emphasize courses and programs that help students explore cultures, life experiences, and worldviews different from their own. These studies—which may address U.S. diversity, world cultures, or both—often explore "difficult differences" such as racial, ethnic, and gender inequality, or continuing struggles around the globe for human rights, freedom, and power. Frequently, intercultural studies are augmented by experiential learning in the community and/or by study abroad.

Service Learning, Community-Based Learning

In these programs, field-based "experiential learning" with community partners is an instructional strategy—and often a required part of the course. The idea is to give students direct experience with issues they are studying in the curriculum and with ongoing efforts to analyze and solve problems in the community. A key element in these programs is the opportunity students have to both *apply* what they are learning in real-world settings and *reflect* in a classroom setting on their service experiences. These programs model the idea that giving something back to the community is an important college outcome and that working with community partners is good preparation for citizenship, work, and life.

Internships

Internships are another increasingly common form of experiential learning. The idea is to provide students with direct experience in a work setting—usually related to their career interests—and to give them the benefit of supervision and coaching from professionals in the field. If the internship is taken for course credit, students complete a project or paper that is approved by a faculty member.

Capstone Courses and Projects

Whether they're called "senior capstones" or some other name, these culminating experiences require students nearing the end of their college years to create a project of some sort that integrates and applies what they've learned. The project might be a research paper, a performance, a portfolio of "best work," or an exhibit of artwork. Capstones are offered both in departmental programs and, increasingly, in general education as well.

Conclusion

To continue to push the community engagement and high-impact practices agenda and purpose forward, we must also continue to examine successful ways to apply our theoretical gains into practice. We offer such tools and opportunities to examine this practice through 21 examples, along with the noted challenges and successes that ultimately build the experience. We recognize and value the contributors' experiences and *personal knowledge* (Polyini, 2015), to give light to the various intricacies that go into developing such meaningful, community and student-focused endeavors. We hope you find a number of ways in which this valuable knowledge can be built upon, adapted, learned from, and replicated.

Helpful Links

Engagement Scholarship Consortium https://engagementscholarship.org/
Calleson, D. C., Jordan, C., & Seifer, S. D. (2005). Community-engaged scholarship: Is faculty work in communities a true academic enterprise? *Academic Medicine, 80*(4), 317-321.
Campus Compact https://compact.org/
International Association for Research on Service-learning and Community Engagement http://www .researchslce.org/
Corporation for National and Community Service- Higher Education Community Service Honor Roll) https://www.nationalservice.gov/special-initiatives/honor-roll
Carnegie's Community Engagement Classification http://www.nerche.org/index.php?option=com_conte & view=article&id=341&Itemid=92
C. Peter Magrath Community Engagement Award http://www.aplu.org/projects-and-initiatives/economic-development-and-community-engagement/W.K.-Kellogg-Foundation-Community-Engagement-Scholarship-Awards-and-C.-Peter-Magrath-Community-Engagement-Scholarship-Awards/index.html
American Association of Public and Land Grant Universities http://www.aplu.org/
Community Campus Partnerships for Health https://ccph.memberclicks.net/

References

Association of American Colleges and Universities. (2017). High Impact Educational Practices. Retrieved October 2, 2017, from https://aacu.org/sites/default/files/files/LEAP/HIP_tables.pdf
Astin, A. (1993). *What Matters in College: Four Critical Years Revisited.* San Francisco: Jossey-Bass.
Bringle, R. G., & Hatcher, J. A. (2000). Institutionalization of service learning in higher education. *The Journal of Higher Education, 71*(3), 273–290.
Boyer, E. L. (1996). The scholarship of engagement. *Bulletin of the American Academy of Arts and Sciences, 49*(7), 18–33.
Butin, D. (2010). *Service-learning in Theory and Practice: The Future of Community Engagement in Higher Education.* New York: Springer.
Butin, D. (2005). *Service-learning in Higher Education: Critical Issues and Directions.* New York: Springer.
Campus Compact. (2016). Creating a Great Campus Civic Action Plan. Retrieved October 2, 2017, from https://compact.org/actionstatement/
Cantor, J. A. (1997). Experiential Learning in Higher Education: Linking Classroom and Community. *ERIC Digest.*
Driscoll, A. (2008). Carnegie's community-engagement classification: Intentions and insights. *Change: The Magazine of Higher Learning, 40*(1), 38–41.
Driscoll, A. (2009). Carnegie's new community engagement classification: Affirming higher education's role in community. *New Directions for Higher Education, 2009*(147), 5–12.

Furco, A. (1996). Service-Learning: A Balanced Approach to Experiential Education. *Service Learning, General*, 128, 3–4

Harkavy, I. (2006). The role of universities in advancing citizenship and social justice in the 21st century. *Education, citizenship and social justice, 1*(1), 5–37.

Hess, D. J., Lanig, H., & Vaughan, W. (2007). Educating for equity and social justice: A conceptual model for cultural engagement. *Multicultural Perspectives, 9*(1), 32–39.

Holland, B. (1997). Analyzing institutional commitment to service: A model of key organizational factors. *Michigan Journal of Community Service Learning, 4*(1), 30–41.

Jacoby, B. (2009). Civic engagement in higher education. *Concepts and Practices.* San Francisco: Jossey-Bass.

Kuh, G. D. (2001). Assessing what really matters to student learning inside the national survey of student engagement. *Change: The Magazine of Higher Learning, 33*(3), 10-17.

Kuh, G. D. (2008a). Why integration and engagement are essential to effective educational practice in the twenty-first century. *Peer Review, 10*(4), 27.

Kuh, G. D. (2008b). Excerpt from *High-impact educational practices: What they are, who has access to them, and why they matter.* Washington, DC: Association of American Colleges and Universities.

Kuh, G. D., Kinzie, J., Schuh, J. H., & Whitt, E. J. (2011). *Student Success in College: Creating Conditions That Matter.* San Francisco, CA: John Wiley & Sons.

Kuh, G. D., Palmer, M., Kish, K., Skipper, T. L., & Argo, R. (2003). *Involvement in campus activities and retention of first-year college students.* Columbia, SC: University of South Carolina.

McInerney, P., Smyth, J., & Down, B. (2011). "Coming to a place near you?" The politics and possibilities of a critical pedagogy of place-based education. *Asia-Pacific Journal of Teacher Education, 39*(1), 3–16.

Miller, R. L., Rycek, R. F., & Fritson, K. (2011). The effects of high impact learning experiences on student engagement. *Procedia-Social and Behavioral Sciences, 15*, 53–59.

New England Resource Center for High Education. (2017). Carnegie Community Engagement Classification. Retrieved October 3, 2017, from http://nerche.org/index.php?option=com_content&view=article&id=341&Itemid=618#CEdef

Pascarella, E., Edison, M., Nora, A., Hagedorn, L., & Terezini, P. (1996). Influences on students' openness to diversity and challenge in the first-year of college. *The Journal of Higher Education, 67*, 174–195.

Polanyi, M. (2015). *Personal knowledge: Towards a post-critical philosophy.* Chicago: University of Chicago Press.

Quaye, S. J., & Harper, S. R. (Eds.). (2015). *Student Engagement in Higher Education: Theoretical Perspectives and Practical Approaches for Diverse Populations.* New York: Routledge.

Sobel, D. (2004). Place-based education: Connecting classroom and community. *Nature and Listening, 4*, 1–7.

Stanton, T. K., Giles Jr, D. E., & Cruz, N. I. (1999). *Service-Learning: A Movement's Pioneers Reflect on Its Origins, Practice, and Future. Jossey-Bass Higher and Adult Education Series.* San Francisco: Jossey-Bass.

Zlotkowski, E. (1998). *Successful Service-Learning Programs. New Models of Excellence in Higher Education.* Bolton, MA: Anker.

Zlotkowski, E. (2015). Twenty years and counting: A framing essay. *Michigan Journal of Community Service Learning, 22*(1), 82–86.

Anthropology

Chapter 1

Anthropology and Service Learning: Building Bridges Across Generations to Challenge the Social Stigmas of Aging

Guillerma G. Núñez, David Josue Lopez, and Corrina Marrufo

SERVICE LEARNING,
COMMUNITY-BASED LEARNING

UNDERGRADUATE RESEARCH

Use these questions to guide your reflection prior to reading the chapter. Use the notes/follow-up section to write your thoughts after you have read the chapter. Your notes can include thoughts in reference to the reflection questions, or general observations about the chapter.

1) What comes to mind when you think of "service" and "learning"?

2) What was your first ever experience interacting or serving your community? What did you learn? What did you experience?

3) What do you think about working across generations? Do you feel you have the knowledge and skills to work with people in different age groups from yours? Why or why not?

Notes/Follow-up:

_____

_____

_____

_____

_____

Introduction

Through a Pedagogy of Engagement, students and faculty can go beyond the classroom to create meaningful and practical experiences while linking academia with the needs and realities of a community (Núñez, 2012; 2014). Participant observation is a signature method of ethnographic research that involves researchers learning in local community settings while being actively involved in their everyday activities. One of the main goals of anthropology is to seek to understand people from their point of view while being mindful of how the researcher is positioned as an outsider. Conducting service-learning and ethnographic research have much in common (Núñez, 2012; 2014), as both involve participant observation, analysis, and critical reflection. Service-learning as a high-impact practice in higher education provides students with the opportunity to learn by being present, participating, and observing others in community settings while linking these experiences to key themes discussed in the university classroom. Through participation in service-learning, students participate in community engagement as a high-impact practice involving learning through direct observation and experience (Kuh, 2008). Like ethnographic research, service-learning also creates the opportunity for critical analysis and reflection of broader structural issues and deep personal held beliefs, values, and practices.

As a professor, I (Gina Núñez) have been offering 20 hours of service-learning as an option in my anthropology courses, including Introduction to Cultural Anthropology, Applied Cultural Anthropology, Urban Anthropology, and Ethnographic Research Methods. In my previous work, I have detailed the ways ethnographic research is aligned with service-learning as a form of community engagement. Ideally, students can have access to diverse and global communities through other high-impact practices such as study abroad and global classroom experiences. However, as other authors in this volume argue, opportunities for students to engage in diverse settings and communities abound in local settings. For this reason, the partnership we highlight in this chapter is one that stemmed as a result of having identified the need to bridge different generations of people in our community together. This work is also part of broader efforts to develop Community-based Participatory Research partnerships that can help eliminate or reduce health disparities within the US—Mexico, particularly among older adults living in El Paso city (Cargo & Mercer, 2008). The concept behind community-based participatory research is to improve community wellbeing through a partnership between researchers and community representatives; it constructs understanding of the surrounding issues and enables community partners to practice a knowledge-based action. Putting knowledge in practice helps counter ageist stereotypes by challenging the attitudes and behaviors of University of Texas (UTEP) students as future health professionals and policymakers (Cargo & Mercer, 2008; Jagosh et al., 2015).

The partnership between the UTEP and the city of El Paso's Parks and Recreational Department began in 2009. This collaboration grew from an effort to promote health and the wellbeing of older adults on the US–Mexico border by engaging students in enrolled anthropology and sociology courses in the Liberal Arts and physical and occupational therapy courses in the Health Sciences. The Partnership between the city of El PAso and the UTEP, aimed to adhere to the goals set by Healthy People 2020 guidelines on aging (Healthy

Contributed by Guillermina G. Núñez, David Josue Lopez, and Corina Marufo. © Kendall Hunt Publishing Company.

People 2020, 2015). These goals were to encourage more physical activity on a broad scale in older adults, to encourage utilization of the numerous senior centers within the El Paso region, and to positively affect the attitudes surrounding seniors that are held by the students working to enter public health professions within the partnership.

For more than 34 years, the city of El Paso, Texas has sponsored the Senior Games in an effort to encourage more physical activity among mature adults as well as to combat stereotypes of aging. In recent years, the College of Health Sciences and College of Liberal Arts at the UTEP at El Paso has partnered with the city to not only give a more well-rounded experience to students who engage in service-learning, but also to help identify why and how future health professionals choose to work with older adult populations or, conversely, why they do not. The Senior Games are a series of events similar to the Olympic Games for adults over the age of 50 to eighty-plus years of age with competitions and awards for various age brackets: 50-54, 55-59, 60-64, 65-59, 70-74, 75-79, 80-84, 85+. Some of the events that are available to participants to compete in are swimming, basketball, volleyball, pickleball, tennis, racquetball, golf, a road race, cycling, and track and field.

In 2012, the dean of the College of Health Sciences provided mini-grants to help support research among the community–university partners. Through this Community and Academic Partnership (CAP1) grant, we developed the "Si Se Puede/Yes We Can!" project to document the experiences of ten senior adult athletes. Through this grant, we were also able to commission an undergraduate student, Diego Davila, to develop a video to help promote the Senior Games (see Senior Games YouTube video at: https://www.youtube.com/watch?v=SYpSV0PxImo).

This small grant served as the seed for us to pursue a State Farm grant in collaboration with the Center for Civic Engagement at UTEP to promote physical activity and community engagement among youth in El Paso high schools. In 2015, we were awarded another Community and Academic Partnership (CAP2) grant, leading to the beginning of the "Building Bridges" project to challenge the stigmas of aging among the residents of El Paso city through the development of educational modules that promoted healthy living practices through proper medication management, physical activity and exercise, fall prevention, and counteracting the social stigmas of aging. The modules were developed by collaborating researchers and have served as main research areas for the continuing partnership based on Service learning opportunities for students.

Service-Learning, Diversity, and Undergraduate Research as High-Impact Practices

Service-learning experiences often serve as a key step towards students selecting a major or defining their career interests such as public health, education, counseling, social work, and social services. Through service-learning experiences, students can develop tacit knowledge while preparing to work directly with populations they will engage with as future professionals. A meta-analysis of 62 studies involving 11,837 students engaged in service-learning has identified significant gains in student outcomes in the areas of attitudes towards self, attitudes towards school and learning, civic engagement, social skills, and academic performance (Celio, Durkal, & Dymnicki, 2011). Gaining valuable hands-on experiences is particularly valuable for students who have a need to work and go to school, who seldom can afford to do an unpaid internship prior to graduation. For students who seek to get out of their comfort zones and to grow personally and professionally, service-learning can be a key event in mapping a professional pathway. Trust, synergy, and consistency in the relationship have been key to the development of the community–university partnership based on service learning opportunities for students.

Although the Senior Games may seem like a great opportunity for seniors or retired peoples to get out of their homes and participate, the Games often suffer from a severe lack of participation and media exposure. While some of this may be due to poor or inadequate advertising, much of the gap in participation seems to occur as a result of overt ageism. That is, that people between the ages of 50 and 69 either abhor the term or do not consider themselves "seniors." In contrast, participants above the age of 70 seem to be consistently more comfortable with the transition to being a senior or mature adult. El Paso, like much of the United States, has a growing "senior population", with over 10% of the population being over the age of 65 in 2013.

While this is slightly below the national statistic of 14%, it is still a significant and identifiable community of people (U.S. Census Bureau, 2015a, 2015b). It is important to understand that the word "senior" carries several meanings in our society. It is a word used in the U.S. to represent the last year of high school as well as older adults in our society. In a capitalist society like the U.S., older adults tend to age out of employment when they reach their late sixties; thus shifting from being seen as "productive" citizens to consumers of high cost services. For many, aging is viewed as a process to be avoided or deferred. Other factors such as media and cartoon representations further add to negative stereotypes of older adults in our society.

Corina Marrufo is a student who has participated in service-learning, independent research, grant-writing, and publications that have involved creative ideas on how to engage university students with older adults. Through the eleven senior centers in our community, students have attended opening ceremonies and an array of competitive athletic events. For students such as Corina and hundreds of others, participation in the Senior Games provided experiences interacting with older adults and getting to learn from their stories and experiences. These experiences have taught students how to care for others, while also reflecting on the benefits of physical activity, exercise, and healthy life choices. One student was quite shocked when an 82-year-old man beat him at mini-golf and at basketball. He walked out of these interactions with a reflection on the need for him to get moving, lose weight, and be healthier. Another student who was seen smoking at one of these events was challenged by one of the senior adult athletes to stop smoking if she wanted to live longer. Students who have participated in the Senior Games learned to see the benefits of physical exercise on a person's mental and physical health over a life span. In their reflections and final papers, they often reflected on their own sedentary lifestyles as students and the importance of adopting a fitness routine as part of a healthier lifestyle shift to live longer. In the end, the senior adult athletes become the teachers and role models for longevity and wellbeing for the students and professors involved.

Case Study: Story of the UTEP Partnership with the El Paso Senior Games as narrated by Gina Núñez

In 2009, I attended a Community–Academic Partnership for Health Sciences Research (CAPSHR) meeting and met David Josue Lopez from the city's Park and Recreation Division, who was seeking to partner with the university to engage students in his programs. I offered to partner with David by providing a service-learning option to my students. Since, then, my students and I participate in the annual Senior Games in the spring semester from February to May.

I invite students to join me in participating in the El Paso Senior Games by attending the opening ceremony and then by attending to a variety of competitions to cheer the senior athletes on. I seek to connect students' experiences in organized sports with the great feeling of having friends and family members support them. I then share a story of my first experience attending a track and field competition and noticing no one was in the bleachers supporting the senior athletes. Together, we work through a creative brainstorming activity to help generate ideas for 1) recruiting more senior adults to participate as athletes, and 2) engaging university students to come out and show their support of senior athletes.

Over the years, students have generated ideas and proposals for showing community support of the senior athletes. My students have included leaders in student government (SGA), clubs, organizations, honor societies, athletics, and the university band. Involving students and their own affinity groups creates a common practice of shared experiences and feel good memories. We get to be together, observing, participating, and hanging out in the community together.

I ask students to work in groups to generate interview questions and engage the various stakeholders who participate in the Senior Games, including athletes, staff, volunteers, and corporate sponsors. By working in teams, students can conduct participant observation, interviews of various stakeholders,

(*Continued*)

qualitative data analysis, report writing, and oral presentations of our research findings to Parks and Recreation staff members.

While out in the "field," students get to know each other outside of the classroom, and they get to bring their friends, their partners, and in some occasions, their family members including parents, grandparents, and children. Hence, this service-learning and engaged research experience serves as a networking opportunity for students to develop social ties beyond the classroom. I personally appreciate getting to know my students outside of class, and seeing them apply research skills learned in class.

An added benefit of having students interview staff and corporate sponsors is that they begin to see our students as potential peers or employees interested in parks and recreations, public health, and health care. It is not uncommon for me to get questions such as "Are these your students? Are they interested in health care? Are they bilingual? When are they graduating?" Students are excited to learn that they are being noticed by potential employers. The City Parks and Recreation department in our city also offers summer employment to students interested in working in community centers and recreational sports facilities.

Another added benefit from participating in the Senior Games involves the relationships that are built between our university students and the adult athletes. Students get to know the athletes by name and begin to show allegiances and support for them during their competitions. Over the length of a semester, students have been known to develop social ties with the athletes they most admire and respect. For example, one undergraduate journalism major learned that one of the athletes competed in track and field competitions in different countries. She decided to interview him for a class project and soon after she would look for him to encourage him and support him during his track and field competitions.

As I engage students in analysis of their observations and personal reflections, I begin to notice students being introspective about their own personal habits and lifestyle choices. Some students recall having time to participate in organized sports or attend the gym regularly, but with school and work, physical activity often gets compromised. Students reflect on the importance of exercise to build strength, resilience, and flexibility. They are often motivated to return to their physical fitness routines or to begin exercising if they have not had a routine in the past. Students in my courses tend to be mindful of their own personal and familial habits and behaviors and how these can lead them to live longer and healthier lives or shorter lifespans.

Hence, the participant observation research that takes place in service-learning experiences generates many lessons for our students and the adult athletes. Athletes often reflect on what has worked for them in the past to prepare for the competitive games, the friendships they have built over the years, and the experiences they have fostered by competing in other states.

The conversations our students have with the athletes, staff, and sponsors helps to generate valuable insights for David and his staff as our community partners. The exchange of success stories, of challenges, and best practices are shared between the senior athletes, the participating students, and parks and recreation staff. Together, we have learned valuable lessons about the benefits of fitness, strength, and determination that help challenge social stigmas of aging across the generations.

What Made This High-Impact Practice Successful?

During the partnership between UTEP and the City of El Paso, a variety of projects have developed following efforts to encourage more physical activity among residents. Over the years, various other faculty and academic units have joined this partnership. For example, in 2015, a professor of Public Relations assigned groups of students to work on a marketing campaign to increase and improve media coverage on the Senior Games. Also that year, students from Anthropology and Sociology engaged in a Rapid Assessment Process at the Senior Games in an effort to provide recommendations for improvement to the El Paso Parks and Recreation Department. A total of 32 students attended the Senior Games, as part of course credit they took field notes and interviewed employees, audience, and senior athletes participating at the event. Field notes and observations of the anthropology students were then gathered and prepared an executive summary for El Paso Senior Games conducted by Ricardo Garza, anthropology student and an intern in the Center for Civic Engagement at UTEP. The executive summary of the Senior Games 2015 was presented to the leadership staff of the city's Parks and Recreation Department. A key recommendation student researchers made was to increase the media coverage of the Senior Games to raise awareness of the games, while also providing a counternarrative of senior adults as actively involved in exercise and competitive athletic events. These visual images and testimonies of older adults participating helped provide a stark contrast to the stereotypes and social stigmas of aging, as active senior adults were shown to be motivated to exercise to be self-reliant and to reduce the probabilities of illnesses and loneliness.

The consistency and stability of this partnership has created opportunities for us to expand our partnership. Most recently, we have partnered with computer science and engineering faculty to conduct surveys of more than 400 older adults in our community to develop a new application for mobile devices to address their transportation needs and promote their physical mobility. As our relationship has developed over time, so has the need to expand beyond our own scope of work to create opportunities for new ideas, projects, and collaborative ideas that can ultimately benefit older adults in our community.

What Were Some of the Challenges?

Extensive research can be found that supports the existence of ageism and stigma surrounding the aging process, not only in the United States, but globally (Binstock, 2010; Kagan & Melendez-Torres, 2015; Kydd, Touhy, Newman, Fagerberg, & Engstrom, 2014; Luo, Zhou, Jin, Newman, & Liang, 2013). Arguably this occurs as a result of a lack of exposure, understanding, and compassion for older adults. Culturally and politically, older adults play important roles in U.S. society. The growing numbers of seniors aging into social welfare benefit programs amidst feelings of economic and political disenfranchisement among younger generations leads to political and philosophical tensions (Binstock, 2010; North & Fiske, 2012). In addition, stereotypes and pejorative language used to describe older adults further propagate the stigmas of aging and the disparaging treatment of older adults (Binstock, 2010; Hollis-Sawyer & Cuevas, 2013). However, these preconceived stigmas can be mitigated in several ways. Evidence has shown that when students or young people are introduced, even with low frequency, to older adults who are healthy, attitudes tend to be much more positive (Bernard, McAuley, Belzer, & Neal, 2003; Thompson & Weaver, 2015). Therefore, throughout our research and partnership efforts, we have sought to increase the occurrence of positive interactions with older adults via student participation in the Senior Games.

Students interviewed during or after the Senior Games expressed surprise towards the physical condition of the "Games" participants. This suggests that their interaction with the participants, combined with their opportunity to witness participants engaging in physical activity, may have altered some bias or stereotypes that those being interviewed had held previous to their involvement in this annual event. In addition, seniors involved in the games challenged social stigmas of aging by showing that, contrary to the popular stereotype, older adults can, in fact, be physically fit and active (Kydd et al., 2014).

One of the major challenges for the city has been recruiting athletes to participate in the Senior Games, primarily because of the social stigmas of the word "senior." Although we cannot modify the official name of the games, we can seek to inform the public that events are organized by generational cohorts. Another challenge involves the need to for the "Games" to recruit more diversity in terms of the local mostly Mexican-origin population, of which 81% of the local population identifies as Hispanic (U.S. Census Bureau, 2015a), yet most participants are predominantly Anglo Americans. This incites an interesting predicament, as Hispanic people tend to experience higher rates of obesity and lower rates of physical activity in adulthood than whites and other minority populations (Neighbors, Marquez, & Marcus, 2008). That being said, research has indicated that people who identify as Mexican-American, in particular, experience a reduction in cognitive decline as they age with physical activity, signaling great benefit (Kim, Lee, Kye, Chung, & Kim, 2015; Ottenbacher et al., 2014). Therefore, it is exceptionally important that the existence of the Senior Games be broadcast rather broadly to increase the participation of athletes of diverse backgrounds.

Conducting Service-Learning in Community Settings

Every semester, students enrolled in Núñez' classes are asked to consider two options for their final paper: 20 hours of service-learning in a community setting or library-based research on a culture or region of the world of their choice. Students are further challenged to venture out of by exploring opportunities that will allow them to grow beyond their comfort zones. By the fourth week in class, students make a decision to engage in service-learning or to begin their library research efforts. Núñez encourages students to choose a non-profit organization that addresses a topic they are interested in to help prepare them in their future careers or one that is close to their hearts.

A key component in developing community–academic partnerships involves the commitment to keep on showing up to the meetings and committing to the relationship. One of the basic problems or challenges for our students is that they work and go to school and they are often pressed for time. So conducting 20 hours of service-learning is a major commitment for students with multiple responsibilities and obligations. Students should be advised to break down their service hours into manageable chunks of time, perhaps 2–3 hours per week until they complete their 20 hours. For students who do not pace themselves over the length of a semester, participation in major events where they can make up their hours in larger blocks of time might be the next best option. Trust and relationship building with my students as they conduct their own service hours. We review expectations we have of each other as we go out into the community representing ourselves, our academic majors, departments, and the university.

To document their observations and reflections, students receive instructions on how to write ethnographic field notes and field jottings. Notes can be written down in short phrases to help trigger their memories in the form of field jottings or short notes. Later, usually within 24 hours of their experience, students should type up their field notes with the time, date, and location of their participation. Over time, students become more observant, more detail oriented, and more critical in their thought process. Field notes are then coded for emerging themes, key events, and representative quotes or narratives shared by the participants. Students submit their field notes along with their final papers for evaluation and assessment purposes. Once students learn to take notes, conduct interviews, and engage with others, they can use these skills in other settings. Students can refer to these experiences in job applications, graduate school applications, and in employment interviews particularly when referencing experiences working with older adults, working in teams, and caring about others. The practice of service-learning, ethnographic research, field note taking, and critical analysis and reflection can be applied in diverse personal and professional settings.

Recommendations For Faculty

Faculty interested in offering service-learning experiences in their courses should think about which organizations they can partner with to incorporate their research, teaching, and service goals. If one organization is not available, faculty could identify community organizations interested in working with students. If your university does not have a centralized office that can coordinate service-learning experiences, faculty can turn to their own networks or their students' networks to identify partnering non-profit organizations, schools, or local government entities. Given the various obligations students might have in any given semester, Núñez offers service-learning as an option and invites students to choose where they want to conduct their service hours. This way, students will know they have agency in their selection and are more likely to be committed to follow through with their 20 hours over the length of a semester. Students who are committed to certain causes might continue with their organization after the course is over, while others will complete their hours and will move on to other commitments.

We encourage faculty to use structured tools for reflection including field notes, and the use of photography and videos when appropriate. Students who are guided with tools for reflection tend to value their service-learning experience more so than not having to write down their observations and experiences. Field notes and the student's final report also serve as evidence of participant observation, critical reflection, and as evidence of hours completed. Ethnographic field notes can then be analyzed and coded for emergent themes that will frame the final paper. Students can be encouraged to document the total number of hours served, as well as key lessons learned during their experience as evidence of student learning. Intellectually and emotionally, students will be able to create knowledge and reflect on this process of engagement and transformation.

In addition to the creation of learning modules, participants in the Senior Games as well as students who volunteered were asked to participate in a semi-structured interview process, which was then analyzed for qualitative trends. These interviews gave researchers a better understanding of what motivates seniors to stay physically active and to participate in the Senior Games. Many of the "Games" participants expressed a desire to remain self-sufficient and independent as they age as a motivator for their involvement. These findings are particularly important because it suggests that by marketing the Senior Games as a way to remain independent among older adults in El Paso, it may encourage more participation. Encouraging physical activity in older adults is especially important for the El Paso region, where 24% of adults are obese and a 39% of the population is identified as overweight in 2010 (Department of Public Health, 2013). Given that adults, and particularly men, tend to slow down after retirement, it is no mystery why the partnership has decided to target older adults (Bell et al., 2014;).

Recommendations For Students

Before we offer the student advice, we'd like to share an example of how Corina benefitted from this experience. Corina Marrufo has participated in the Senior Games by doing service-learning. She has also conducted independent research, worked on grants and publications, and has helped generate creative ideas on how to engage university students with older adults. Through the eleven senior centers in our community, students have attended opening ceremonies and an array of competitive athletic events. For students such as Corina and hundreds of others, participation in the Senior Games provided experiences interacting with older adults and getting to learn from their interactions, stories, and experiences. These experiences have taught students how to care for others, while also reflecting on the benefits of physical activity, exercise, and healthy life choices.

Students are asked to commit to 20 hours for the length of a semester. This is roughly the equivalent of 2 hours a week over 10 weeks. Initially some students might want to do service-learning at various agencies and organizations in the community. The importance thing is to pick one community partner and to be aware of the time commitments required to follow through. Perhaps the most stressful part of doing service-learning is getting started and making a connection with the community partner. As a good rule of thumb, We recommend student prepare their personal statement, where they outline their specific skills and talents, and the reason they would like to do service-learning with a particular partner. Then it is important to decide on a schedule when students can attend events or participate in an agency to build relationships over time.

Students are encouraged to bring their skills, experiences, and talents to the forefront to build on this community–university partnership. One student, Diego Davila, created a short video of the Senior Games applying his multimedia communication skills. Another student helped conduct interviews as a sociology student. Two other students helped prepare a small grant application to promote physical fitness among university and high school students (one of these students went on to graduate school and the other went on to do international marketing for a famous brand of energy drinks). Both of these students were able to document their service-learning experiences and their grant-writing experiences in their resumes and personal statements as evidence of their engagement and service-leadership efforts. Students often refer to these experiences and the empathy and compassion they have developed for others in their personal statements when they apply for graduate school and for employment. In essence, students will have invested in developing meaningful experiences before graduation that can translate into assets they can build upon moving forward. As one student indicated, "I was a psychology major and criminal justice minor in college, but it was not until I took an anthropology course that I started to learn about and care for others through a service-learning experience. I went on to work in health care and now I am preparing to become a counselor." Thus, by incorporating service-learning into curriculums, students gain interpersonal skills and experience working with diverse populations.

The partnership between the university and the Park and Recreation Department have challenged the stigmas and stereotypes of several students. For Corina, this experience prepared her to work with older adults. She recalls having no interest in working with older adults prior to this experience. Later, as she completed her internship at a mental health hospital, she found the gerontology unit the most rewarding and describes the population as being "supportive towards each other and energetic compared to other populations." Service-learning takes students out of their comfort zones into trying new experiences that enriches their education.

Recommendations For Community

Community members seeking to develop community–university partners should reach out to individual faculty members or groups who are interested in research and practices in which a mutually beneficial relationship can be developed. Once a relationship is developed with a faculty member, new relationships can be built over time with other faculty and academic units who have other skills and interests working with your population or areas of service. For example, David with City Parks and Recreation has developed relationships with faculty in pharmacy, physical and occupational therapy, public relations, communications, and kinesiology. Most recently, because of our relationship, we have expanded our ties with engineering and computer science to conduct surveys in the city's senior centers to develop a mobile phone application (an app) to address older adults' transportation and mobility needs via a Department of Transportation grant.

To formalize the partnership, we developed an interagency agreement to collaborate and be supported by our respective units (the city and the university). This agreement was discussed and reviewed by various units including our legal offices to formalize our partnership, while expressing our disposition to collaborating in research and grant-seeking efforts, and educationally related service activities. Having this mutual agreement allows for city employees to step out of their usual routines and commitments to attend monthly meetings to build on this community–university partnership. The community benefits from having access to faculty whose research foci align with the populations being served and to students who are equipped with computer skills, social media/social networking skills, and a variety of other strengths and interests.

The relationship we have developed between the city and the university has also yielded other opportunities for lifelong learning and personal growth. We have attended and have presented at conferences together to learn about other community–university partnerships and their best practices. We have gone through community engagement training and have been recognized for our long-standing relationship and commitment to engaged scholarship efforts at the city and the university. As a community partner, David has reached out to the university to seek support for communication and conflict resolution workshops for staff members, as well as a workshop that focused on identifying assets and partners to expand services for parks and recreation services.

Conclusions and Lessons Learned

The goal of this chapter is to challenge the social stigmas of aging by documenting and understanding the positive impacts interaction with El Paso senior athletes has on students and service learners. In reflecting on the partnership between the UTEP and Parks and Recreation Department, we have learned about the importance of building healthy partnerships. Throughout these past years, the partnership has been solidified by a mutual commitment to our partnership and sustaining our mission and priorities. Cargo and Mercer (2008) have identified engagement and sustainability, formalization, and maintenance as the key elements to initiate a partnership and strengthening the relationship. Each partner has identified key skills that can be utilized to promote healthy behaviors and physical activities among older adults in El Paso. This is a step closer towards diminishing the gap of health disparities in the US–Mexico border region affecting older adults while preparing students professionally to work with aging populations.

In addition, over the years, students participating in the Seniors Games have learned and have modified their perceptions and willingness to work with older adults. Contrary to the general stereotypes, senior athletes participating in the Senior Games are energetic, physically active, and very competitive. Senior adults are not homogenous and have their own generational differences and commonalities, for example, older adults between the ages of 50 and 60 do not usually see themselves or identify as as senior citizens, while seniors in their 70s and 80s are more accepting of their identities as older adults. These nuances are important to consider in teaching, researching, and providing services to older adults. Horowitz, Tagliarino, and Look (2014) identified that education on gerontology, service-learning experience, positive contacts with older adults, and intergenerational experiences tend to generate positive attitudes towards older adults among students. Having positive experiences increases the students' willingness to build positive habits at an early age that will contribute to their longevity and wellbeing in the future.

A Few Selected Resources and Tools

The following reflective questions are useful at the beginning of every project formed in collaboration with a community partner:

1. What motivated you to choose the service-learning option?
2. What skills, talents, or experiences do you bring to the service-learning experience and how might you be able to contribute to the community partners' mission and goals?
3. What are your career goals and aspirations, and how might this service-learning experience help you build experiences for you to move forward?
4. What is your schedule? When do you plan on attending events or doing your site visits in the community?

Writing Field Notes

Date	
Time	
Location	
Observations and direct quotes of what people said	Reflections and interpretations

References

Bell, C. L., Chen, R., Masaki, K., Yee, P., He, Q., Grove, J., & Willcox, B. J. (2014). Late-life factors associated with healthy aging in older men. *Journal of the American Geriatrics Society, 62*(5), 880–888.

Bernard, M. A., McAuley, W. J., Belzer, J. A., & Neal, K. S. (2003). An evaluation of a low-intensity intervention to introduce medical students to healthy older people. *Journal of the American Geriatrics Society, 51*(3), 419–423.

Binstock, R. H. (2010). From compassionate ageism to intergenerational conflict? *The Gerontologist, 50*(5), 574–585.

Cargo, M., & Mercer, S. L. (2008). The value and challenges of participatory research: Strengthening its practice. *Annual Review of Public Health, 29*, 325–350.

Celio, C. I., Durkal, J., & Dymnicki, A. (2011). A meta-analysis of the impact of service-learning on students. *Journal of Experiential Education, 34*(2), 164–181.

Department of Public Health. (2013). *Community health assessment: Final report.* Retrieved from https://www.elpasotexas.gov/~/media/files/coep/public%20health/community%20health%20assessment%20final%20report.ashx?la=en

Healthy People 2020. (2015). *Physical activity.* Retrieved from https://www.healthypeople.gov/2020/topics-objectives/topic/physical-activity

Hollis-Sawyer, L., & Cuevas, L. (2013). Mirror, mirror on the wall: Ageist and sexist double jeopardy portrayals in children's picture books. *Educational Gerontology, 39*(12), 902–914.

Horowitz, B. P., Tagliarino, J., & Look, K. (2014). Occupational therapy education, attitudes on aging, and occupational therapy students and therapists interest in gerontology practice. *Physical & Occupational Therapy in Geriatrics, 32*(2), 136–151.

Jagosh, J., Bush, P. L., Salsberg, J., Macaulay, A. C., Greenhalgh, T., Wong, G., & Pluye, P. (2015). A realist evaluation of community-based participatory research: Partnership synergy, trust building and related ripple effects. *BMC Public Health, 15*(1), 725.

Kagan, S. H., & Melendez-Torres, G. J. (2015). Ageism in nursing. *Journal of Nursing Management, 23*(5), 644–650.

Kim, J., Lee, Y., Kye, S., Chung, Y. S., & Kim, K. M. (2015). Association between healthy diet and exercise and greater muscle mass in older adults. *Journal of the American Geriatrics Society, 63*(5), 886–892.

Kuh, G. D. (2008). *Excerpt from high-impact educational practices: What they are, who has access to them, and why they matter.* Washington, DC: Association of American Colleges and Universities.

Kydd, A., Touhy, T., Newman, D., Fagerberg, I., & Engstrom, G. (2014). Attitudes towards caring for older people in Scotland, Sweden and the United States: Angela Kydd and colleagues compare data from three countries to assess what staff think about working in the specialty. *Nursing Older People, 26*(2), 33–40.

Luo, B., Zhou, K., Jin, E. J., Newman, A., & Liang, J. (2013). Ageism among college students: A comparative study between US and China. *Journal of cross-cultural gerontology, 28*(1), 49–63.

Neighbors, C. J., Marquez, D. X., & Marcus, B. H. (2008). Leisure-time physical activity disparities among Hispanic subgroups in the United States. *American Journal of Public Health, 98*(8), 1460–1464.

North, M. S., & Fiske, S. T. (2012). An inconvenienced youth? Ageism and its potential intergenerational roots. *Psychological Bulletin, 138*(5), 982.

Núñez, G. (2012). Writing while participating: Incorporating ethnography in service-learning practicums across the curriculum. In I. Baca (Ed.), *Paving the way to literacy(ies): Writing and learning through community engagement* (pp.83–105). Boston, MA: Brill by Isabel Baca.

Núñez, G. (2014). Engaging scholarship with community. *Journal of Hispanic Higher Education, 3*(2), 95–115.

Ottenbacher, A. J., Snih, S. A., Bindawas, S. M., Markides, K. S., Graham, J. E., Samper-Ternent, R., & Ottenbacher, K. J. (2014). Role of physical activity in reducing cognitive decline in older Mexican-American adults. *Journal of the American Geriatrics Society, 62*(9), 1786–1791.

Thompson Jr, E. H., & Weaver, A. J. (2015). Making connections: The legacy of an intergenerational program. *The Gerontologist, 56*(5), 909–918.

U.S. Census Bureau. (2015a). *Quick Facts: El Paso County QuickFacts.* Retrieved from http://quickfacts.census.gov/qfd/states/48/48141.html

U.S. Census Bureau. (2015b). *American Month Facts for Features.* Retrieved from https://www.census.gov/newsroom/facts-for-features/2015/cb15-ff09.html

Communications

Chapter 2

Service-Learning as a Collaborative Assignment: Possibilities and Practices

Sarah De Los Santos Upton, PhD

CAPSTONE COURSES
AND PROJECTS

SERVICE LEARNING,
COMMUNITY-BASED LEARNING

WRITING-INTENSIVE
COURSES

Pre-Reading Reflection Questions   Chapter 2

Use these questions to guide your reflection prior to reading the chapter. Use the notes/follow-up section to write your thoughts after you have read the chapter. Your notes can include thoughts in reference to the reflection questions, or general observations about the chapter.

1) Describe a time when working on an assignment as a member of a collaborative team gave you positive results? What made it successful or what could have made it successful?

2) Why would collaboration be important among people when working with community?

3) What community issue would you most like to see addressed through collaboration?

Notes/Follow-up:

_____

_____

_____

_____

_____

Introduction

Collaborative assignments and projects are considered a high-impact practice because they encourage students to work together towards a common goal for course credit, while at the same time strengthening their communication, problem-solving, team-building, and leadership skills. This high-impact practice is typically carried out through the use of group presentations, papers, and other types of creative projects. Service-learning as a high-impact practice allows students to learn academic course content while at the same time meeting a community need through direct or indirect service. When combined with service-learning, collaborative assignments and projects allow students to work with stakeholders outside of the university on issues that are important to the community, exposing them to a diversity of thought and creating opportunities for experiential learning that only exist outside of textbooks and classrooms. Through service-learning, collaborative projects and assignments enrich student understanding and application of course concepts, while at the same time providing opportunities to practice relationship development and negotiation. Students are also able to experience the important community-based concept of reciprocity, exchanging their time and service for the unique learning opportunities available in the community.

As an undergraduate, I had the opportunity to participate in several collaborative assignments and projects through service-learning, and these experiences allowed me to apply the concepts and ideas I was learning in class to real issues in my community. As result, the lessons learned through these assignments stand out as the most important of my undergraduate career, and still shape the way I view the world around me to this day. I believe that academic course content becomes more meaningful when it can be used to make a difference outside of the classroom. Inspired by these experiences, much of my research as a faculty member is community-based, and I now assign collaborative assignments and projects through service-learning in a majority of my courses. I have found that when students are able to apply what they are learning in the classroom to real-world issues, especially those that impact their community, they become more engaged in the learning process. New kinds of relationships are developed with their peers, professors, and community members, and as a professor I have enjoyed watching my students bloom through this process.

The communication discipline offers unique opportunities for exploring how human beings use symbols to share meanings with one another. In my courses, I focus specifically on how people communicate within and across cultures, how they use communication to develop relationships with others, ways they are impacted by mass media, and methods for designing and pursuing qualitative research within the discipline. In the following section, I offer three case studies of ways I have incorporated service-learning as collaborative projects in three such courses. The first describes a course on Border Communication, in which students collaboratively designed and implemented a service-learning project to meet a need they identified in our border community. The second focuses on a group project from my Mass Media and Society course, where students created media literacy lessons for elementary, middle, and high school students. The final case study outlines a research project in my Qualitative Research Methods course where students worked with a community organization to design and conduct research on a community issue.

Service-Learning as a Collaborative Assignment: Three Case Studies

Border Communication: Final Exam

In our course on Border Communication, my students and I explored various issues that impact our border community. We questioned how people create a sense of identity when they live between two countries, cultures, and languages. We discussed the rhetoric surrounding immigration. We analyzed how popular media represent the border we call home. Finally, we observed the unique forms of resistance and social movements that are born from border communities.

While students came to class equipped with a genuine pride and love for their border community, during the course of the semester they became increasingly aware of, and concerned by, issues our community faces. When we arrived at the section on social movements, students began questioning what they could do to make a difference in their community. I originally assigned a final paper asking students to reflect on their views of the border resulting from lived experiences and course content; however, one student asked me if instead of writing their final papers, the class could put together a service project as a final exam.

I agreed that this project would be an excellent way to apply what they learned in our class in service to their community, and they quickly began researching nonprofit organizations. As a group, they decided to address the issue of food insecurity in our community, choosing to partner with Mustard Seed Café, a pay-what-you-can restaurant in El Paso's Rio Grande Historic District.

On a Wednesday morning during the finals week, my students and I met in Mustard Seed's community garden where we worked digging holes for soon-to-be-planted fruit trees that will eventually supplement produce in the café. After working all morning, we sat down to share lunch in the café, and discussed the ways in which this organization, and our service project, connected to borderland issues we covered during the semester. Students explained that instead of feeling defeated by some of the more difficult border issues we covered that semester, they felt a sense of pride by being able to make a meaningful contribution to their community.

Mass Media and Society: Group Project

My Mass Media and Society course focuses specifically on becoming more media literate. In other words, we analyze and evaluate media by questioning who creates media and for what purpose/audience, what underlying messages are present in any given media text, and how media represent issues of race, gender, and ethnicity. In an effort to increase media literacy in our community, my students have been able to collaborate with Latinitas, a local nonprofit aimed at empowering young Latinas through media and technology.

Based on our course focus of media literacy, the director of Latinitas requested that my students create media literacy lessons for use in their afterschool programs. Drawing from course content and in response to Latinitas' needs, the director and I worked together to identify five key topics for these media literacy lessons: stereotypes of women in media, body image, leadership and role models, ethnic stereotypes in media, and diversity in media.

The director of Latinitas visited our class to talk to students about their afterschool programs, and based on the topic areas we identified, we asked students to break into groups of five to begin brainstorming for their media literacy lessons while the director was present to answer questions. Working in groups of five, students researched and organized information about their given topics over the course of the semester to create bilingual media literacy lessons. These lessons consisted of a PowerPoint presentation and poster, which students shared to an audience of school-aged Latinas at a Latinitas' event called "Chica Power Fest" that took place at the end of the semester. Students also created individual lesson plans and handouts for use by Latinitas in their afterschool programs. These media literacy lessons required students to tap into the knowledge they developed over the course of the semester, conduct research to further their understandings of course concepts, and share their knowledge in ways that were accessible to elementary, middle, and high school-aged students.

Qualitative Research Methods

Research Paper

My graduate course on Qualitative Research Methods focuses on introducing students to the process of designing, planning, and conducting qualitative research projects, as well as effectively negotiating research relationships with participants. In an effort to provide students with hands-on research experiences, I have developed a partnership with Ciudad Nueva, a community development organization in El Paso's Rio Grande Historic District. Ciudad Nueva is interested in understanding how community members, real estate agents, and business owners understand and/or experience change in the Rio Grande Historic District. As students in my course develop skills like data collection and analysis, they are able to work with staff at Ciudad Nueva to explore how people in the historic district understand and experience change. In addition, this partnership allows students to experience the process of developing and negotiating research relationships.

Before the beginning of the semester, I worked alongside the director and other staff members of Ciudad Nueva to create and submit an Internal Review Board (IRB) proposal so that students would be able to use their research for conference presentations and publications in the future. The director attended our first class meeting to help me introduce our collaborative project and brainstorm individual research topics alongside students, and returned multiple times during the semester to check in on student progress and offer support. Students developed community asset maps and conducted interviews with neighborhood residents, business owners, and real estate agents, finding that tensions exist between excitement for new development projects and a fear of being displaced by neighborhood changes.

At the end of the semester, students wrote up their findings in a research paper and we held a dinner to share what we found with Ciudad Nueva. Students expressed that this approach to research made their projects more meaningful. Brenda explains "through the initial coursework and readings, I was able to understand the technical side of research, the methodologies that better fit a situation or a group of people, but through active service-learning I was able to relate that academic knowledge to true life situations and my experience was enriched" (Upton & Bravo, forthcoming).

What Made This High-Impact Practice Successful?

Using service-learning as an approach to collaborative assignments has been successful for two main reasons; first, it has created opportunities for different kinds of collaborations, and second, it has allowed students to apply learning to address issues in their community. Each of the three projects discussed earlier allowed students to work with one another and with community members to varying degrees. For the final exam in Border Communication, students worked together to brainstorm service opportunities, then reached out to Mustard Seed Café to choose a day, time, and activity that would work for members of the organization and the class. The group project in Mass Media and Society focused on students working together to research media literacy concepts, and develop and deliver presentations for Latinitas. The research project in Qualitative Research Methods allowed students to work collaboratively with Ciudad Nueva to identify research needs, desires, and goals and conduct research to specifically address these and lay a foundation for future community action.

Collaborative assignments through service-learning also gave students the opportunity to apply course material to community issues. Because Mass Media and Society covered issues in media literacy, students were able to collect, organize, and share their knowledge with Latina youth, which in turn reinforced their own learning.

In Qualitative Research Methods, students learned about the research process while simultaneously practicing research in a community setting. In addition, they learned to effectively negotiate reciprocal research relationships with community members. Perhaps the best example of applying course content to community issues came from Border Communication. Instead of feeling powerless while learning about the unique issues and concerns impacting their border community, students learned how to apply what they learned in class and channel their concerns productively into action through their service-learning final exam. They ultimately learned more through experiential learning, organizing with one another and community members, than they could have from writing a paper. In all three cases, class material became more real for students as they moved through their service experiences.

What Were Some of the Challenges?

Collaborative assignments using service-learning have presented two main challenges: logistics and IRB approval. In my experience, logistical challenges can often be remedied with planning, flexibility, and experience. In the case of the Border Communication course, because we did not plan for service-learning as a final exam until late in the semester, students felt rushed to identify an organization to partner with. Once they chose to work with Mustard Seed, the café's limited hours of operation, coupled with my student's complicated work and final exam schedules, limited their possible dates for service. In the future, this option could be built into the syllabus from day one, and students could begin planning from the beginning of the semester. Additionally, if one date and time does not work for all students, they may split up and pursue different opportunities as one student in my course chose to do because of his work schedule.

In Mass Media and Society, the group project with Latinitas presented logistical challenges as well. Latinitas held the "Chica Power Fest" at our university, and because of complications reserving space, they had a difficult time pinning down an exact date and time for the event. Because many of my students' work, it became difficult for them to plan their schedules around their final presentations at the festival. To remedy this, students worked together to break up responsibilities. Those who could not attend the event were able to take on larger roles in developing presentations, while those with more flexible schedules committed to representing their groups at "Chica Power Fest."

Finally, the research project in Qualitative Research Methods presented challenges around IRB approval. During the first semester where I used service-learning as an approach to teaching Qualitative Research Methods, I contacted a representative from the IRB and was told that students could collect research for class purposes without an IRB. Students were able to work with Ciudad Nueva to create research questions and come up with plans for data collection and analysis. Because they did not have IRB approval, however, students were not able to present their results at conferences or submit them for publication. To remedy this, I worked with Ciudad Nueva to create an IRB proposal and obtain IRB approval before I taught the course again the following year. Students from that class are now able to share their results in various academic formats; however, they were not able to play as big of a role in the initial planning process with Ciudad Nueva and had to work within the parameters of the project we proposed in advance.

Moving Forward with Service-Learning as a Collaborative Assignment

Through the case studies described earlier, I learned that service-learning as a collaborative assignment can be approached in two different ways: as student-led assignments and preplanned assignments. My hope for this section is to demonstrate that faculty and students play a variety of roles in designing and implementing this type of project, and readers should be able to choose an approach that will work best for the needs of their class moving forward.

Student-led assignments

The final exam in my Border Communication course was an example of a student-led assignment, in that students planned, organized, and carried out the service-learning project. The beauty of a student-led assignment is that there are multiple ways to include it in a course. In my case, students approached me with a great idea for connecting course concepts with community action. By making this request, students showed me that they were not only critically reflecting on the border issues we covered in class, but they were also self-motivated to use the knowledge they gained to make a positive impact in their community and the world around them. This desire was of course something I hoped our course could instill in them, but it was not something I could assign as a reading, teach in a lecture, or require in a final paper. Therefore, I was open to allowing them to explore the service option for course credit.

Student-led assignments can also be built in to the syllabus as an option from the very beginning of a course, and there are two different ways to approach this. First, the service-learning final exam can be a required assignment for every student in the course, making it clear that this is something they will be working towards from day one. Second, the service-learning final exam could be offered as one of many options. Students could elect to participate in the service-learning final exam pursuing a project they have planned individually, or as a group, or they could write a final paper or take a written exam.

When using service-learning as a student-led assignment, it is important to set clear expectations that the service experience will fulfill a need, desire, and/or goal identified by the community organization, and at the same time align with concepts from the course. Students should be evaluated on their projects ability to meet these two criteria.

Preplanned assignments

The media literacy presentations in my Mass Media and Society course and the research papers in my Qualitative Research Methods course were examples of preplanned assignments. For service-learning to run smoothly in these courses, it was important to plan collaboratively with the community organization in order to set clear expectations for desired outcomes of each assignment. In addition, members of each organization came to class early in the semester to meet students and negotiate expectations in person. When organizations were willing/able to make follow-up visits to class, it was helpful for tracking progress and making sure that community needs, desires, and/or goals were guiding assignments at every stage. I also included in-class workshops for working through issues that came up as students developed their presentations and research projects. Students were given clear guidelines for presenting assignments to the organizations, such as the length, format, and style expected of each.

In the case of preplanned assignments that involve research with human subjects, it is important to review your universities guidelines. Because my university allows research projects to be conducted for course purposes without IRB approval, but requires IRB approval for academic use outside the course, it is important to decide what the focus of the research project should be in terms of learning objectives. In other words, is it more important that students play a role in, and learn from, the planning process of a research project? Is it more important that they have IRB approval so that they are able to use data from their research projects in future academic conferences and publications? These decisions, along with university requirements, will guide the way you approach the design of research projects, and so they are an important step in the planning process.

Preplanned assignments should ultimately be assessed on their ability to meet the guidelines and criteria negotiated between the community organization, professor, and student.

Recommendations For Faculty

Service-learning as a collaborative assignment allows you as a faculty member to design curriculum based on active learning that meets course objectives. At the same time, by using this high-impact practice you are providing students with real-world experiences and equipping them with tools for developing reciprocal relationships with their classmates and members of community organizations. The following are a few tips and recommendations for getting started:

- Get to know your students and the community around your university. What unique assets do they bring to your learning environment? What needs, desires, and/or goals do they have? How can service-learning as a collaborative project meet these?

- Find ways to incorporate course learning objectives into the collaborative service-learning experience. For example, in my department ,written and oral presentation skills are important learning outcomes, and each of my collaborative service-learning assignments allows students to practice these skills.
- When planning lectures, discussions, and activities, look for ways to connect concepts from course to the service opportunity.
- Holding a reflection session at the end of the course can help facilitate student learning by allowing students to think about, and articulate moments of learning throughout their service, and identify major takeaways from the experience.
- Be flexible. It is important to remember that during any type of collaboration, things may not always go as planned, and/or people may have different ideas for the direction of the project. Keep an open mind.
- Be patient. Working with a community organization means that things cannot always be planned around strict university timelines. Remember that the organization is working with their own set of deadlines, and may not be familiar with the way time is scheduled at the university.
- Communicate expectations effectively with students and the organization you are collaborating with.

Recommendations For Students

As a student, collaborating with others on a service-learning project allows you to gain real-world experience; learn to work effectively in group settings and build professional connections, while at the same time making an impact in the world around you. Course concepts become more valuable as you find connections between what you are learning in class and issues in your community. The following are some tips and recommendations for beginning service-learning and getting the most out of your service experience:

- Even if you have not been offered service-learning as an assignment, if you are interested in pursuing this approach, talk to professors about the possibility of doing alternative assignments. You never know until you ask!
- Find ways to incorporate service-learning into collaborative assignments you already have to do. For example, if you are assigned a research paper, find ways to make your research about a community issue and partner with a community organization.
- Always take your service-learning collaboration seriously. You are working directly with a community organization on an issue that is important to them.
- This could be a career opportunity for you. Several of my students have been offered internships and jobs as a direct result of their service-learning experience.
- Communicate expectations effectively with your professor and the organization you are collaborating with.
- Service-learning can lead to better letters of recommendation. In my experience as a professor, service-learning has allowed me to work one-on-one with students and write better letters of recommendation through my ability to highlight their successes inside and outside of the classroom.
- Be flexible. It is important to remember that during any type of collaboration things may not always go as planned, and/or people may have different ideas for the direction of the project. Keep an open mind.
- Be patient. Working with a community organization means that things cannot always be planned around strict university timelines. Remember that the organization is working with their own set of deadlines, and may not be familiar with the way time is scheduled at the university.

Recommendations For Community

Partnering with faculty and students on collaborative service-learning assignments can provide your community organization with more than just volunteers. Students bring curiosity and new ideas informed by what they are learning in their classes, and they can apply this knowledge and desire for learning to help with day-to-day tasks, larger projects, and the development of promotional and educational materials for your organization, among other things. I have listed a few tips and recommendations for pursuing service-learning projects with students and faculty as follows:

- If you have a specific need, desire, or goal that you think students may be able to help you with, find and reach out to faculty members who teach in these areas. Some universities have centers for community engagement and service-learning that can help connect you with interested faculty, but if you are not able to find such a center, you can browse faculty profiles to look for their areas of interest and courses they teach.
- If time allows, play an active role in the course. Coming to meetings, brainstorming sessions, and other events can solidify relationships with faculty and students, and help ensure that everyone is on the same page.
- Communicate expectations effectively with the faculty member and students you are collaborating with. Don't be afraid to specify exactly what you are looking for out of the collaboration, or voice concerns when expectations are not being met.
- Be flexible. It is important to remember that during any type of collaboration things may not always go as planned, and/or people may have different ideas for the direction of the project. Keep an open mind.
- Be patient. Working with students means that they are sometimes held to strict university timelines in addition to jobs and other extracurricular activities.

Selected Resources

At the end of each service-learning collaborative assignment I offer students an in-class session to facilitate their reflection on the experience. During this session, I guide discussions using liberating structures such as *9 Whys* and *Fishbowl*.

9 Whys

Students pair up and take turns interviewing one another about their service-learning experiences. The first student will ask a question such as "why did you pick . . . as your service-learning site?" and follow-up with some version of a *why* question after each response. The students then switch roles. The purpose of this activity is to uncover deeply held reasons for choosing to engage with communities in particular ways, and pushes students to reflect deeply on the ways their service impacts the community.

Fishbowl

After completing the *9 Whys* activity, I ask students to participate in a *Fishbowl*. Three to seven chairs are placed in the middle of the room, and these "fish" serve as representatives of the course, discussing their experiences with service-learning as a collaborative assignment while the other students look on. The rest of the class may choose to observe, ask questions, make comments, or join the fishbowl themselves. Through this activity, students are able to build off of the experiences of one another, and make stronger connections between their collaborative service-learning projects and course material.

For more information on this, and other liberating structures please see: http://www.liberatingstructures.com/

Conclusion

Service-learning as a collaborative assignment or project is a rewarding experience for students, faculty, and community organizations alike. To ensure the success of this experience, it is important to plan with intention and communicate expectations effectively. Using service-learning as an approach to collaborative assignments offers students a richer understanding of course content through experience, which can lead to life-long learning. When service-learning is truly community-centered, it offers greater opportunities for reciprocity. Students are able to apply what they are learning in class to meet the needs, goals, and desires of their community organization. This chapter has shared just a few ideas and examples, but there are an unlimited number of ways to use service-learning for collaborative assignments.

Note

For more information on how I designed and implemented service-learning as a research project at the graduate level, as well as the differences in obtaining IRB approval in advance vs. conducting research strictly for class and community purposes, please see my chapter in *Community Engagement Best Practices Across the Disciplines: Applying Course Content to Community Needs* edited by Heather K. Evans.

Upton, S., & Bravo, B. (2017). Teaching research for a greater purpose: Incorporating community engagement into a Graduate Qualitative Research Methods Course. In. H. Evans (Ed.), *Community engagement across the disciplines: Applying course content to community needs.* Lanham, MA: Rowman & Littlefield.

Feel free to contact me at smupton@utep.edu for more information about how I designed these projects, example syllabi, or other questions.

Communications

Chapter 3

Entering Students Practicing Social Justice and Activism through Research, Service Learning, and Documentary Film Making

DeAnna Kay Varela

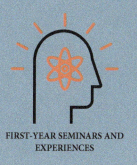

FIRST-YEAR SEMINARS AND
EXPERIENCES

SERVICE LEARNING,
COMMUNITY-BASED LEARNING

Use these questions to guide your reflection prior to reading the chapter. Use the notes/follow-up section to write your thoughts after you have read the chapter. Your notes can include thoughts in reference to the reflection questions, or general observations about the chapter.

1) What experiences were most meaningful to you in your first year of college?

2) Were these experiences organized by the university or college, or were these informal experiences?

3) What does Social Justice mean to you?

4) How can developing documentaries and utilizing film making serve the community or the public good?

Notes/Follow-up:

_____

_____

_____

_____

_____

Introduction

I am a high-school dropout. Announcing this on the first day of class surely gets my student's attention. And it's true; I struggled as a teenager coming from a home surrounded by violence and poverty. These struggles are what motivated me to get an education. First, I earned my General Education Diploma and then pursued a BA in Psychology and Spanish. In addition, as an undergrad, I volunteered with the Big Brother Big Sister program of Central Texas as a mentor. After I earned my BA and returned home, I was a substitute teacher until I was hired full time as a case manager, and eventually interim director, to help establish the first Big Brother Big Sister of El Paso chapter. I later completed an MA in Communication, with an additional certificate in Women & Gender Studies. Today, I am a lecturer with The Entering Student Program at The University of Texas at El Paso. The experiences that led me to earning my current position have not been forgotten and are integral to how I teach and interact with my students. I know that a student's first-year experience (FYE) will similarly shape their perception of education and their ability to succeed in it.

The first-year program I teach in "focuses on assisting entering first-year and transfer students with their successful transition" into the university by offering a core curriculum course entitled "Seminar in Critical Inquiry" (Entering Student Program, 2017). This is also known as University Studies [UNIV]—an interdisciplinary seminar using various academic and professional themes proposed and taught by faculty in order to achieve UNIV learning outcomes. Along with the goals and objectives set forth in this seminar, I believe it is important to bridge the first-year experience between academics, professional preparation, and civic engagement. There is little doubt that my early educational and community experiences are what have influenced my passion for education, social justice, and activism—and inspired me to connect my teaching to the community through service-learning.

Contributed by DeAnna Kay Varela. © Kendall Hunt Publishing Company.

Case Study: Integrating Service-Learning into the First-Year Experience

The overall success of a formalized, FYE curriculum in higher education has been studied since the late 1980s, particularly reflected by positive student retention and degree completion rates. The University of South Carolina–Columbia, for example, found that students "who participated in their first-year seminar between 1973 and 1996 were more likely to persist into their sophomore year than students who did not participate in the seminar" (Goodman & Pascarella, 2016). In addition, Pascarella and Terenzini (2005) stated that those who participated in a FYE course had "statistically significant and substantial, positive effects on a student's successful transition to college and the likelihood of persistence into the second year, as well as on academic performance while in college and on a considerable array of other college experiences known to be related directly and indirectly to bachelor's degree completion" (p. 403).

The FYE program at my institution is similarly structured to facilitate skills and values inherent to student success, such as leadership, academic, and transitional strategies necessary for success in their academic, career, and life goals, research and critical thinking skills, and engagement in campus and community activities. UNIV 1301 seminar classes deliver the core curriculum for the FYE program. These classes are designed to increase student–instructor interactions to provide a more personal learning experience and foster student participation in other high-impact practices such as learning communities, undergraduate research, diversity/global learning, capstone courses and projects, internships, and service-learning/community-based learning.

Students in my class are achieving the learning outcomes set forth by the FYE program by combining a themed course, in this case, *Social Justice and Activism,* with 20 service-learning hours. Scholarly texts and short pieces of media over select movements are organized into modules for the course. For each module, students prepare a guided written response to the material covered. This includes the main idea of the reading or media, a question that they have about the movement or issues involved, and a personal connection that they can make to better understand key systems of power and oppression within social institutions. Through this assignment, students are also asked during discussion to make connections with how service-learning can be a form of equity-building, activism, and justice. Students are paired with organizations that connect to the concepts and areas of inquiry discussed in the course, such as their understanding of gender, race, class, sexuality, ability, and culture. By combining service-learning into the FYE of my students, they are more exposed to academic skills (such as research, writing, and critical analysis), technical skills (such as online research, academic blogging, film making, storyboarding, scripting and editing), as well as professional development skills (such as time management, communication, personal responsibility, working with others, work–life balance, leadership skills, and conflict management) in an immersive, active learning environment. Kuh (2008) has argued that the highest-quality FYEs place a strong emphasis on critical inquiry, frequent writing, information literacy, collaborative learning, and other skills that develop students' intellectual and practical competencies, particularly when high-impact areas are combined.

My courses are designed to include this service-learning component, because this "enables students to achieve learning goals, engages students in active learning, integrates disciplinary theory and knowledge with practice, deepens understanding of the complex causes of social problems, and creates new knowledge" (Howard, 2001). First-year students have many opportunities in the UNIV seminar to succeed as active learners because they get practice in being *active citizens* through service-learning. It is important for students to apply what they learn in the classroom in a community setting because this provides a chance to put concepts and theory into practice in a safe environment. For many students, this is the first time they are exposed to ideas and voices less known in mainstream education, as found in, for example, the Women's, Chicana, Environmental, or Animal Rights movements. They are able to see firsthand the underlying history and issues of the people or ideas that service-learning sites are addressing in the community. As a student and participant of a mentored and guided experience, this helps bridge the academic and professional environments. It offers work experience earlier in their college career, which may help provide internships and jobs in their junior or senior years, gives them experiences and insight into professional settings that they may have not known before, helps them to build a resume, as well as helps students discover what they are truly passionate about. They also have behind-the-scene access to how organizations function, have the opportunity to practice their interpersonal communication skills, network with stakeholders in areas of their professional interest, and can become part of community solutions.

Service-Learning Success

Several students from courses I have taught have been offered internships and/or jobs with some of the organizations they served with. Other students have been inspired to earn graduate degrees to become educators themselves or work in sectors connected with social justice such as the Democratic National Committee in Washington, DC. I have even had students start their own successful nonprofit organizations and campaigns including *West Fund*, which is a nonprofit organization assisting with reproductive justice in the El Paso area. Another student who relocated to San Diego, California started *Music Life Change,* a creative agency that cultivates social revolutions through the influence of music. These are just a few of my students who have gone on to be very successful.

Participating in service-learning and courses surrounding social justice issues gave them an early start to learning, exploring, and practicing skills in their academic career. In six-course sections, over three semesters, students have completed an estimated 2,700 service-learning hours to the community. The impact that this has had goes beyond the grade they receive in the class. Some of them choose to continue volunteering at their site after the course has ended, and as previously mentioned, some students go on to work for the organization. This is the result, in part, because service-learning projects contribute to meaningful, life-long learning, and allow students to be part of something bigger than themselves.

Service-Learning Challenges

Incorporating service-learning into the FYE offers many positive outcomes for students, but it does come with some challenges. Service-learning takes a lot of faculty planning before, during, and after implementation. This begins with designing and planning how the learning outcomes are connected to service-learning in the first-year classroom, and how these goals will be accomplished and assessed. Next, it is necessary to build a team by establishing relationships with community partners or campus resources to coordinate service projects, hours, and expectations for everyone involved. Lastly, students must be matched with a site that meets the needs of the course requirements and their personal interests. Even with good planning, things do not always go smoothly, and adjustments have to be made. This can cause some frustration for faculty, staff, students, as well as the community partners.

Time management and student commitment are also challenges. Balancing coursework, college activities such as involvement in athletics or other extracurricular activities, personal responsibilities, or student employment can make it difficult for a student to schedule in service-learning hours. In addition, some students are resistant to being in the UNIV seminar as a required course. By adding in the requirement of 20 service-learning hours impacts the challenge of being committed to the course and service-learning. However, in my experience, by clearly disseminating the process of service-learning, having open, clear communication with students, and being flexible to issues of time management, some of these challenges can be overcome. As long as the service-learning opportunity is scaffolded and integrated into the learning of the class, and not used as an "addition" to the course, students will be able to see the value of service-learning, and not as a separate, extraneous component to the class.

For example, my class demonstrates this integration through a final project about the student's service-learning experience. There are three components:

1. Completing 20 service-earning hours at a community site.
2. Writing a literature review on a topic related to the course theme and the mission of the service-learning site.
3. Creating a mini-documentary that communicates the service-learning and research visually to demonstrate what a student has learned.

While the literature review gives students practice in research, critical thinking, writing, and further connection of theory and methodology in relation to social justice and activism, the student's documentary film serves as a tool for reflection, representation, and assessment of each student's learning experience. This final project allows students to apply course materials and lessons to the real world and develop practical life skills and knowledge.

My first step in facilitating student success for this final project was to design and plan around the goals and objectives of the UNIV seminar. This included course materials, assignments, activities, assessment and reflection tools, and building a student-centered support team for the final project. At my institution, the FYE program assigns a peer leader, librarian, and academic advisor to all UNIV 1301 courses. Peer leaders assist in and out of the classroom throughout the semester in a mentorship role, day-to-day course-related tasks, and general support. The assigned librarian assists students in learning about credible research and where to find sources. Next, I built a resource team to support the work in the class.

Students utilize resources such as the university writing center, which is available for students to have their work reviewed before submitting it in class. The service-learning coordinating structure also has well-established community partnerships and an easy-to-use service-learning management system. They provide training, track hours, assist students when choosing a service-learning site, as well as conduct a reflection session at the end of the semester. It is also important to have technological support—for students to have workstations and staff to help troubleshoot when there are issues with the video-editing process or software students use to produce their mini-documentaries. These are all campus resources to connect with and direct students to utilize.

Once my team is in place, I coordinate training and workshop dates with these campus resources. Lessons and detailed directions covering service-learning, the literature review, and filmmaking are given in class before training. Once directions, training, and lessons are given, checkpoints for the final project are broken down into manageable steps for completion. Here is a visual representation of this process (Figure 1) Service-learning Integration Steps

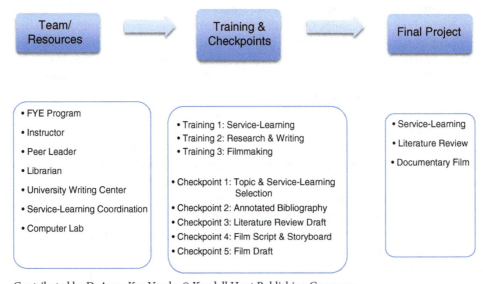

Contributed by DeAnna Kay Varela. © Kendall Hunt Publishing Company.

Figure 1 Service-learning Integration Steps

Students are allowed to complete the literature review and film portions of the final project individually, with a partner, or in a group of three. This allows students to share the workload, practice teamwork, time management, personal responsibility, and communication skills. The part of the final project that cannot be shared is the service-learning hours. Each student must complete their own 20 hours at their chosen site. This allows each student the opportunity for a full service-learning experience. Students may group together based on the sites they work with and/or the topic they wish to research. For example, if students wish to research the importance of mentoring and three students are completing hours with a local Boys and Girls Club of El Paso they may form a group, complete the checkpoints, literature review, and film together, but will each being responsible for completing the 20 service-learning hours.

Student progress is assessed at each checkpoint with clear, straightforward rubric. Feedback and guidance is provided to allow the student opportunity for planning, understanding, as well as making necessary edits towards the final project. The final literature review, service-learning, and film each have their own rubrics, and all three must be completed in order to receive a grade for the final project as a whole. It is important to have very detailed directions and rubrics so that students know what the expectations are up front and can refer back to them as needed. Having students report out, present, or prepare a creative representation of their work and experiences based on their service-learning will help them to communicate the connections they've made through this method of active learning. By using various assessment tools and a reflection exercise, faculty will be able to establish student's educational, intellectual, and emotional outcomes.

This project can be incorporated into other disciplines and courses to fit the needs of the students. For example, the research piece could be an informative report, an augmentative paper, or a more formal study. The service-learning hours can be done with one community partner, on campus, such as institution-based days of service, new student orientation activities, or an institutionally organized service project. The amount of service-learning can be modified to fit the course structure and educational needs. Lastly, the technology piece can be substituted with other multimedia projects such as a podcast, an e-portfolio, or student-created website. The possibilities for incorporating service-learning are many and can be modified to the needs of the students, course, and discipline.

Recommendations for Faculty

Faculty who want to incorporate service-learning should start planning early—take time to gather information, contacts, and resources on and off campus. Once you have these in place, the details of how service-learning will work for your students can be defined. It's important to schedule any training, workshops, presentations, and reflection sessions before the semester begins, so that facilitation of the service-learning may run as smoothly as possible over the course of the semester.

When incorporating service-learning into a course, it is important to be patient and flexible. Assignments, due dates, training dates, community sites, etc., may change. Working with others takes a lot of coordination, but it is helpful to have a good understanding of what each part of a team contributes and what kind of backup plan may be needed to facilitate the project when hiccups occur. One semester, for example, I had a small group of students, who due to schedule and work issues, were not able to attend presentations that provided the foundational information needed for this service-learning integration.

As faculty, we need to anticipate issues like this. I, therefore, strongly recommend utilizing your institution's learning management system to create and provide online modules students are able to access on their own time, with all the context and information needed. Having online support enables students to utilize the technology they typically have and use frequently, such as their mobile devices, so that your classroom extends beyond the building—much like service-learning.

Recommendations for Students

My main recommendations for students pertain to time management, being present, and being open to new ways of thinking and experiences, not only in relation to service-learning, but also to college in general. One of the most pressing challenges students face as entering students is time management. There are simple and creative ways to address this. One is to have an academic planner to refer to during the course of the year. I also recommend students refer to the course syllabus and calendar regularly to stay on top of things. Lastly, if given a large assignment, such as this final service-learning project, it is best to break it down into manageable pieces with self-imposed deadlines (if they are not already given). Creating and practicing time management early on makes a big impact on student success.

Attendance and participation are also instrumental to success. Showing up for class whether it is face-to-face or an online course matters. Being present should not be mistaken for simply sitting in class—it is participating mentally, emotionally, and vocally as an active learner. Students need every opportunity to hear, see, and take ownership in their education, so being "present" is a must.

Lastly, students should be open to new ways of thinking and experiences. Entering students will be introduced to new ideas, teaching methods, ways of learning, and opportunities they may not have experienced before. It is important to be open-minded, willing to learn, and to think critically about topics, ideas, and even people who may be different. Growth comes from going outside of one's comfort zone.

Recommendations for Community

Service-learning is a fantastic opportunity for the community to have access to the emerging talent at the university. You have the chance to mentor young people and possibly even prepare them for future positions in their own organization. When working with college students who have little to no work experience, I recommend that there be clear guidelines as to what the student will do at the organization, who will supervise them, and how their work will be evaluated. Their duties should be meaningful, educational, and focused on the mission and values of the community organization. Providing consistent, positive guidance and feedback will help students work at their highest potential and make the most of their time during the experience.

Community partners should keep in mind that the students will be sharing their service-learning experience with their professors, peers, family, friends, service-learning coordinating services, and possibly public venues such as conferences. These are terrific opportunities to bring awareness to the organization's purpose, secure future volunteers, and possibly even financial support.

Conclusion

Service-learning in the FYE has been shown to be a high-impact practice with benefits linked to student success including retention and graduation, developing academic, personal, and professional skills, and meaningful learning and citizenship. With careful planning, seeking out campus and community partners, and engaging students through active learning methods, these high-impact practices can be incorporated into courses across the disciplines.

I have had several students and even peer leaders from my program share their experiences, personal growth, and professional success in relation to what they have learned in my courses. The pursuit of social justice through education and service-learning continues to inspire me to grow as an instructor and individual. As a high-school dropout, I never imagined how far I would go with higher education or as an activist. I am truly inspired and humbled by my students' work within the classroom and beyond.

Resources

The following are recommended readings, websites, and student sample films for review.

Readings

Dolgon, C., Mitchell, T. D., & Eatman, T. K. (Eds.). (2017). *The Cambridge Handbook of Service Learning and Community Engagement.* New York, NY: Cambridge University Press.

Websites

National Resource Center for First-Year Experience and Students in Transition. Retrieved from http://www.sc.edu/fye/

The Entering Student Program. Retrieved from http://academics.utep.edu/Default.aspx?alias=academics.utep.edu/esp

Center for Civic Engagement. Retrieved from http://academics.utep.edu/Default.aspx?alias=academics.utep.edu/cce

Student Film Samples

Arts Education and Creative Kids by Naomi Ingram. Retrieved from https://www.youtube.com/watch?v=y6ahfr6IWgg&t=2s

Educational Disparities Among Different Racial Groups by William Chapa. Retrieved from https://www.youtube.com/watch?v=KdEhNQR5l0c&t=188s

Activism by Charles Corner. Retrieved from https://vimeo.com/112427619

References

Entering Student Program. (2017, March 5). Retrieved from http://academics.utep.edu/Default.aspx?alias=academics.utep.edu/esp

Goodman, K., & Pascarella, E. T. (2006) First-year seminars increase persistence and retention: A summary of the evidence from how college affects students. *Peer Review Summer, 8*(3), 26–28.

Howard, J. (2001). *Service-learning course design workbook.* Ann Arbor, MI: OCSL Press.

Kuh, G. D. (2008). *High-impact educational practices: What they are, who has access to them, and why they matter* (p. 34). Washington, DC: AAC&U.

Pascarella, E. T., & Terenzini, P. T. (2005). *How college affects students. Volume 2: A third decade of research.* San Francisco, CA: Jossey-Bass.

Education

Chapter 4

Collaboration Creation of an Air Quality Curriculum That Promotes Community Based Learning

Elaine Hampton, Cynthia Ontiveros, Amy Canales, Monica Chavez, Manuel Pina Jr., W.L. Hargrove, Wen-Whai Li, Susan Brown, Bora Simmons, and Jennifer M. Lujan

SERVICE LEARNING,
COMMUNITY-BASED LEARNING

COLLABORATIVE
ASSIGNMENTS AND PROJECTS

Pre-Reading Reflection Questions

Chapter 4

Use these questions to guide your reflection prior to reading the chapter. Use the notes/follow-up section to write your thoughts after you have read the chapter. Your notes can include thoughts in reference to the reflection questions, or general observations about the chapter.

1) Who do you know or think designs and decides what is taught in a k-12 classroom?

2) What comes to mind when you think of "air quality"?

3) Is there a role to play by all individuals when it comes to air quality? If so, what is that role?

Notes/Follow-up:

____

____

____

____

____

Introduction

With funding from the U.S. Environmental Protection Agency, the University of Texas at El Paso's (UTEP) Center for Environmental Research Management established a US–Mexico border environmental education partnership entitled *Buen Ambiente-Buena Salud*, (*Good Environment-Good Health*) focusing on air quality, environmental health, and environmental justice. The partnership included UTEP, a leading Hispanic-Serving Institution located on the border, and, as principal partner, the El Paso Independent School District (EPISD), a metropolitan school district serving over 60,000 students. The partnership also involved the YWCA El Paso del Norte, state and national leaders in environmental education, and government and private sector partners, all committed to education and outreach aimed at improving air quality on the border. The long-term goal of the program was to train and retain border-area professionals to address air quality issues and impacts in the border region.

This chapter provides an overview of one major goal of this project, the development of an environmental science curriculum about local air pollution issues, environmental health, and environmental justice. EPISD teachers who led successful science programs (master teachers) teamed with UTEP faculty to design the curriculum. The curriculum design also allowed students in the district to implement service learning projects in their community.

The curriculum design was founded in the problem-based approach to learning defined by the environmental education community's *Guidelines for Learning* (North American Association for Environmental Education, 2010). These best practices include teaching across disciplines to prepare well-informed citizens to confront integrated social and environmental issues. In this approach, the learner and teacher are active participants in acquiring environmental knowledge and skills and then applying them. The learning begins at home and in the community, where local relevance intersects active and meaningful learning through investigation, problem-solving, and critical thinking. With such place-based learning (learning that is relevant to the local community), students are more interested in the educational experiences and are eventually more prepared to become life-long learners and responsible environmental citizens.

Contributed by Elaine Hampton, Cynthia Ontiveros, Amy Canales, Monica Chavez, Manuel Piña Jr., W.L. Hargrove, Wen-Whai Li, Susan Brown, Bora Simmons, and Jennifer M. Lujan. © Kendall Hunt Publishing Company.

Case Study

Brief History of this High Impact Practice

Two detrimental gaps affect quality of education in public schools: 1) the gap that exists between teacher professional development programs at the university level *and* the teachers' needs for immediate and practical approaches, and 2) the gap that exists between the border communities' needs to understand its environmental setting and how to interact in a sustainable manner *and* strict curriculum demands that leave little room for learning beyond a set of core content and skills (Hampton, 2004; Valenzuela, 1999).

A strong partnership including UTEP faculty and EPISD administrators, teachers, and students bridged these two gaps through a multiyear, community-based, collaborative learning project. The university and public school participants developed and enjoyed mutual learning experiences as they worked together in curriculum design teams to research best learning practices relevant to the air quality theme. They implemented those best practices and assessed their impact and revised and implemented improved lessons over several iterations of curriculum design. Community involvement was embedded in the curriculum as the EPISD students designed and conducted information sessions and environmental improvement projects in their communities.

The curriculum project was led by the 25 master teachers from EPISD, four district curriculum leaders, two university science and engineering educators, and five university faculty with expertise in environmental sciences. Joining the team were some 3,000 students (grades 3–12), whose experiences with the lessons guided the design and redesign of the curriculum.

In the later part of the project, UTEP students, guided by the Center for Civic Engagement, used components of the curriculum modules to create learning activities for elementary children, which they taught in afterschool programs sponsored by the YWCA.

Collaborative Creation of a District Curriculum

In the first 4 years of the 5-year project, the curriculum teams developed, tested, and implemented ten problem-based, inquiry-rich curriculum units on air quality, environmental health, and environmental justice for grades 3–12. The modules were tested and revised in two cycles, and embedded in the district's curriculum. The leaders in the curriculum division at EPISD were enthusiastic partners, and they designed a model framework of content that was aligned with each grade's state science requirements so that these modules could become components in the teachers' approved curriculum. The process for designing this curriculum framework occurred in the first year and involved selecting appropriate content for each grade level, recruiting master teachers to help in designing, piloting, and disseminating, and aligning with state standards and environmental education's *Guidelines for Learning*.

Writing curriculum is complex, but the wealth of information and lessons available on relevant and reliable environmental education websites made this manageable. A list of some of these resources for environmental education is available at the project website for the Border Air Quality Project, *http:// BAQed.utep.edu*, under the tab for *Support Documents*.

The main steps for creating and implementing the curriculum included the following actions:

1. Scientists and community experts met with teachers to provide overview of important environmental concepts relevant to the border setting.
2. Curriculum writers worked with each grade-level team of teachers to select, modify, or write lesson modules.
3. These teams, in a professional learning setting, analyzed the first pilot and revised as appropriate, implemented the lessons again, analyzed, and revised again, and implemented a third time. This resulted in a reiterative process of improvement.
4. The writing teams evaluated the curriculum modules by examining student products and comparing evidence of learning with the lesson objectives.
5. The curriculum writers worked closely with the web designer to create the freely accessible website where lessons and other support materials are posted.

6. The modules were translated into Spanish and posted on the website.
7. The master teachers trained their colleagues to implement the lessons in the fourth year of the project. The curriculum administrators at the district ensured that the lesson modules were embedded in the district's online curriculum so that all of the teachers now have access to and an understanding of the Border Air Quality Curriculum.
8. Experts reviewed each iteration of the modules and provided quality assurance and suggestions for improvements.
9. The writing teams also created the following support documents, which are available on the website: 1) *Smelter in the City: The American Smelting and Refining Company (ASARCO) Case Study,* which includes the history, lesson plans, and resources for teaching about the large copper smelter and its history of air pollution, and 2) two sets of guidelines, *Ways to Reduce Greenhouse Gas Emissions* and *Activities for Greener Schools,* which assist students in designing activities for civic responsibility.

What Made this High-Impact Practice Successful?

Elements of Success

The expertise of practicing K-12 educators and UTEP faculty guided the project activities to bring the best of both teams to make this high-impact practice successful.

- The purpose and process of the project were created in collaboration between the two institutions who worked as an effective team for the duration of the project.
- The district donated the expertise of their science curriculum leaders (coauthors Ontiveros, Canales, and Chavez) who gave expert guidance about teachers needs and logistics to ensure the collaborative curriculum creation progressed smoothly.
- The iterative review of curriculum was based in formative evaluation and analysis of the quality of the impact of the curriculum drawn from the student's work and responses.
- The content was high interest as it responded to and addressed real-world conditions in the local area.
- Project leader (coauthor Hampton) had extensive education background and experience in environmental curriculum writing and teaching.
- The lessons were designed as discrete modules (about 2 weeks of instruction time) based in a specific air quality content theme. This allowed the lessons to be inserted into broader curriculum and to be useful to the online audience.

Evidence of Success from Positive Outcomes

Because civic responsibility and actionable steps for improving air quality permeated the curriculum, the project resulted in positive environmental actions.

Monitoring air quality in every school: The U.S. Environmental Protection Agency provides information about a world-wide *Air Quality Index* based on a standard measurement of pollutants in the air (more information is available at https://waqi.info/). The interpretation of the index is divided into levels of health concerns. Low levels of pollutants, measuring up to 100 on the index, indicate that the air is relatively clean and those levels are colored on the Air Quality Index chart as green and yellow. Higher levels of pollutants are rated as *Unhealthy for Sensitive Groups, Unhealthy, Very Unhealthy, and Hazardous* and are charted with colors ranging from orange to maroon.

The district administrators provided these Air Quality Index charts to every school. Teachers taught the elementary students how to read the Air Quality Index chart and how to use the website to find the air quality levels for cities across the globe. All students regularly charted ozone alert days for the border area. Third-grade children taught first graders about the Air Quality Index. They became reading buddies sharing the book, *Why is Coco Orange*, a colorful children's book about a chameleon who has asthma (available free at https://www3.epa.gov/airnow/picturebook/cocos-orange-day-web.pdf).

Asthma education: Because asthma and other respiratory problems are exacerbated in the region's dry environment with its many sources of pollution, middle-school students studied causes of asthma, created surveys and interviews to examine rates of asthma, and learned how to avoid air quality problems that pose health risks.

Activities to reduce carbon emissions: Students created and presented public service announcements about reducing carbon emissions. Some schools created no-idle zones and implemented "walking school buses" (an adult accompanies a group of children from a community to walk together to school rather than drive in cars) to reduce pollution around the school campus.

Reduced pollution on military base: Students learning about air pollution led to a significant change to improve air quality at an elementary school located on the Fort Bliss Army Base. During recess one day, third-grade children showed the teacher how black residue in the air, which was generated by military vehicles involved in training exercises, accumulated on the school's fence and other surfaces on the playground. With involvement and support from parents, the teachers brought this to the attention to the school's military liaison who, in turn, brought it to the attention of commanders in charge of the training exercises. Within a few weeks, the exercises were relocated to areas away from the school and rescheduled to avoid school hours.

Environmental science in local history: Teachers in the high schools worked to keep alive an important part of the border-area's environmental history, one of the worst air pollution stories over decades, the ASARCO, a large copper smelter that is now closed. These students measured soil samples for toxins that were evident in the smelter's pollution. In chemistry class, students performed an experiment demonstrating a chemical reaction that separates a metal from a compound, similar to metal smelting, and then examined the leftover chemicals. Some students produced podcasts that explained important aspects of the smelter's history. They worked in teams to find authentic stories from the smelter years and, using the free program, *Audacity*, they produced NPR-style podcasts in Spanish and English and then posted them on their teacher's webpage.

Learning about wind and justice: High school students also learned to use wind direction and wind speed data from air monitoring stations to create a *wind rose*, a historical record of prevailing winds expressed as a vector diagram. The students were not only able to analyze the data but also critically assess it and concluded that wind and pollutants from El Paso go into Ciudad Juárez as well, countering the assertion that the air pollution in El Paso is coming only from Ciudad Juárez, Mexico.

Evidence of Success from External Evaluation

External evaluator, Manuel Piña, Jr.'s evaluation of the program over the 5 years provided data about of the impacts of the curriculum design and implementation. The evaluation provided evidence of a significant increase in interest, participation, and professional growth from the master teachers. These teachers reported growth in 1) the ideas for lessons and activities, 2) raising awareness about the importance of air quality, 3) access to experts on air quality issues and science, 4) working in teams, and 5) curriculum vertical alignment. The master teachers also reported that addressing prevailing social justice issues, enabling their students to have hands-on experiences, doing independent research, and having the liberty to think and act "outside the box" bolstered their ability to train other teachers. Teachers stated that the lessons were particularly valuable for the students because they permitted the students to actively engage in learning, to increase their awareness of environmental issues, and to extend their learning through interaction with their families and communities. One hundred percent of the teachers agreed or strongly agreed that their understanding of teaching through inquiry and/or problem-solving had improved.

The value of embedding local environmental issues into the curriculum and making the curriculum community-based was evident by how teachers responded to the curriculum. Following are six statements made by teachers regarding the value of community-based learning about the impacts of the ASARCO smelter in El Paso.

1. I learned how ASARCO influenced El Paso in so many bad ways. They provided a good economy but at a cost to so many people and the environment.
2. This opened my eyes to how ASARCO affected the city and the environment. I felt responsible for our kids and the future for not caring or not considering the damage on the environment.

3. I noticed right away that as the project progressed my students began to care more and more about their environment. As an educator I want my students to become global citizens and this project is an excellent way to get started. By the time we finished I had people who were willing to learn more to help our city.

4. I will try to implement more local science and history into my lessons.

5. It is projects like this that as an educator we welcome. Something different that makes a personal impact on my students' thought process.

6. Students were able to understand how important and dangerous ASARCO was and how it is an example for how hazardous waste cannot be discarded or neglected. This made me want to mention environmental concerns in all my classes.

The evaluation data also showed evidence that the K-12 students involved in the program acquired a better understanding about the broad aspects of air quality, indicated an interest in learning more about air quality-related careers and air and environmental issues, and had increased knowledge about reducing enery use to reduce air pollution.

The teachers gave high rating to the depth of understanding about curriculum development and content relevant to air quality issues that developed as the teachers and UTEP faculty worked together in a partnership. Teachers learned to look critically at their practice and UTEP faculty learned to respect the constraints that teachers must negotiate. University educators might consider additional ways to partner with teachers to develop relevant lessons for local schools.

What were Some of the Challenges?

This project was, in its conception, designed to overcome some of the large challenges in an educational collaborative—time and money. There was ample time to write and pilot the modules. The teachers were compensated for their contributions. The district provided materials, teacher time, and meeting space. Yet, the teachers still struggled to fit new lessons into the state and district demands for class time. In addition, the 2-week modules do not allow for the desired depth of content knowledge. That was evident as students in elememtary and middle schools had challenges with the finer details of air quality content.

The project advanced toward the goal of educational modules that are steeped in the problem-based approach to learning defined by the environmental education community's *Guidelines for Learning*. However, this level of excellence demands a systemic change where schools and universities rethink and revise constraints such as testing, scheduling, teachers' roles, professional development, and community involvement. This will always be a challenge for future teachers and curriculum developers, but for students who aspire to teach, participating in a process like this will prepare them to exercise leadership to make needed changes in prevailing curricula.

Making this Work in Other Settings

Faculty: The value of a collaboration between the university and a school district is worth the effort of searching for external funding, as long as the planning and the proposal process are conducted in a horizontal collaboration where both sets of participants value and appreciate the other's skills and contributions, and resulting resources from the external funding are shared in collaboration. However, even without external funding, an informal partnership with a school would allow university students to enter local K-12 classrooms to experience teaching in the local setting and to assist local teachers in teaching about important and relevant environmental concepts.

University students can design their own community-learning experiences by collaborating with local K-12 schools. The lessons provided in the BAQed curriculum are easy to teach in a classroom or in an afterschool setting. Visit with a local teacher to see if you might introduce the students to the important realm of air quality education. Be sure to assist the students to take steps to improve their own environmental footprint.

K-12 Educators: As the lessons are readily available on a public website in English and Spanish, educators can take any aspect of the lessons or the support documents and modify these to fit their needs and their situations. The curriculum includes some 40 lessons related to air quality, valuable background information for teachers and students, a list of resources, the ASARCO case study for educators, and various support documents.

Conclusion and Recommendations

The partnership was successful because community engagement was a core of the initial design of the project and was a required component of the learning experiences for the local school children. The project also drew upon place-based learning by developing educational modules that incorporated local air quality issues, local pollution sources, and local environmental justice challenges.

Community engagement is foundational for a sustainable project; be it sustainable environmental practices, sustainable teaching practices; sustainable business practices; or sustainable engineering practices. The community—the people who implement the practices and the people who are impacted by the implementation of the practices—have vast understanding of the context, the history, the needs, and the limitations of any intervention. Curriculum writers, in this setting, worked in equal partnership with the teachers who observed and listened to their students to understand this new approach in an ethic of continual improvement. Good business leaders listen carefully to their employees and incorporate their knowledge into the business's improvement. Good engineers search for information from members of the community that their project will impact and listen carefully to the technical staff who implement the engineering designs. And good educators work closely with their community to improve education from preschool through higher education based on the strengths and constraints in the area. Community engagement in many fields of study allows for projects to be more successful and more sustainable.

The consensus among the scientific community about global warming and escalating changes in climate brings urgency to our educational programs to shift to accommodate environmental understandings. The border region's education system should be the source for emerging national leaders in border-related environmental understandings and civic actions to protect our air, land, and waters. Including more community collaborations in the K-12 schools, collaborations that lead to learning while doing environmental sciences and environmental health, would help prepare our citizens to address border environmental issues.

Relevant and Useful Resources

Air Quality Index Toolkit for Teachers. U.S. Environmental Protection Agency. Retrieved from https://airnow.gov/index.cfm?action=resources.aqi_toolkit and https://www3.epa.gov/airnow/aqi_brochure_02_14.pdf

Bullard, R. (1994). Overcoming racism in environmental decision making. *Environment*, 36(4), 10–44.

Clark-Reyna, S., Grinesky, S. E., & Collins, T. W. (2016). Residential exposure of air toxics is linked to lower grade point averages among school children in El Paso, Texas. *Population and Environment*, 37(3), 319–340.

Collins, T. (2014). *Bordering authority, circumventing resistance: ASARCO and the search for environmental justice in the Paso del Norte*. Public Political Ecology Lab. Retrieved from http://ppel.arizona.edu/?p=592

Environmental Protection Agency. *Why is Coco Orange?* Retrieved from Airnow website: https://www3.epa.gov/airnow/picturebook/cocos-orange-day-web.pdf

Fischel, A., & Nelson, L. Retrieved from www.theirminesourstories.org

Hampton, E. (2004). Standardized or sterilized? Divergent perspectives on the effects of high-stakes testing in West Texas. In Valenzuela, A. (Ed.), *Leaving children behind: Why Texas-style accountability fails Latino youth* (pp. 179–200). Albany, NY: State University of New York Press.

National Environmental Education Foundation. (2015). *Environmental Literacy in the United States: An Agenda for Leadership in the 21st Century*. Washington, DC: National Environmental Education Foundation.

North American Association for Environmental Education. (2010). *Excellence in Environmental Education: Guidelines for Learning (K-12)*. Washington, DC: North American Association for Environmental Education.

Ontiveros, C. (2015). *Latin@ High School Students' Standpoint on Environmental Justice in a Border Community: A Phenomenological Study* (Doctoral dissertation). Retrieved from Proquest (Document ID 1732168419).

Smelter in the City: The ASARCO Case Study. Retrieved from BAQed.utep.edu under 'Support Documents.'

Valenzuela, A. (1999). *Subtractive schooling: U.S.-Mexican youth and the politics of caring.* New York, NY: State University of New York Press.

Special Appreciation to the EPISD Master Teachers: Katherine Mullane-Erlick, Donna Gray, Jessica Favela-Casillas, Francisco Casillas, Eric Pichardo, John Thomas, Sarah Escandon, Maria Reyna, Sylvia Montoya, Nancy Barraza, Jeanette Cubillos-Dominguez, Teresa Pena, Luis Diaz, Blanche Herrera, Roxanne Ramos, Ronnie Allen, Theresa Turner, Lacey Bustamante, Rosetta Baquera, Summer Steele, Adriana Herrera, Ernesto Herrera, Mariano Silva, and Elizabeth Keith.

Chapter 5

Using a Service-Learning Project to Overcome the Fear of Arthropods and Instill an Awareness of the Sixth Mass Extinction in Future Teachers and Elementary Children

Ron Wagler

SERVICE LEARNING,
COMMUNITY-BASED LEARNING

Pre-Reading Reflection Questions

Use these questions to guide your reflection prior to reading the chapter. Use the notes/follow-up section to write your thoughts after you have read the chapter. Your notes can include thoughts in reference to the reflection questions, or general observations about the chapter.

1) From the title of this chapter, what do you think it is about?

2) What issues or commonly known fears do you believe community engagement might help alleviate?

3) What are your assumptions about education when it is tailored for elementary school children?

Notes/Follow-up:

_____

_____

_____

_____

_____

Introduction

As a professor that teaches science education and environmental education courses for future teachers, I find myself in an interesting time in Earth's history. We are in the midst of a mass extinction. Mass extinctions are characterized by an enormous loss of life in a relatively short period of time (Wagler, 2012). The last time humans lived in the midst of a mass extinction was . . . well . . . never. The last mass extinction happened approximately 65 million years ago and humans were obviously not there to witness it. In the past, there have been five mass extinctions. Because of this, the current mass extinction is often referred to as the Sixth Mass Extinction. The Sixth Mass Extinction is defined as an ongoing current event where a large number of living species are threatened with extinction or are going extinct because of the environmentally destructive activities of humans (Wagler, 2016). Now we find ourselves in the midst of the Sixth Mass Extinction, and unlike the five-pass mass extinctions, we are the ones causing this mass extinction. From an educational standpoint, the Sixth Mass Extinction provides the best way for people to *fully* understand the environmental impact we are having on Earth because it encompasses *all* of the major human activities driving global environmental degradation. These large-scale global human activities are the spread of invasive species and genes; over-exploitation of species; habitat modification, fragmentation and destruction; pollution and climate change (Wagler, 2011a, 2011b, 2012, 2013, 2016, 2017).

Sadly, the Sixth Mass Extinction has received little media coverage. The vast majority of people I encounter are unaware that we are in the midst of a mass extinction, and they are often equally surprised to find out that we are causing it. As an environmental educator I believe that education can play a role in reducing the impact humans are having on nature. I also feel a strong sense of responsibility to educate the next generation of teachers and children about the ongoing mass extinction with the hope that humanity can live a sustainable existence in the future. The importance of educating future generations about this topic cannot be overemphasized as the very fate of humanity and Earth's ecosystems may very well hang in the balance. This chapter explains a very unique service-learning project (Kuh, 2008) that used an unlikely group of animals, living arthropods (i.e., bugs), as a vehicle to attempt to instill an awareness of the Sixth Mass Extinction in both future teachers and elementary school children. Figure 1 shows one of the many species of captive-bred living arthropods that were used in the service-learning project.

Contributed by Ron Wagler. © Kendall Hunt Publishing Company.

Contributed by Ron Wagler © Kendall Hunt Publishing Company.

Figure 1   A Captive-Bred *Damon diadema* (Tanzanian Amblypygid) with Her Young on Her Abdomen

Case Study

A Description of the Service Learning Project

This service-learning project involved the living arthropods from my university laboratory (see example species in Figure 1), the local zoo, local elementary school children, and my university undergraduate students (i.e., future elementary school teachers). All of the living arthropods used in the project were captive-bred as to not remove further species from their already fragile ecosystems, and some of the captive-bred living arthropods were Critically Endangered or Extinct in the Wild. The project began in my university course "Science Teaching in the Elementary School," which has a strong focus on developing effective inquiry-based science activities for elementary school children. The university students that were enrolled in my course were preparing to be elementary school teachers and none of them had ever taught science before. We began the semester by performing Sixth Mass Extinction activities together that educated my university students about the Sixth Mass Extinction and the science pedagogy techniques they would need to effectively teach concepts associated with the Sixth Mass Extinction to elementary school children. Please see the Appendix for these resources. These activities were, at first, purposefully very simple but progressively became more complex so that I could instill a sense of confidence in my students that they could effectively teach science to elementary school children. My unpublished research shows that my students enter my course and, because of their past experiences with learning science, do not enjoy science. I have found that if we can perform and develop age-appropriate elementary school level science activities together in a positive "safe" environment, where they receive frequent constructive feedback from their peers and their professor, their level of science teaching confidence increases, they enjoy science, they enjoy teaching science, and they become effective at teaching science.

After this phase of the project, my students, again under my guidance, developed Sixth Mass Extinction science activities that utilized the living arthropods from my university laboratory. All of the activities had a component that showed how the arthropods were essential to nature, allowed the elementary school children to intact with the living arthropods, incorporated concepts about the Sixth Mass Extinction, and taught actions they and others could take to reduce their impact on Earth. Once the activities were developed, the students taught them to one another. All of the activities were then critiqued by the students and me. Based on these recommendations, the activities were modified and improved. During this time, my university students and I also met with people at the local zoo to see if it was possible to teach the activities they were developing at the zoo. A series of logistic meetings occurred where we developed a plan that allowed my students to teach the activities at the zoo throughout the semester. Once my students were ready to teach their activities, we went to the zoo and they taught their activities to local elementary school children that had come to the zoo. Throughout the semester, I also conducted ongoing "debriefing and brainstorming sessions" in my university elementary school science education course, where we addressed any ongoing problems with the service-learning project, developed ways to solve these problems, talked about ongoing positive outcomes associated with the project, and reviewed what we would be doing in the next phase of the service-learning project.

The Success of the Service-Learning Project

The service-learning project was a very successful venture between the university and the zoo. Both groups wanted to cooperatively develop an innovative way to teach environmental concepts to the two groups of students we worked with. We also wanted to develop a service-learning project that would allow both groups to learn from one another by interacting together. My university students, as future teachers, learned from the elementary school children because they developed and taught age-appropriate environmental education activities to children that simultaneously educated them about the Sixth Mass Extinction. These teaching events gave them real-world experiences before they had even stepped foot into an elementary school classroom. Likewise, the elementary school children at the zoo learned from my university students by becoming aware of the Sixth Mass Extinction and ways they could reduce their impact on Earth. My university students and the elementary school children both commented on how the service-learning project was an enjoyable experience.

As an environmental educator, I also wanted to assess the service-learning project from a research perspective. Both of the participating groups of the service-learning project, my university students and the elementary school children, were assessed before the service-learning project began and after the service-learning project was completed. Before the service-learning project began, both groups had very high levels of fear toward most arthropods and had no desire to save arthropods (e.g., spiders and roaches) that are on the edge of extinction due to the environmentally destructive activities of humans. Both groups also had minimal awareness of the Sixth Mass Extinction. Most had moderate-to-minimal awareness of effective actions they and others could take to reduce their impact on Earth. After my university students taught their activities to the children, both groups showed changes in these areas. Both groups now displayed much lower levels of fear toward arthropods and now possessed a much stronger desire to save the arthropods that are on the edge of extinction. Both groups also displayed a much stronger awareness of the Sixth Mass Extinction. Lastly, the participants in both groups showed a greater awareness of actions they and others could take to reduce their impact on Earth.

The Challenges of the Service-Learning Project

The challenges of the service-learning project were minimal. All of the groups involved were glad to work together because we shared a common goal that we believed could be reached in an innovative, exciting, and fun way. With any service-learning project that has multiple groups involved, as in the service-learning project described here, quick communication to deal with small logistical issues is important. We found one of the best ways to address these small issues and keep the project running smoothly was to have frequent face-to-face meetings, phone calls, and online communication as needed.

When I develop service-learning projects that focus on the Sixth Mass Extinction, the biggest challenge I have faced is skepticism or unbelief from adults (associated with the project) that do not believe the Sixth Mass Extinction is occurring, or do not believe we are causing the Sixth Mass Extinction, or do not believe certain aspects of the Sixth Mass Extinction, such as human-induced climate change, are real. These adults can be community partners, my adult students, or parents of children involved in the service-learning project. In my experiences with talking to many children about the Sixth Mass Extinction, I have not encountered children that have these beliefs. The children I talk to are often very excited to learn about the Sixth Mass Extinction but at the same time are very vocal once they learn what we are doing to Earth. It is common for them to tell me that it is "wrong what we are doing" and "we need to do something right now" to fix the problem! This often leads to discussions with the children on things they can do to reduce their impact on Earth.

Integrating the Sixth Mass Extinction into Other Service-Learning Projects

Even though this service-learning project occurred in a specific university course with future teachers and used living arthropods as a vehicle to convey the current mass extinction, the Sixth Mass Extinction theme can be used by any educator in any service-learning project that occurs in any educational setting. The Sixth Mass Extinction will increasingly impact many areas of humanity, so there is the potential to integrate the Sixth Mass Extinction theme into other disciplines beyond science. For example, the Sixth Mass Extinction theme can be easily integrated into the arts, engineering, the humanities, mathematics, political sciences, or multicultural studies service-learning projects and could occur in public or private schools, museums, science centers, nature centers, community centers, or anywhere the community gathers.

Recommendations for Faculty

As a university faculty member you may or may not (depending on your area of expertise) be knowledgeable about the Sixth Mass Extinction and the science pedagogy techniques you will need to effectively integrate the Sixth Mass Extinction theme into your service-learning project. Use the Sixth Mass Extinction resources that are provided in the Appendix to educate yourself and your university students about the Sixth Mass Extinction. This wealth of resources will provide you and your students with the science content and pedagogy knowledge you will need to effectively integrate the Sixth Mass Extinction theme into your existing service-learning project. If you would like to fully implement the service-learning project I conducted instead of just integrating the Sixth Mass Extinction theme into your existing service-learning project and you do not have access to living arthropods, consider purchasing captive-bred species online. If you do not have funds to purchase living arthropods, contact a local nature center, local zoo, or a colleague at your university or another university and see if you can have some of their excess captive-bred living arthropods. Please contact me for a full list of the captive-bred arthropods used in this service-learning project, free care guides for captive-bred living arthropods, and my free curriculum that integrates captive-bred living arthropods and the Sixth Mass Extinction.

During my first class period with my university students, I introduced the Sixth Mass Extinction service-learning project that we would be doing during the semester and I had a very small number of students that did not want to participate in the service-learning project because they did not believe that the Sixth Mass Extinction was occurring or that it was human-induced. I talked to these students individually and asked them if they would be willing to participate in the initial activities and they agreed. Based on my interaction with these students, it became apparent to me that their initial level of scientific literacy associated with basic ecological processes, such as a food chain, was very low. As they participated in the initial activities, I noticed a change in their attitude toward the science behind the Sixth Mass Extinction and eventually many of these students asked if they could participate in the service-learning project because they began to believe that humans *may* be causing the Sixth Mass Extinction. I recommend that if you have students that do not want to participate in the Sixth Mass Extinction service-learning project, ask them if they would be willing to participate in the initial activities. If they will not agree, then I would recommend that you provide an alternative assignment of equal effort. I would have them work on this assignment during class time with the other students that are working on the Sixth Mass Extinction service-learning project. The group interaction that occurs between the students working on the Sixth Mass Extinction service-learning project and those working on the alternate assignment has also been instrumental in students choosing to participate in the service-learning project. I would not recommend engaging the student and attempting to explain the scientific research associated with the Sixth Mass Extinction with the hope that this will change the students' mind. This, in my experience, is a very ineffective way to convince the student for participation in the service-learning project. Please do not force students to participate in the service-learning project if they have no desire to participate.

I also strongly recommend that you include your university students (or a small representative group of your students) at the initial and ongoing planning meetings that will occur with your community partner. I invited my students, and their feedback and ideas during these meetings was very insightful, and ultimately their ideas made the service-learning project better. I also found that their collective level of creativity was often greater than mine, and they brought a fresh perspective to the discussions that occurred during the meetings. Lastly, I would strongly suggest that you conduct ongoing "debriefing and brainstorming sessions" with your university students. These sessions were fundamental in keeping the service-learning project running smoothly and provided a place where my students could reflect on their service experience. Lastly, as a university professor, it is always important to maintain open lines of communication with your university students and your community partners throughout the service-learning project.

Recommendations for Students

As a student, the idea of your professor informing you that you will be doing a service-learning project can be stressful. I understand your concern. It just seems like one more assignment in an already very busy and full semester. Yes, it can be a lot of work but the rewards are great. The positive real-world experiences you will have and the long-lasting community friendships you will make have the potential to enrich your life and career far more than any in-class assignment ever will. That is not to say that as a university student participating in a service-learning project, everything will go smoothly all of the time. There may be times when you find the project difficult, and I would encourage you to communicate with your professor and your peers frequently so that as problems arise they can be dealt with quickly.

Your professor will be conducting initial and ongoing meetings with your community partners that you will be working with on the service-learning project. You will be invited to these meetings, and I would encourage you to freely share your ideas about how the service-learning project should be conducted and your concerns about problems that may arise. You provide a fresh perspective that is valued and important to the success of the service-learning project. Often, as a professor, I have a very definitive idea about how I am going to conduct a service-learning project, and by listening to my student's ideas, the service-learning project takes on a new and innovative approach that I would not have developed on my own. Your professor will also be conducting ongoing "debriefing and brainstorming sessions" in your university course. These sessions also provide you with an opportunity to bring fresh ideas to the service-learning project and make the project more successful. These sessions will also provide an opportunity for you to reflect on your service-learning experience. Do not be afraid to share your ideas with your professor. Your professor values your ideas and wants to maintain open communication with you and everyone involved in the service-learning project.

Recommendations for Community Partners

As a community partner, you may have been approached by a university faculty member or you may have approached a university faculty member to cooperatively implement a service-learning project that has an integrated focus on the Sixth Mass Extinction. In either case, you will find that it is a rewarding and educational experience. As a community partner, your interaction with the public will occur quite frequently during the service-learning project. You will also encounter members of the community that oppose the idea of the Sixth Mass Extinction. For example, you may encounter parents that do not want their children to learn about the Sixth Mass Extinction, other community partners that do not want to partner in a service-learning project that deals with an environmental topic, or resistance from members of the general public. Take the time to educate yourself about the Sixth Mass Extinction using the resources provided (see Appendix). If the person seems open to learning about this topic, share the resources from this chapter with them. In my experience, people from the community that may be disagreeable at first but are open to learning from you can often be your greatest future advocates and partners.

Conclusion

My hope is that by educating the next generation about the ongoing Sixth Mass Extinction they will become teachers, scientists, and citizens that can participate in the reduction of the destruction of Earth. The sad truth is that if the effects of the current human-induced Sixth Mass Extinction are not reduced (and they currently show no signs of slowing), 1 day the vast majority of Earth's ecosystems will be gone and the future of our own species will be in question. Even though some would paint a grim picture of humanities future and believe there is nothing we can do *now* to change our future course, I still have hope. I believe that there is still time for us to collectively work together and to reverse the course we are on. And I believe education is a tool that can play an important part in reaching that goal *if* we do not wait too long. As humans, we find ourselves at a unique window in time where we have the skills and knowledge needed to bring humanity back into a sustainable relationship with Earth. I invite you to be part of making this vision a reality. Let's not wait too long and let this moment slip away.

References

Kuh, G. D. (2008). *High-impact educational practices: What they are, who has access to them, and why they matter.* Report from the Association of American Colleges and Universities, Washington, DC.

Wagler, R. (2011a). The anthropocene mass extinction: An emerging curriculum theme for science educators. *The American Biology Teacher, 73*(2), 78–83.

Wagler, R. (2011b). The impact of human activities on biological evolution: A topic of consideration for evolution educators. *Evolution: Education and Outreach, 4*(2), 343–347.

Wagler, R. (2012). The sixth great mass extinction. *Science Scope, 35*(7), 48–55.

Wagler, R. (2013). Incorporating the current sixth great mass extinction theme into evolution education, science education and environmental education research and standards. *Evolution: Education and Outreach, 6*, 9.

Wagler, R. (2016). *Anthropocene extinction.* New York, NY: McGraw-Hill Education Board AccessScience Article Series.

Wagler, R. (2017). 6th Mass Extinction. Encyclopedia of the Anthropocene: Biodiversity Volume, Elsevier (In Press).

APPENDIX

Sixth Mass Extinction Resources for Educators

Below are resources that will provide you with many opportunities to integrate the Sixth Mass Extinction into your specific service-learning project. These resources can be used by educators to teach concepts associated with the Sixth Mass Extinction, bring about awareness of the Sixth Mass Extinction, and instill habits of sustainability within others. A key is provided that indicates the type of resource.

Key for Sixth Great Mass Extinction Resources

Symbol	Description
a	Sixth Mass Extinction Curriculum and Scientific Information
b	Interactive Website for Teacher Guided, Student Generated Question-based Investigations associated with the Sixth Mass Extinction
c	Scientific Information or Scientific Report for Teacher Guided, Student Generated Question-based Investigations associated with the Sixth Mass Extinction
d	Scientific Study associated with the Sixth Mass Extinction for Incorporation into Teacher Guided Discussions
e	Science Pedagogy Techniques

[a]Wagler, R. (2011a). The anthropocene mass extinction: An emerging curriculum theme for science educators. *The American Biology Teacher, 73*(2), 78–83.

[a]Wagler, R. (2011b). The impact of human activities on biological evolution: A topic of consideration for evolution educators. *Evolution: Education and Outreach, 4*(2), 343–347.

[a]Wagler, R. (2012). The sixth great mass extinction. *Science Scope, 35*(7), 48–55.

[a]Wagler, R. (2013). Incorporating the current sixth great mass extinction theme into evolution education, science education and environmental education research and standards. *Evolution: Education and Outreach, 6, 9.*

[a]Wagler, R. (2016). *Anthropocene extinction.* New York, NY: McGraw-Hill Education Board AccessScience Article Series.

[a]Wagler, R. (2017). 6th Mass Extinction. Encyclopedia of the Anthropocene: Biodiversity Volume, Elsevier (In Press).

[b]Air Pollution: View air pollution levels around the world. Retrieved from http://aqicn.org/

[b]Global Footprint Network: Calculate your personal ecological footprint and much more. Retrieved from http://www.footprintnetwork.org/

[b]Google Earth Blog: Source for interactive environmental activities utilizing Google Earth Blog. Retrieved from http://www.gearthblog.com/ Download Google Earth: http://earth.google.com/

[b]The Habitable Planet: A wealth of information and interactive activities on Earth. Retrieved from http://www.learner.org/courses/envsci/unit/index.php

[b]TOXMAP: Use this interactive website to find out what toxins the government allows entities to release near you and the health effects of these toxins. Retrieved from http://toxmap.nlm.nih.gov/toxmap/main/index.jsp

[b]US Environmental Protection Agency. (2016). Use this interactive website to explore environmental issues anywhere in the US. Retrieved from http://www.epa.gov/myenvironment/

[b]US Environmental Protection Agency. (2016). Use this interactive website to learn about superfund sites and where they exist. Retrieved from http://www.epa.gov/superfund/

[b]Worldometer. (2016). Use this interactive website to find statistics about current human population and environmental degradation. Retrieved from http://www.worldometers.info/

[c]Center for Biological Diversity: The Extinction Crisis. Retrieved from http://www.biologicaldiversity.org/programs/biodiversity/elements_of_biodiversity/extinction_crisis

[c]Millennium Ecosystem Assessment. (2005). *Millennium ecosystem assessment.* Retrieved from www.millenniumassessment.org

[c]The IUNC Red List of Threatened Species: View the conservation status of Earth's species and more. Retrieved from http://www.iucnredlist.org/

[c]United Nations. (2011). As world passes 7 billion milestone, UN urges action to meet key challenges. Retrieved from http://www.un.org/apps/news/story.asp?NewsID=40257

[c]World Wide Fund for Nature. (2016). *Living Planet Report 2016.* Retrieved from http://wwf.panda.org/about_our_earth/all_publications/lpr_2016/

[d]Alroy, J. (2008). Dynamics of origination and extinction in the marine fossil record. *Proceedings of the National Academy of Sciences, 105*(1), 11536–11542. Retrieved from http://www.pnas.org/content/105/Supplement_1/11536.full

[d]Erwin, D. H. (2001). Lessons from the past: Biotic recoveries from mass extinctions. *Proceedings of the National Academy of Sciences, 98,* 5399–5403. Retrieved from http://www.pnas.org/content/98/10/5399.full

[d]Jackson, J. B. C. (2008). Ecological extinction and evolution in the brave new ocean. *Proceedings of the National Academy of Sciences, 105,* 11458–11465. Retrieved from http://www.pnas.org/content/105/Supplement_1/11458.full.pdf

[d]Rohr, J. R., Raffel, T. R., Romansic, J. M., McCallum, H., & Hudson, P. J. (2008). Evaluating the links between climate, disease spread, and amphibian declines. *Proceedings of the National Academy of Sciences, 105*(45), 17436–17441. Retrieved from http://www.pnas.org/content/105/45/17436.full

[d]Wake, D. B., & Vredenburg, V. T. (2008). Are we in the midst of the sixth mass extinction? A view from the world of amphibians. *Proceedings of the National Academy of Sciences, 105,* 11466–11473. Retrieved from https://www.ncbi.nlm.nih.gov/books/NBK214887/

[d]Zalasiewicz, J., Williams, M., Steffen, W., & Crutzen, P. (2010). The new world of the anthropocene. *Environmental Science & Technology, 44*(7), 2228–2231. Retrieved from http://pubs.acs.org/doi/abs/10.1021/es903118j

[e]National Research Council. (1996). *National science education standards.* Washington, DC: National Academy Press. Retrieved from http://www.nap.edu/openbook.php?record_id=4962

[e]National Research Council. (2009). *Learning science in informal environments: People, places and pursuits.* Washington, DC: National Academy Press. Retrieved from http://www.nap.edu/catalog.php?record_id=12190#toc

[e]National Research Council. (2011). A framework for K-12 science education: Practices, crosscutting concepts, and core ideas. Washington, DC: National Academy Press. Retrieved from http://www.nap.edu/catalog.php?record_id=13165

[e]NGSS Lead States. (2013). *Next Generation Science Standards: For states, by states.* Washington, DC: National Academies Press. Retrieved from http://www.nextgenscience.org/

Engineering

Chapter 6

Community Engagement in Civil Engineering Senior Capstone Design

Ivonne Santiago

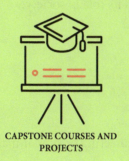

CAPSTONE COURSES AND
PROJECTS

UNDERGRADUATE RESEARCH

Pre-Reading Reflection Questions

Use these questions to guide your reflection prior to reading the chapter. Use the notes/follow-up section to write your thoughts after you have read the chapter. Your notes can include thoughts in reference to the reflection questions, or general observations about the chapter.

1) What is your understanding of capstone experiences in college? How are they helpful or beneficial to your education?

2) What is your understanding of civil engineering and its role in society?

3) How can community engagement enhance civil engineering or similar majors or disciplines?

Notes/Follow-up:

______

______

______

______

______

Introduction

A Senior Capstone project provides the practicum evidence that students are ready to put their education into practice. This course can be viewed as the last opportunity to reinforce in the student the sense of professional and social responsibility, ethics, and life-long learning skills that they should uphold for the rest of their personal and professional lives (Figure 1).

The main approach for the Capstone project in a successful Civil Engineering Department at University of Texas at El Paso (UTEP) is a magnet approach or discipline-specific approach for Civil Engineering that incorporates an interdisciplinary perspective, with an architectural point of view, and service-learning coming together at the conclusion of the design project. The service-learning component is inherent in Civil Engineering, as this is a "people-serving profession." Design projects are developed in teams; in this way, students are exposed to working with a larger group of people and begin to appreciate the dynamics of teamwork used in engineering workplaces today.

For the completion of their Engineering projects, students seek primarily mentors who are consultants in their local communities, in our case, the El Paso region. The local chapters of the American Society of Civil Engineering as well as the local chapter of the American Council of Engineering Companies have been an effective reference for students. It is noteworthy to mention that this is used as a mentorship tool to encourage students to become active in the student chapters of the professional organizations. Some students have chosen faculty members that are registered professional engineers as mentors as well. Although students seek external advice for their design, the project is still self-directed, team-based, problem-based, collaborative, and intended mainly as an out-of-class curricular experience.

By the conclusion of the Senior Design project, each student should be able to generate a design and report the results in a written and oral report. This ultimate experience should be a crucial milestone that enables the student to begin a career as a Civil Engineer that is aware of his/her social, ethical, and professional responsibilities.

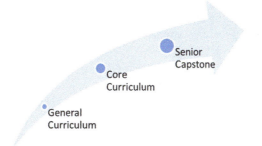

Figure 1 Culminating Experience with Senior Capstone

Chapter and Figure 1 contributed by Ivonne Santiago. © Kendall Hunt Publishing Company

Case Study: Designing Facilities for Our Communities

The Senior Design course is a one-year/two-semester course with projects that consist of real-case design scenarios that involve an element of service-learning and/or community service. Some projects selected were in collaboration with the City of El Paso, the County of El Paso, and other non-profit organizations. Students work in teams of five to six members in a competition-type format where all student groups have the same project.

In the first semester, students develop the conceptual design with an architect mentor of their choice. The requirements for that first semester include the delivery of:

1. **Architectural**—Floor plan and site plan design in compliance with applicable requirements and regulations:
   a. Scope
   b. Codes and regulations (United States Green Building Council Leadership in Energy and Environmental Design, Green Globes, Smart Code, City Codes, International Building Code, American Disabilities Act, other Federal codes)
   c. Area for art, if applicable
   d. Easements
2. **Topographic map**—During the first 2 weeks of the second semester, the students must make a formal oral group presentation to an architect selected by the instructor. The second semester students then complete the engineering design by incorporating all five disciplines offered by the program: namely, structural, geotechnical, environmental, construction management, and transportation, with engineer mentors. They will complete a final written report and technical presentation. The minimum requirements for the second semester include the following components:
   1. Environmental (assessment, stormwater management, and green design)
   2. Transportation (traffic and pedestrian flow inside and around the facility)
   3. Structural
   4. Geotechnical (foundation and pavements)
   5. Construction Management (cost and scheduling)
   6. Socioeconomic impact

Following is a list of some of the projects developed by the students with a brief description of each. It should be noted that throughout the years, the element of community engagement became more prominent:

- Smart Design Fire Station 513 (Fall 2011–Spring 2012). City requirements for the project include a 14,000 square feet fire station with seven drive-thru apparatus parking bays. It also requires sleeping accommodation for 22 on duty personnel and a total capacity of 66 for the three shifts.
- East Side Transit Terminal (Spring 2012–Fall 2012). The project consisted of designing a new Transit Terminal Facility approximately 4,000 square feet in size.
- Consolidated Rental Car ("ConRAC") (Fall 2012–Spring 2013). The ConRAC facility consisted of a 3-level ready/return vehicle parking structure containing approximately 650–700 dedicated parking stalls.
- Erosion control project at non-profit Paisano Summer Camp (Fall 2012–Spring 2013). The purpose of the project was to halt arroyo-flow erosion and protect the camp school.
- Rain water harvesting at UTEP (Fall 2012–Spring 2013). As part of UTEP's centennial celebration, students created an innovative green infrastructure design for a site on the UTEP campus showing how managing storm water at its source can benefit the campus community and the environment.
- Water Campus Project (Fall 2015–Spring 2016). El Paso Water challenged students to provide ideas and designs for a Water Supply and Resource Recovery Campus in a 500-acre area surrounding the Rio Bosque Wetlands Park, the Jonathan Roberts Water Treatment Plant, and the Sergio Bustamante

Wastewater Treatment Plant. The facilities include a Learning Center, water retention ponds, and other improvements throughout the 500-acre property where people with diverse technical background can gain an understanding and appreciation of our city's outstanding water utility system and diversified water portfolio as well as provide recreational opportunities for El Paso and Juarez residents.

- Ascarate Park Project (Fall 2016–Spring 2017) This is part of a project with the Civil Engineering Senior Design students resulting from a Memorandum of Understanding between UTEP and the County Commissioner's Court. The Commissioners provided the students with five charges:
  - Restoring Lake water quality and protecting it from golden algae blooms and fish kill. This component provided the students with an opportunity for undergraduate research for phytoremediation, the direct use of living green plants for *in situ*, or in place, removal, degradation, or containment of contaminants. Different types of plants needed to be tested for removal of nitrate and phosphate to control algae blooms to be implemented in floating islands in and around the lake.
  - Making walking/hiking trails ADA compliant (accessible for people with disabilities).
  - Locating and designing soccer fields.
  - Resolving the stormwater ponding issues.
  - Design a scenic event amphitheater.
- Solar-powered water purification system for a community in Po Ploom, Haiti; a project was funded by a private donor through a church in Tennessee. Students were charged with the design of a water purification system for a community of about 500 people with no electricity whose only water source is brackish. Since there is no electricity, the system must be solar powered. Students will help install the system in the Fall 2017.

What Made this High-Impact Practice Successful?

In engineering, we refer to learning outcomes as student outcomes, which is the standard notation used by ABET, the non-profit and non-governmental accrediting agency for academic programs in the disciplines of applied science, computing, engineering, and engineering technology (http://www.abet.org). Under the ABET accreditation, as of 2017, the Civil Engineering Department has adopted these 13 student outcomes—skills that Civil Engineering students will need to have at the time of graduation. At their graduation, our graduates should possess the ability and knowledge to:

a. Apply mathematics, science, and engineering principles;
b. Design and conduct experiments and interpret data;
c. Design a system, component, or process to meet desired needs;
d. Function on multidisciplinary teams;
e. Identify, formulate, and solve engineering problems;
f. Understand professional and ethical responsibility;
g. Communicate effectively;
h. Understand the impact of engineering solutions in a global context;
i. Recognize the need for, and an ability to engage in life-long learning;
j. Understand contemporary issues;
k. Use the techniques, skills, and modern engineering tools necessary for engineering practice; and
l. Understand Professional practice.

These outcomes are a guiding light for assessment, not only for ABET accreditation purposes, but also for the Civil Engineering Body of Knowledge for the 21st Century, endorsed by the American Society of Civil Engineers. These define the following: What the knowledge, skills, and attitudes need to be to enter into professional practice; How the Body of Knowledge can be fulfilled by tomorrow's aspiring engineers; and Who should guide the learning of the engineering student and engineering intern.

The main goal of the Senior Design project is to give the students a real world, first-hand knowledge of how an engineering design works in a simulated client/consultant environment with a strong component of community service and/or service-learning. The course objectives are related to immediate, intermediate, and long-term outcomes, as shown in the logic map presented in Figure 2.

The emphasis of the Senior Design course is on further developing and refining the students' primary capabilities in the three categories that are based on The Transferable Integrated Design Engineering Education consortium of design educators at Washington State University (http://www.tidee.wsu.edu/)

1. **Design Process**: When assigned a significant design project, students will be able to manage, assess, and improve their design efforts to conceive, create, evaluate, and deliver a design to satisfy the needs of a diverse set of clients.
2. **Teamwork**: When a team is given a collective responsibility, the team will be able to organize and develop a cohesive, energized team; plan, execute, critique, and improve team processes; and produce required deliverables within allotted resources.
3. **Communication**: When students work in design teams, they will be able to establish and implement communication processes to effectively record, critique, and exchange information inside and outside the team for quality performance.

Short-term goals are connected to course objectives so that student outcomes will be assessed for accreditation purposes as shown in Table 1.

Service-learning projects promote student learning in the form of experiential education and can be a useful teaching method for accomplishing the learning objectives set forth by the instructor and by ABET (Ropers-Huilman, Carwile, & Lima, 2005). In this course, a systems approach that combines engineering, technology, and personal/interpersonal skills also aligned well with ABET (2007) engineering outcomes criteria (a–k) especially outcomes f, h, and j (e.g., analyze complex situations involving multiple professional and ethical interests, understand the impact of engineering solutions in a global and societal context, and

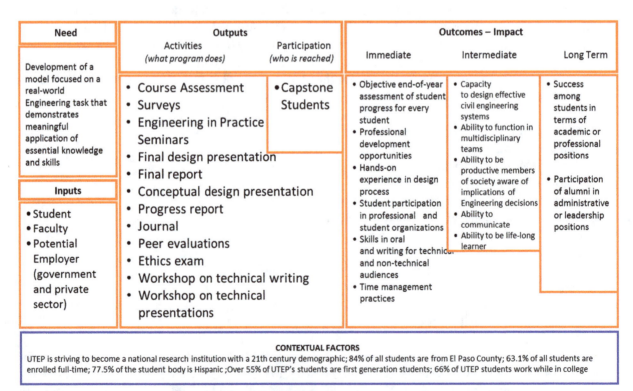

Contributed by Ivonne Santiago. © Kendall Hunt Publishing Company

Figure 2 Logic Model for Assessment of Capstone Course

Table 1 Course Objectives and Students' Outcomes Assessed in Capstone Course

Course Objectives	a	b	C	d	e	f	g	h	i	j	k	l
DESIGN PROCESS								h	I	j		
Design a system, component, or process to meet desired needs			X									
Demonstrate knowledge of a professional code of ethics						X						
COMMUNICATION							X					
Prepare a well-written final report												X
Make an effective oral presentation												
TEAM WORK												
Work effectively as team/group				X								

have a knowledge of contemporary issues). Additionally, previous studies have shown positive effects of service-learning on a wide variety of cognitive and affective measures, many of which match the criteria of ABET that were satisfactorily met in the Senior Design course, namely those dealing with interdisciplinary teams (d) and effective communication (g). Fundamentally, this systems approach that incorporates environmental, social, political, regulatory, and economic issues when identifying, defining, and solving engineering problems (Lathem, Newmann, & Hayden, 2011) provides the unique opportunity of a real-life scenario for people-serving professionals.

Student surveys indicate they gained the most learning from designing with real-life scope constraints, using professional design standards, interacting with engineers and architects, experience at time management, learning to compromise and resolve conflicts, and preparing of oral and written presentations. The surveys also indicated that the project helped develop the following attributes:

- Motivation—Motivated and takes action to complete assignments on time.
- Technical competence—Competent in knowledge and tools of engineering.
- Judgment and decision-making—Able to make sound engineering decisions.

The projects helped meet the following objectives:

- Learned to produce a design that met desired needs, including socioeconomic needs.
- Learned to work effectively as a team/group member in benefit of local and international communities.
- Learned to make an effective oral presentation.
- Gained knowledge of professional practice and the professional code of ethics.

Also, Figure 3 shows some of the skills gained, according to the students themselves.
Some of the particularly successful projects include:

- Smart Design Fire Station 513 (Fall 2011–Spring 2012). This project won the 2012 NCEES Engineering Award for Connecting Professional Practice and Education as shown in the following figures. This award was established to promote understanding of the value of licensure and to encourage partnerships between the engineering profession and education.
- Ascarate Park Project (Fall 2016–Spring 2017) The students provided the Commissioners' Court of the County of El Paso with recommendations to restore the quality of the Lake. These recommendations will be implemented and continued to be monitored by students as volunteer undergraduate research opportunities.
- Solar-powered water purification system for a community in Po Ploom, Haiti to be installed in the Fall 2017. It should be noted that international humanitarian international service-learning experiences can also help meet ABET criterion while providing a transformational experience to the students by helping needy populations in the world (Budny & Gradoville, 2011).

AREA OF EXPERTISE	WHAT WAS DONE?		KNOWLEDGE AND SKILLS GAINED	
Architecture	• Design Floor plan and site layout • Assess required permits		• Design process from beginning to end • Building and Smart codes	• Green building design and LEED Silver Certification
Construction Management	• Scheduling and cost estimate		• Construction process • Cost estimate of a building project	• Use of Primavera software
Geotechnical	• Parking Lot Design • Concrete Design	• Foundations design • Site Preparation	• Design Foundations based on loading • Site preparation for construction	• Cut and fill calculations
Structural	• Placement of Columns • Design of Beams, Columns, Trusses		• Use of STAAD software • Required loadings	
Transportation	• Reconstruction of Roads • Traffic Flow	• Light Systems	• Take into account use-specific condition, such as turning radius of fire trucks • Regulatory and legal requirements for adding a traffic light to a major street	

Contributed by Ivonne Santiago. © Kendall Hunt Publishing Company

Figure 3 Students' Views of Knowledge and Skills Gained in Senior Design

As a result of the success of these larger projects, we have been sought for collaboration from other organizations. Although this has occasionally resulted in a slight deviation from the same-project-competition format, we believe that the students have tremendously benefited from these real-life experiences in the context of the client/consultant environment. Smaller projects such as an erosion control project at non-profit Paisano Summer Camp (Fall 2012–Spring 2013) were also beneficial. The students' recommendations were successfully implemented by the Administration of the camp.

What were Some of the Challenges?

The selection of a real-life project where the "client" is willing to provide all the information that fulfills most of the following requirements can be challenging.

- The project should be multidisciplinary; therefore, it should incorporate the five areas of engineering taught in our program (environmental, geotechnical, structural, transportation, and construction management) in addition to an architectural, surveying, and legal component.
- The project should provide a Client/Consultant environment.
- The project must have an element of community service or service-learning that provides socioeconomic benefits to the community by engaging with partners and stakeholders in either individual interviews or focus groups.
- The project should integrate different standards (Architectural and Engineering).

According to student surveys, the biggest challenges students faced in their Senior Capstone courses were the following: time management, team coordination, and gathering information for design.

Another challenge is ensuring that the students understand clearly the goals and deliverables of the course, which should be clearly defined in the course syllabus as well as:

- Fairly comprehensive information covering issues such as providing the students with some of my background; rules of conduct in the classroom and as a professional; resources available; expectations; my personal philosophy on the course; and academic and professional success.
- Resources beyond the classroom for them to gain the needed knowledge and skills to be able to complete a successful final design.
- Information on the course objectives and goals, making sure they understand that it is a challenging course, and as such it will be very demanding on their time and effort.
- Information on the role of the mentor(s) they choose so they understand that the mentor(s) will "guide" them in the design process, but not do the design for them.
- Last but not least, consistently finding community partners that provide opportunities that challenge the students technically and that also provides a service-learning experience is not always easy. There should be an ongoing effort to network and partner with government, non-government, and private organizations to understand and be updated on the needs of the community that would benefit from an Engineering intervention.

Applying this Methodology in Other Settings

Although this high-impact practice focuses on a Civil Engineering Capstone design project, these practices can provide key lessons to other non-Engineering professions that are linked to the success of any project namely: interdisciplinary team-building experiences, communication with technical and nontechnical audiences at all levels, social responsibility, global and socioeconomic impacts, and contemporary issues.

The Civil Engineering Senior Design course is inherently team-based, so all the team-building activities and peer-assessment activities would be applicable in any team-based course. For example, during the first part of the year-long course, a series of team-building exercises are performed to ensure that teams are well balanced. We seek to have diverse team members communicate, participate, and resolve effectively. Students start by doing the Myers & Briggs type Indicator Test (MBTI) to prepare them to form balanced teams (http://www.myersbriggs.org/my-mbti-personality-type/mbti-basics/). With some flexibility and wherever possible, background (e.g., military, parents, works outside of school), ethnic, and gender balance is sought along with diverse approaches to design as a visionary, an idealist, a conductor, or a troubleshooter personality.

Team formation is followed by creating different scenarios and brainstorming solutions using Liberating Structures (http://www.liberatingstructures.com/) that allow the students to:

- Tap and share the collective knowledge and experiences that make up a good team; and
- Collect ideas on how to effectively solve problems and complete the design.

The team-building activities are followed by a team contract where students describe specifically the expectations from each other and procedures to deal with challenges and issues within the team. At least twice per semester, a Team Peer evaluation is done based on work-related performance as well as work-related interactions with others. The results from this evaluation allow the professor to design appropriate interventions and conflict resolution strategies.

Recommendations For Faculty

The assessment for a Senior Capstone course has a triple purpose: Program Criteria for Curriculum, Student Outcomes, and Continuous Quality Improvement (Figure 4). According to curricular requirements from ABET: *"Students must be prepared for engineering practice through a curriculum culminating in a major design experience based on the knowledge and skills acquired in earlier course work and incorporating appropriate engineering standards and multiple realistic constraints."*

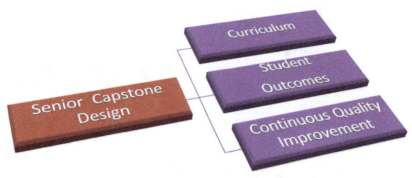

Contributed by Invonne Santiago. © Kendall Hunt Publishing Company

Figure 4 Goals of Assessment in Senior Capstone Design

As stated earlier, during the first 2 weeks of the second semester, the students must make a formal oral group presentation of their conceptual design, which is used to assess their technical and nontechnical verbal communication skills. General Presentation (attire, volume, organization, vocabulary, and understanding) and specific design features (originality of floor plan, quality of site plan, adequate research, documentation, compliance with codes, namely IBC, City Codes, Smart Design, and Green Design concepts).

In the second semester of the Capstone Course, Senior II, the students are required to complete their engineering design. To that effect, the topics of seminars and classes are geared towards the understanding of professional practice and tools such as use of software, site constraints, and finding a compromise between different standards and requirements (e.g., LEED and Green Globes versus Smart Code). At the end of the second semester, all design teams are required to submit a final written report and to present their design in an open forum, which is used to assess their technical and nontechnical written and verbal communication skills. There is an evaluating panel composed of at least five external engineering consultants and one CE professor. This panel does the evaluation of both the final report and the presentation. At least one of the engineers in the panel is a representative of the City of El Paso and often has a stake in the implementation of the results of the project. Most importantly, using a systems approach for their design, students incorporate not only the technical fundamentals, but also the social, political, regulatory, and economic issues in their design. The rubrics for evaluation include but are not limited to the following:

- Presentation. Content, comprehension, enthusiasm, preparedness, and grammar.
- Report. Organization, amount and type of information, sources, diagrams and illustrations, grammar, and syntax.
- Ability to design to meet desired needs. Design process, awareness of customer in the design, identify project objectives based on client requirements, and synthesis of ideas.
- Consideration of relevant constraints. Economic, environmental, buildability, health and safety, compliance with codes and regulations, and professional ethics and responsibility.
- Professional practice. Integration of client scope, design, codes, and engineering principles.
- Social and economic impacts of engineering design on the community at the local and city level.

Specific learning outcomes are shown in Figure 5 for the different activities. These activities and student outcomes are applicable in other areas of Science and Engineering.

Recommendations For Students

Senior Capstone experiences are part of a well-designed curriculum where, as students move to more advanced courses, they develop higher-order learning skills and more advanced understanding of the discipline. In addition, the Senior Design course serves as a transition from student to professional or any post baccalaureate

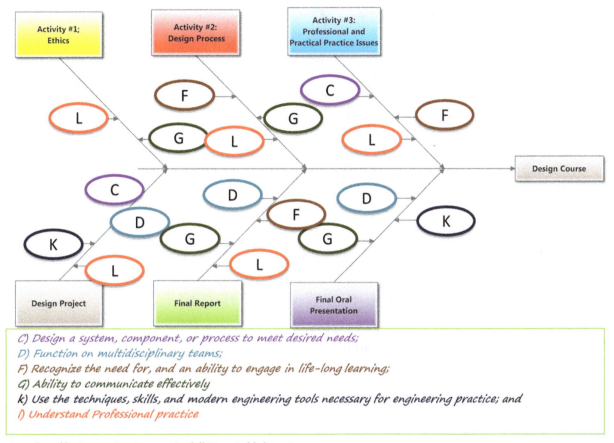

C) Design a system, component, or process to meet desired needs;
D) Function on multidisciplinary teams;
F) Recognize the need for, and an ability to engage in life-long learning;
G) Ability to communicate effectively
k) Use the techniques, skills, and modern engineering tools necessary for engineering practice; and
l) Understand Professional practice

Contributed by Ivonne Santiago. © Kendall Hunt Publishing Company

Figure 5 Connection of Activities to Student Outcomes in Design Course

role. In a well-designed curriculum, students will develop basic learning skills and acquire foundation knowledge in their earliest courses. In other words, students will apply previously acquired knowledge rather than acquiring new knowledge. For Civil Engineering students, the Senior Design Capstone Course is the culminating major design experience where they incorporate the following:

- Knowledge from earlier courses.
- Appropriate engineering standards.
- Realistic political, environmental, and socioeconomic constraints.

Recommendations For Community

As stated earlier, the project must have an element of service-learning that provides socioeconomic benefits to the community by engaging with partners and stakeholders in either individual interviews or focus groups. The community benefits from the partnership by:

- Providing opportunities for mentorship.
- Providing opportunities to develop potential engineers and/or leaders for their own organizations or the community in general.
- Gaining support in their efforts to address social issues.
- Gaining public awareness about the communities' work among university students, staff, and faculty.
- Gaining access to resources that are normally available at the university.

A Few Selected Readings, Resources and Tools

- MBTI Test to prepare them to form balanced teams (http://www.myersbriggs.org/my-mbti-personality-type/mbti-basics/). With some flexibility and wherever possible, background (e.g., military, parents, works outside of school), ethnic, and gender balance is sought along with diverse approaches to design as a visionary, an idealist, a conductor, or a troubleshooter personality.
- Team formation is followed by creating different scenarios and brainstorming solutions using Liberating Structures (http://www.liberatingstructures.com/). The most commonly used structures are Mad Hatter.

Suggested Guiding Questions

The following reflective questions are useful at the beginning of every project formed in collaboration with a community partner:

1. What are the needs of the partner that would require a Civil Engineer?
2. Who are the stakeholders and why?
3. Is there a government or private enterprise that plans to solve the need of the partner?
4. Who will decide if the project will move forward?
5. What is the timeline for completion?
6. Who are the points of contact for the partner?
7. Who will benefit from the project?

Conclusions

First and foremost, the service-learning partnerships can support student outcomes and provide opportunities for new approaches to teaching and learning technical and nontechnical skills outside the context of the classroom.

Embedding the Senior Capstone design with community partners puts students in a situation that they have to engage face-to-face and develop relationships with the public and other professionals and mentors that are vested in student success. Because of this, the students experience interactions with a diverse group of people outside of the campus that deal with contemporary issues and that will challenge and help them broaden their way of thinking beyond their own engineering mindset.

Service-learning activities provide the students with opportunities to converge their technical and intellectual tools to give them the confidence they will need in the real world. Additionally, and just as important, the Senior Capstone design course can change students' perceptions of engineers' social responsibilities locally, regionally, and internationally. In turn, the community partners benefit by establishing a network of future professionals committed to improving their communities. Our partnership with the City of El Paso has been fruitful and has opened the doors to other interested parties that wanted to partner with us. Other partnerships include the County of El Paso, as well as non-profit and religious organizations.

References

Budny, D., & Gradoville, R. T. (2011). International service learning design projects: Educating tomorrow's engineers, serving the global community, and helping to meet abet criterion. *International Journal for Service Learning in Engineering, 6*(2), 98–117.

Lathem, S. A., Newmann, M. D., & Hayden, N. (2011). The socially responsible engineer: Assessing student attitudes of roles and responsibilities. *Journal of Engineering Education, 100*(3), 444–474.

Ropers-Huilman, B., Carwile, L., & Lima, M. (2005). Service-learning in engineering: A valuable pedagogy for meeting learning objectives. *European Journal of Engineering Education, 30*(2), 155–165.

English

Chapter 7

Leveraging Assets Through Appreciative Interviews in Classrooms and Communities

Lucia Dura

COMMON INTELLECTUAL
EXPERIENCES

COLLABORATIVE
ASSIGNMENTS AND PROJECTS

Pre-Reading Reflection Questions

Chapter 7

Use these questions to guide your reflection prior to reading the chapter. Use the notes/follow-up section to write your thoughts after you have read the chapter. Your notes can include thoughts in reference to the reflection questions, or general observations about the chapter.

1) Describe a time when you had to serve as a problem solver. What skills are necessary to be a good problem-solver?

2) Has there ever been a time you decided to take on a different approach to an issue or problem than was expected of you? If so, how did it feel to take on a different risk?

3) If you could change higher education, what would make your college education more interesting or exciting?

Notes/Follow-up:

____

____

____

____

____

Introduction: A Problem Well Put Is Half Solved

Whether we are practitioners or academics engaged in inquiry, and whether that inquiry is formal or informal, we likely recognize the power of a good question. If it is true that "a problem well put is half solved," as attributed to educational reformer John Dewey, well stated questions can take us to solutions better, as well as faster. Yet sometimes, no matter how good we get at wording questions, we still fall prey to what Dewey called "occupational psychosis." As problem-solvers, we get really good at asking questions to the tune of *what are the gaps, needs, and causes?* In essence, we tend to ask, *what's wrong and how can we fix it?* And why wouldn't we ask these questions as problem-solvers, right? But problem-solving as a trained incapacity translates to trapping ourselves in "deficit" mode and engaging in conversations that focus on money, time, and outside resources. This chapter is about challenging our trained incapacities by asking strengths-based questions in problem-solving situations, both in the classroom and in community settings. This means looking at what's working, i.e., leveraging the assets stakeholders bring to the table. One way to do this is through the high-impact practice (HIP) of Appreciative Interviews (AI/AIs).

AIs are derived from an asset-based community development model called Appreciative Inquiry. Appreciative Inquiry "involves systematic discovery of what gives 'life' to a living system when it is most alive, most effective, and most constructively capable in economic, ecological, and human terms" (Cooperrider, Whitney, & Stavros, 2008, p. 101). Appreciative Inquiry can take weeks or months to implement in an organization. AIs compress Appreciative Inquiry into a "positive question" aimed at revealing hidden success stories within an organization or group in a very short time frame, e.g. 1 hour (McCandless & Lipmanowicz, 2014). This compressed version acts as a Liberating Structure. Liberating Structures are group facilitation techniques that aim to unleash creativity and maximize participation (see www.liberatingstructures.com). They are based on complexity leadership principles, which emphasize relationships, emergence, and adaptability (Sullivan, 2011), and are being used increasingly in business, education, healthcare, and non-governmental sectors (Gorski, 2016; Singhal, 2016). As a HIP, AIs bring to the surface social proof of past success, local innovations, and promising prototypes (McCandless & Lipmanowicz, 2014). In essence, they change the stories people tell about themselves, and in doing so, they expand notions of what is, what is good, and what is possible. Adding an appreciative dimension in a problem-solving situation has profound effects on stakeholders' dispositions, making them more likely to take ownership, and therefore contributing to deep learning and more sustainable outcomes. I started using AIs, along with other Liberating Structures, to facilitate "flipped" classroom discussions. In this chapter, I present a case study on my use of AIs during the first week of class as a way to bring students' strengths to ground the semester in a narrative of possibility and accountability.

Case Study: Asking the Appreciative Question in the Classroom to Establish a Different Kind of Baseline

Every semester on the first day of class, I invite students to talk in pairs about the greatest challenges they have as writers. This is not an uncommon practice in writing classes. Commiserating with each other around their challenges makes students feel that they are not alone in the perils of writing. In three Speed Networking (http://www.liberatingstructures.com/2-impromptu-networking/) rounds, students are able to acknowledge that they are not alone in their negative experiences with writing. Whether students are graduates or undergraduates, some of the most cited examples of challenges around writing are the following:

- "Getting my thoughts on paper."
- "Organizing my ideas."
- "I don't have a lot to say, and my professors always tell me to expand or develop my ideas. But I don't understand how."
- "I have a hard time being concise and getting to the point."
- "I'm not very good with English grammar or punctuation."

Brainstorming challenges serves as a diagnostic that alerts me as their instructor to the "big scaries" they face as writers or what has been emphasized the most by other writing instructors.

The problem is that if we stop here, we begin our work together with the assumption that the students have problems or challenges and I (and the course materials) have answers. Not only that, but the expected answers or solutions are assumed to be able to address wordiness *and* expansion, content *and* grammar, organization *and* development—for all students and all in one semester. So, students in my courses tend to be surprised by my second prompt: "Think about a good writing experience you have had in your life, and tell a partner the story of this experience."

Hence begin the AIs, which generate conversations about positive writing experiences, i.e., what has worked for them in the past, revealing hidden success stories and patterns among "non-experts." I add to the storytelling prompt a listening component: "As a partner, your job is to listen to the story and be able to tell it to another pair of students when I put you in groups of four." I give them about four minutes for each story, and I emphasize the structure of the story: A story has a beginning, a middle, and an end. It includes details about who was there, where did it take place, what sights, smells, sounds, and tastes do you recall? If we go back to the essence of Appreciative Inquiry as a community-based approach, we are looking for peak moments, and these can be conveyed more vividly as stories than as abstract facts.

Once students have told their own stories and their partners' stories in groups of four—*a la* think-pair-share—I prompt them to look for what made success possible. "What patterns do you see across stories" I ask. "What anomalies?" We then work together to create a collective list of "tried and true" practices that we know have helped us achieve success in writing. These are published on our class learning management system online as a reminder that we have succeeded in the past, and that we come to the table with positive experiences and ideas that we can implement right away (see Figure 1 for an example). Parallel to the diagnostic based on challenges, AIs give me a different kind of baseline: one based on strengths that students bring to the table and that we can draw from to continue to build on where they are in their lives as writers.

What Made this HIP Successful?

By sharing their challenges with respect to writing with each other, students feel less alone and build empathy. Yet, their assumptions about writing remain the same: it is a mysterious art that some are good at and some are not. When students see the collective list of successful practices that have led them to

---

CHARACTERISTICS OF A GOOD WRITING EXPERIENCE

- *Writing about something that you are interested in*
- *Practice makes better: multiple drafts or simply writing "a lot"*
- *Seeing writing as a process: going from a "bad" draft to a good final product*
- *Time: multiple drafts, multiple eyes to review*

Contributed by Lucia Dura. © Kendall Hunt Publishing Company.

Figure 1 Student-Generated List of Patterns for Success in a Writing Experience—Posted in Online Learning Management System

positive writing experiences (see Figure 1), they tend to smile, nod, and express that they are pleasantly surprised.

AIs remind students that they are capable of navigating writing challenges, overcoming them, and even coming up with innovative practices, which contributes to their sense of self-efficacy. In other words, the asset-based narrative helps to replace, or at minimum complement, the deficit-based narrative influencing students' perception of themselves as writers. Research on positive affect and emotions tells us that asset-based thinking engages the imaginative neocortex, enabling flexible, responsive problem-solving (Isen, 2004). In this sense, changing the stories we tell ourselves about our perceived reality changes how we respond to the challenges we face.

Further, students are often taken aback by the idea they might have something to learn from their classmates, especially if they have had mostly negative group experiences or tend to be the ones who "do all the work." Conducting AIs in groups, instead of simply integrating the question into a lecture or individual response, puts into practice the idea that knowledge is produced in interaction with others, i.e., what Vygotsky called the zone of proximal development (1978, p. 32). The instructions for AIs embed storytelling, listening, repeating, and pattern recognition, which are sophisticated research mechanisms involved in the more expansive process of Appreciative Inquiry.

What Were Some of the Challenges?

Trying something new or deviating from the traditional teaching practices and behaviors can be risky, especially for those in contingent or junior positions. A typical university practice is to hand out a syllabus and to review it on the first day of class. Some professors ask students to review the syllabus on their own time and dive right into the course material. At most in addition to this, some professors throw in introductions or icebreakers. So spending an entire class period talking about challenges and successes is an unexpected twist. Such a twist can seem strange to students. They may not be thrilled about reading the syllabus on the first day or about getting straight to work, but they have come to expect it. And their expectation can override the need for variety or adventure. Furthermore, as a professor, not delivering the usual can be risk enough—what if it's a waste of time? What if they don't read the syllabus later? What if the activities simply flop?

In my first year designing classroom interactions with Liberating Structures, I confessed these fears to a seasoned mentor who responded with a sentence that comes to mind every time I plan something unconventional: "You can only measure the success of what you will do against the alternative. And most of the time, you know as little or as much about how well the alternative works as you do about what you're about to do." On the first day of class, do you know that students gain more from (a) introducing themselves and their majors or hobbies and reading the syllabus, (b) diving straight into the course material, or (c) reflecting collaboratively on their challenges and strengths? The truth is that any of these can work, depending on the purpose. AIs tend to work best when the purpose is to discover and build on the root causes of success. If that is your purpose, I would hedge my bet that option (c) will be most appropriate.

Most of us are not in the habit of asking positive questions, so another challenge of this HIP can be wording. In the classroom case as aforementioned, I have asked, different variations of the questions, ranging from asking students to think of a good writing experience to asking them to *think of the absolute best writing experience*. And I have also changed the wording to *describe a writing experience where you were successful*. And to *talk about a time you felt like you overcame a writing challenge*. In playing with the wording every semester I have yet to discover a "perfect" sequence—usually I aim to be as universal as possible, but I never know how my audience will respond. For example, students may ask, *what if we've never been successful?* Or, *what if the last experience I can remember was in first grade?* When I get questions such as these, I tend to go for the kernel of what I am asking: *Think of a time when you have been at your best with respect to writing, tell your partner the story of that time. When was it? Where were you? Who was a part of this experience?* Asking a good question—one that will yield robust results—and giving instructions can be overwhelming, even in the best of cases. So, my advice is, whether you do a practice run with someone you trust or you see each opportunity as a chance to prototype and refine your question/instructions, know that for most of us, getting the wording just right is a matter of time and of audience feedback. Remember that in many ways, asset-based framing runs counter to our habitual ways of problem-solving, and changing our habits takes practice and repetition; changing habits is another way of risk-taking.

Moving Forward: Cultivating Appreciative Dispositions in Community Settings

Upon gaining experience with AIs in my classes, I began using them to design conversations in community-based settings where the focus was on deficits, problems, gaps, and where experts were brought in to problem-solve. The purpose of AIs in community settings is the same as in classroom settings: sharing and understanding information about the root causes for success. But different contexts call for different wording and might emphasize research language, e.g., data collection, analysis, results, or community-based language, as well as goal-setting, programming, and outcomes. Table 1 (Dura, Salas, Medina-Jerez, & Hill, 2015) illustrates these adaptations of AIs for a community-based participatory action research setting. The purpose of this program, which we came to call the "Escuelita" was to create and test an afterschool curriculum at one of our city's public housing community centers. Through the program, we aimed to bridge home and school knowledge and literacy practices using food-based pedagogies. In essence, in this project, we would use food as a conversation anchor and imagination catalyst so that students and their parents could make meaningful connections between their funds of knowledge, i.e., the knowledge they gain from their families and communities (Gonzales, Moll, & Amanti, 2005; Moll, 1992) and what is taught in school.

Table 1 Appreciative Interview

Appreciative Interview Instructions (www.liberatingstructures.com)	Adaptations for Escuelita Program in a Community-Based Setting (Dura et al., 2015)
1. Tell a story about a time when you worked on a particular challenge and are proud of what you accomplished. 2. Tell your partner's story to another pair. 3. Engage in sense-making about patterns for success and what made the success possible.	1. In pairs, tell your partner (preferably someone you don't know or whom you know the least) a story about your favorite food or recipe growing up. Who cooked it? When did you eat it? What made it special? 2. In fours, tell your partner's story to the group. 3. Once everyone has told their story, talk about the patterns and the differences among yourselves. 4. At the end of this session, the research "harvests" top patterns and insights from each group.

The AIs employed in the Escuelita yielded important information about the families that we might have had trouble accessing in other ways. In less than an hour, we (facilitators, community partners, and participants alike) learned about where participants were born or had lived. We learned about the influence of gender roles in the preparation of foods. We learned about parents' intricate skills in traditional Mexican cooking techniques such as cooking outside or using a *metate* to grind corn. We also learned about participants' sense of time as something expressed in seasons and based on events rather than numbers (e.g., during the time of a particular president vs. a particular year). Similar to the classroom example, the application of AIs here emphasized strengths, cultural wealth, and co-learning. Co-learning was happening not only across participants in a horizontal sense; it was happening across the organizational hierarchy. Program participants, traditionally positioned in a client role that assumes deficits were the experts, and teachers from local schools, public housing coordinators, and professors with higher levels of formal education were the non-experts. In the sections that follow, I provide broader conclusions and applications for implementing AIs in classroom and community settings.

Recommendations For Classroom Settings

Faculty can use AIs across their roles in teaching, research, service, and administration. As I hope I have illustrated, AIs work particularly well on the first day of class when they are strung with the Impromptu Networking structure and discussion of challenges in the subject matter. I like to scaffold them with another string of Liberating Structures: 25 Gets You 10 and TRIZ, which you can read about on www.liberatingstructures.com. 25 Gets You 10 helps us articulate our class goals—the outcomes of which we put on the syllabus. And TRIZ asks, *What must you stop doing to achieve your purpose?* This combination has worked well for me time and time again. When using these strings, be prepared for the kind of reflexivity and accountability that makes learning transformational, i.e., beyond "what the instructor wants" and outside the limitations of grades! In weekly reflections and end-of-semester evaluations, students remarked on the fact that this activity changed their expectations about the course and about themselves. It reminded them that they had gotten this far for a reason—they had been successful in the past, and so had their peers. Since Liberating Structures are licensed under Creative Commons, anyone can use them, including students. It's just a matter of practice!

Recommendations For Community-Based Participatory Action Research Settings

Any time you are problem-solving from a deficit-based perspective, students, faculty, and practitioners alike can test the possibility of asking a question from the point of view of assets. When I adapt AIs for research and need them to function as formal data collection methods, I keep the instructions the same but put mechanisms in place for recording, such as handouts and chart paper, where participants record patterns and interpretations. I am not listening to individual conversations, but I am relying on group sense-making. My role as the facilitator is to ask probing questions when I walk around the room and at the larger group level.

Recommendations For Meeting Design

I make similar adaptations when I use AIs in meetings at the research and service levels. At a program retreat, for example, I used AIs to help dig into the strengths that we value the most in our work lives. I applied the same string of Liberating Structures (www.liberatingstructures.com) that I do in the classroom:

- Start with Impromptu Networking to articulate challenges.
- Add AIs to remind ourselves of strengths or successful moments and their characteristics.
- Use 25 Gets You 10 or a related structure to establish a clear sense of purpose.
- End with TRIZ to come up with a list of must do's and must not do's when working towards our purpose.

A Few Selected Readings, Resources, and Tools

Ais and Liberating Structures

You can find step-by-step instructions on the use of AIs on the Liberating Structures website: www.liberatingstructures.com. There you will also find information on riffs and variations, user stories, and similar tools for all 36 Liberating Structures. And you will find information on workshops and communities of practice worldwide. If you want a more nuanced perspective, the book by McCandless and Lipmanowicz (2014) can help take you further and deeper.

Appreciative Inquiry and Other Asset-Based Inquiry Approaches

If you are more interested in the nature and practice of AI, the website on appreciative inquiry lists a wealth of resources: https://appreciativeinquiry.case.edu/intro/whatisai.cfm

You might also find interesting other asset-based inquiry structures such as Discovery and Action Dialogues (also on www.liberatingstructures.com and in McCandless and Lipmanowicz (2014), which like AIs are inspired by the more comprehensive model of positive deviance: www.positivedeviance.org

Frequently Asked Questions and Tips:

1. I'm nervous about inserting this into my work processes. It is very different from how my institution operates.

   Remember that doing something different can be risky. Discomfort and fear are normal, but they can shatter confidence. Move forward with confidence knowing that what you are doing is probably just as effective as (but hopefully better than) the alternative. It's worth a try. And practice. Assumptions are hard to change. We can attempt to do so theoretically, but AIs as a practice facilitate a "doing is believing" approach. The more you practice with AIs and related frameworks, the more effective they will begin to seem. This goes both for facilitators and participants.

2. What if someone doesn't have a story? What if participants don't follow directions? What if someone doesn't want to participate?

   We can't control everything; we can only design with the best intentions. If a person doesn't have a story (even after you offer gentle prompts) or doesn't want to participate or follow directions, you can ask them if they would participate by listening. One of the premises of Liberating Structures is that you can't "force" participation. If someone wants to opt out, they can do so at any time.

3. How do I know if I'm doing this right?

   You can follow the structure guidelines, and you can still make mistakes. Nonetheless, you will probably still achieve a good outcome: bringing out patterns of success. Beyond practice, getting feedback from a peer can help. Many Liberating Structures practitioners have a "buddy" that they call upon for advice during the design process and after implementation. In addition to the website and finding practitioners in your area, you can connect with other users on social media, e.g., LinkedIn and Slack.

Conclusion

AI are simple ways of leveraging assets in a variety of settings. In the same time, space, and with the same people where deficit-based problem-solving takes place—they facilitate discussions around proven strengths and infuse participants with positive dispositions towards their purpose, enabling more creative and responsive problem-solving. AIs point to the importance of structure: the arrangement of people in a given space for a given amount of time and the structure of the question asked. They also point to the importance of adaptability based on context. AIs, as is the case with other Liberating Structures, have been tested in group settings worldwide and in a variety of contexts, but they are not exhaustive and are meant to be adapted by users.

References

Cooperrider, D., Whitney, D., & Stavros, J. (2008). *Appreciative inquiry handbook* (2nd Ed.). Brunswick, OH: Crown Custom Publishing, Inc.

Dura, L., Salas, C., Medina-Jerez, W., Hill, V. (2015). De aquí y de allá: Changing perceptions of literacy through food pedagogy, asset-based narratives, and hybrid spaces. *Community Literacy Journal*, 10(1) pp. 21-39.

Gonzalez, N., Moll, L., & Amanti, C. (2005). Funds of knowledge: Theorizing practices in households. New York, NY: Routledge.

Gorski, P. (2016). Rethinking the role of "culture" in educational equity: From cultural competence to equity literacy. *Multicultural Perspectives*, *18*(4), 221–226.

Isen (2004). Some perspectives on positive feelings and emotions: Positive affect facilitates thinking and problem solving. In A. Manstead, N. Frijda, & A. Fischer (Eds.), *Feelings and emotions: The Amsterdam symposium* (pp. 263–280). Cambridge, UK: Cambridge University Press.

McCandless, K., & Lipmanowicz, H. (2014). *The surprising power of Liberating Structures: Simple rules to unleash a culture of innovation*. Seattle, WA: Liberating Structures Press.

Moll, L. (1992). *Vygotsky and education: Instructional implication and applications of sociohistorical psychology* (pp. 319–348). London: Cambridge University Press.

Singhal, A. (2016). Creative content and inclusive classrooms to transform student learning: Liberating Structures for mathematics educators. *Journal of Mathematics Education*, *9*(2), 132-140.

Sullivan, T. (2011). Embracing complexity. Harvard Business Review, September. Retrieved from https://hbr .org/2011/09/embracing-complexity

Vygotsky, L. (1978). Interaction between learning and development. In *Mind and society* (pp. 79–91). Cambridge, MA: Harvard University Press.

Acknowledgments

I am indebted to Amy Wagler and Laura Gonzales for their feedback on this manuscript. I am also indebted to the students, colleagues, and collaborators who have trusted me as a facilitator and to my LS buddies worldwide for their mentorship, friendship, and support. This is a practice of many, and I am humbled to be able to write about our work.

English

Chapter 8

The Value of Internships in a College Education

Isabel Baca

SERVICE LEARNING,
COMMUNITY-BASED LEARNING

WRITING-INTENSIVE
COURSES

Pre-Reading Reflection Questions

Chapter 8

Use these questions to guide your reflection prior to reading the chapter. Use the notes/follow-up section to write your thoughts after you have read the chapter. Your notes can include thoughts in reference to the reflection questions, or general observations about the chapter.

1) Think of a time that you realized that your initial perception or opinion about something was wrong. How did you come to realize this? Did you like this realization? Why or why not?

2) How important is it for those around you to think the way that you do about issues of importance to you?

3) How do you feel about dialogue, conflict and debates? How do you approach challenging conversations? Do you feel skilled to do this? Why or why not?

Notes/Follow-up:

___

___

___

___

___

Introduction

A common complaint of college graduates upon graduating is that employers seek employees with work experience. They ask themselves: How can I have experience if I have been in school working on my degree required for employment? It seems that the job search is a Catch-22: How am I to gain experience (to be hired for a job) if I am constantly turned down for not having any? Internships are the answer. Another common situation is for new college students to be unsure of what they want to study. Without knowing what is entailed in the careers that interest them, these students may find themselves feeling lost and confused. What can be done to help these students? Internships, again, are the answer since these can help students determine what direction to take. Thus, internships fill two major purposes: they provide work experience and offer career guidance.

Internships, according to George D. Kuh (2008), are a form of experiential learning that allows students to gain direct experience in a work setting typically related to their major/career. Internships derive from the medieval apprenticeship in which "skilled laborers (often craftsmen) would teach a young person their trade and, in exchange, that person would agree to work for the teacher for a certain length of time" (internships.com, 2017). However, internships are more exploratory and not as rigid. You are not required to work for your internship supervisor once the internship is over, and you can use the internship to explore your career interests and to build your experience.

Internships can be paid or unpaid, and they usually last several months. Internships, if connected to a college course, can last a semester or they can be summer internships. Internships are offered in different ways: An internship can be a course where students get college credit for completing it; an internship can be identified much like a job, through Career Services at the university or college, and college students can also seek internships by approaching employers and professionals in their field of study.

According to Nancy O'Neill (2010), Director of Integrative Programs and the LEAP Campus Action Network of the Association of American Colleges and Universities (AACU), an internship at the beginning of your college education can help you choose a major or help you identify career interests. In fact, an internship can also help you discover what you don't want to do. If you are more advanced in your studies and have a clearer sense of what career you want to pursue, an internship will help you apply what you are learning in your college courses, particularly your upper-division courses focusing on your major/minor, in a real workplace setting. This way, you gain work experience in your intended career, and you can develop a network of professionals in your field of interest. O'Neill (2010) goes on to say that internships can also help you establish short-term and long-term plans for your career, and they can help you decide on a second major or minor. Based on the purpose for which students want to do an internship, students should intern at the beginning of their college education for career guidance or close to the end of their studies to gain work experience and practice what they have learned.

Internships then allow you to apply your knowledge and skills in new settings that extend outside the university or college. Internships provide a high-impact learning experience because they integrate learning and real-world experience. Internships can be viewed as the longer version of service-learning courses where students apply what they are learning in a specific course in a real workplace setting, typically by working with a nonprofit organization or community agency. Both service-learning and internships can be described as community-based learning, all identified as high-impact practices in higher education because they lead to numerous educational outcomes, such as student retention, student engagement, and improvement in several learning outcomes (Kuh, 2008). Internships could also be identified as community-based internships when they serve a community purpose.

No matter what career you are pursuing or interested in pursuing, you can do and should do an internship. The purpose of this chapter is to give you advice on the do's and don'ts of internships, discuss the benefits that come from doing an internship, and address possible challenges you may face when doing an internship. The chapter focuses on a specific internship, the community literacy internship, to illustrate how internships should be structured, monitored, and evaluated, making them a high-impact practice in higher education and beneficial to students, faculty, and community partners (the internship supervisor/agency mentor).

Case Study: The Community Literacy Internship

The community literacy internship is taught as a graduate course in the Rhetoric and Writing Studies (RWS) Program in the Department of English at the University of Texas at El Paso (UTEP). Students in the RWS graduate programs take this course to apply what they have learned in their graduate studies in a real workplace setting, more specifically by working as writers, communicators, researchers, webpage developers, and even at times, as translators in nonprofit organizations. This course, however, could be easily offered at the undergraduate level as well. The goal would be the same by having undergraduates majoring or minoring in RWS practice what they have learned in their upper-division courses in a real workplace setting. The course would be structured, monitored, and evaluated the same way. Undergraduates, earlier in their studies, can also do an internship to determine if they wish to pursue such a degree.

Structuring the Internship

To provide structure to an internship, objectives and measurable outcomes should be developed. In the case of this course, the instructor would do this, but the internship supervisor (called agency mentor in this course) can assist with this by working with the instructor in establishing such objectives and outcomes. This course accomplishes this by having the students create an internship contract. See the sample contract in Appendix A.

The contract should be negotiated between the agency mentor and the student. They both decide on the internship purpose, projects, tasks, and timelines. The contract should also list the responsibilities of both the student and the agency mentor. The instructor must approve the contract, making sure that tasks and projects relate to the student's major/minor (in this case to RWS). Thus, to make the contract official, all three signatures are required: the student's, the agency mentor's, and the instructor's.

Monitoring the Internship

Once the contract has been approved and signed by all three parties, the student begins the internship. Throughout the internship, the instructor asks for different kinds of progress reports from the student. Progress reports can be written and submitted to the instructor. The instructor can have an individual conference with the student to discuss the internship, and/or the instructor can hold a class meeting where all the course students report on their progress in their internships. Students can also keep an internship journal where they list the date, the tasks performed, and a reflection on how the tasks/ projects performed that day connect to their studies/course, and/or they can also address how they feel about the work they did that day and any observations from that day's work. Each day they work at their internship site or do work for their internship, they include an entry in their journal. Guiding questions for these progress reports include the following:

1. Based on your internship contract, what have you specifically completed?
2. Based on your internship contract, what specifically remains to be done?
3. How would you describe the communication with your agency mentor?
4. Have you received any feedback from your agency mentor? If so, describe his/her feedback. If not, how do you feel about this? If you want feedback from your agency mentor and you are not getting any, how should you approach this situation?
5. What challenges, if any, have you faced in your internship? How have you resolved these? If you haven't, what do you plan to do?
6. Have you done any additional tasks or projects not listed in your contract? If yes, what are these tasks/projects? How do they relate to your studies? If they don't, have they taught you anything? What specifically?
7. Have you met all your deadlines so far? If not, what have you done to make up for this? Have there been any consequences to this?
8. Do you feel confident or concerned about finishing your internship? Why?

Evaluating the Internship

At the end of the internship, students and agency mentors must evaluate the internship experience. The student completes an evaluation form as does the agency mentor. See Appendixes B and C for sample evaluation forms. In addition, the instructor asks the student to give a final internship presentation to the class, making sure the agency mentor is invited to this presentation. This way, the instructor, gets the student's and the agency mentor's perspectives on how successful the internship was. These evaluations help assess the identified learning outcomes of the internship.

What Makes this Internship Successful?

The community literacy internship has been successful because it has provided students with real-world experience, and they have been able to apply their learning in real workplace settings. Students have been able to network with professionals, have gained work experience, and have contributed to meeting community literacy needs by working with nonprofit organizations. For example, in this internship course, students have created English-Spanish newsletters for community nonprofits, such as for Centro Mujeres de la Esperanza, a center focused on empowering women in the region. Students have worked with other nonprofits, such as the Reynold's Home (a shelter), AVANCE (a family literacy program), Villa Maria (a women's shelter), the local chapter of the National Alliance on Mental Illness, the El Paso Hispanic Chamber of Commerce, and the El Paso District Attorney's Office. Students have written grants, researched funding opportunities, created and edited manuals, policies, brochures, pamphlets, PowerPoint presentations, and curricula, developed webpages, translated such documents and texts, and managed social media platforms for these and other nonprofit organizations.

Furthermore, many times, students, upon completing their internship, are asked or they ask to continue working with the organization as interns. Some students have even been offered jobs upon completion of their internships. For some students, their internships have confirmed or clarified their career choices: One student decided that working with nonprofits was what she wanted as a career while another realized that teaching was not what she wanted to do. Internships pave the way for careers by allowing students to practice their learning and skills and allowing students to explore other possibilities.

What Are Some of the Challenges?

No internship is perfect. Internships can present challenges. The most common challenges identified by community literacy internship students, agency mentors (internship supervisors), and the course instructor include the following:

1. Agency mentor does not understand the purpose of the internship and has the student intern perform tasks not related to his/her studies, the course, and/or his/her career interests.
2. The student receives no guidance or supervision. In the case of the community literacy internship course, some students may not receive feedback from their agency mentor on the writing they completed or the feedback is given too late.
3. When students are doing the internship as a course, they, more than likely, are taking other courses too. Time management for students can be a challenge.
4. Communication between the student intern and the agency mentor is poor, limited, or nonexistent.
5. Students may have a difficult time saying "no" to additional tasks/projects not listed in their internship contract.

These challenges can be addressed and resolved, for the most part, by creating a contract between the student intern and the agency mentor as referenced earlier. When the internship is connected to a course, the instructor should approve the internship contract. The internship contract should do the following:

1. List the specific duties, tasks, and projects to be completed by the student intern.
2. Provide specific deadlines for projects and tasks.
3. Address how and how often the student intern and the agency mentor will meet to discuss progress, performance, and any concerns the student intern or agency mentor may have.
4. State how and how often the agency mentor will provide feedback to the student intern on the work completed. In the case of the community literacy internship, student interns must receive feedback on the writing they complete (first draft), so they revise and edit accordingly.
5. State what the student will not do or any limitations and scope of the internship.
6. State the starting date and completion date of the internship.
7. Provide the contact information and signature lines for the student intern, agency mentor, and if applicable, the course instructor.
8. State how the internship will be assessed upon its completion.
9. When applicable, list any specific training and/or orientation required by the agency for the student to complete.

The student intern and agency mentor must recognize the value of the work performed by the student intern. If they negotiate the contract and the tasks and projects to be performed, this is more likely to happen and contributes to making the internship successful for both the student intern and the agency mentor.

Internships in Other Careers/Majors and Implemented in Other Work Settings

Not all internships have to be with nonprofit organizations, but community-based internships give back to the community by meeting needs that typically cannot be funded by these organizations. However, internships can be done with for-profit organizations, companies, and industry. Internships can be done in any field of study; some of these internships, however, are set up differently and their requirements are more extensive, such as with the medical and health sciences fields. But no matter what kind of internship you do or where you do it, all successful internships share the following characteristics:

1. Effective communication between student intern and intern supervisor, and when applicable, with the instructor,
2. Trust and respect,

3. Responsibility,
4. Professionalism,
5. Established objectives and purpose,
6. Measurable outcomes,
7. Monitoring,
8. Assessment/Evaluation.

These characteristics help internships be a high-impact practice in higher education. In addition, when these characteristics are present and practiced by the student intern and the intern supervisor, both benefit and the internship outcomes can extend to benefit the internship site and the community.

Recommendations for Faculty

Faculty can contribute to making internships a high-impact practice in higher education. Recognizing how internships contribute to students' learning experience and professional development is crucial. In the *Peer Review* article "New Research on Internships and Experiential Learning Programs" (2010), findings from several surveys and studies along with their sources are listed to support the exigency of having students do internships.

1. Nearly three-quarters of employers (73%) surveyed would like colleges and universities to emphasize more the ability to apply knowledge and skills to real-world settings through internships or other hands-on experiences (*How Should Colleges Prepare Students to Succeed in Today's Global Economy?* AAC&U/Peter D. Hart Research Associates, 2007.)
2. More than four in five employers believe that completion of a supervised and evaluated internship or community-based project would be very or fairly effective in ensuring that recent college graduates possess the skills and knowledge needed for success at their company. *(How Should Colleges Assess and Improve Student Learning? Employers' Views on the Accountability Challenge*, AAC&U/Peter D. Hart Research Associates, 2008).
3. More than two-thirds of employers (67%) believe that a faculty supervisor's assessment of a student's internship or community-based project would be very or fairly useful to them in evaluating college graduates' potential for success. (*How Should Colleges Assess and Improve Student Learning? Employers' Views on the Accountability Challenge*, AAC&U/Peter D. Hart Research Associates, 2008).
4. Four in five employers (79%) want colleges to place more emphasis on internships or community-based field projects that teach students to apply knowledge and skills in real-world settings. (*Raising the Bar: Employers' Views On College Learning in the Wake of the Economic Downturn*, AAC&U/Hart Research Associates, 2010).

To help make internships successful and contribute to students' learning and professional development, faculty may find the following recommendations helpful:

1. If offering the internship for course credit, the instructor should provide a syllabus that states the internship's purpose, objectives, desired outcomes, and assessment criteria.
2. Instructor should require students to create an internship contract that must be signed by the student, internship supervisor, and the instructor, upon his/her approval. The instructor must make sure that the internship connects to the student's studies or career interests.
3. Instructor should provide venues for students to report their internship progress, such as written or oral progress reports.
4. Instructor should establish how the internship will be evaluated and how the outcomes will be assessed. See Appendixes B and C.
5. Instructor can serve as the liaison between the student intern and the internship supervisor by making himself/herself available to both the student intern and internship supervisor when issues, questions, or concerns arise regarding the internship.

6. Instructor can create an Internship Directory listing internship sites and their corresponding supervisors by connecting and networking with professionals in the community. As students complete their internships or when students find their own internship sites, these can be added to the Internship Directory.
7. Instructor can provide helpful readings on internships to the student.
8. Instructor should provide a platform for students to showcase their internship work and experience.

Recommendations for Students

Many of the recommendations given to faculty can apply to you as a student intern, particularly if you are doing the internship on your own. You must create a contract as discussed throughout this chapter. See Appendix A. Make sure that you and your internship supervisor agree on the purpose and the objectives of the internship. Remember that an internship should help you strengthen your professional skills and allow you to explore your career interests and/or apply what you have learned in your studies. The internship should also help you practice interpersonal communication in a professional setting. Most important, and particularly when the internship is not for course credit, you must want this experience. In addition, consider the following recommendations:

1. Manage your time wisely.
2. Be assertive. Know when to say "no" and do not be afraid to ask questions.
3. Ask for feedback on your work/performance.
4. Meet all of your internship supervisor's requirements: training, orientation, etc.
5. Treat the internships as a real job: Be on time, follow the agency's dress code, meet deadlines, etc.
6. Upon completion of your internship, write a thank you letter to your internship supervisor. Don't be afraid to ask your internship supervisor if he/she is willing to serve as a professional reference in the future.

Following these recommendations can make a difference on how you are viewed as a future employee and professional in the field you are pursuing, and they can open doors of opportunity.

Resources and Guiding Questions for Students

As students, you should take advantage of your campus Career Services. They tend to not only have lists of job openings but of internship opportunities as well. Your university or college may also have a community engagement or community service office or center. In the case of the UTEP, for example, students have the Center for Civic Engagement. This center provides students with venues to become engaged with their communities through community service projects, service-learning courses, and internship opportunities. Other resources may include faculty in your major; they may know employers or organizations that need, seek, or are open to having student interns.

If your internship is not connected to a course or is not for course credit, you can take the initiative and seek internships on your own. Let the following questions guide you:

1. What have I learned in the classroom and how can I apply this in a workplace setting?
2. What new skills will I learn or hope to learn during the internship?
3. What is the purpose of this internship? What are my expectations?
4. What should the internship outcomes be?
5. How will I benefit personally, academically, and/or professionally from the internship experience?

These questions can assist you when seeking an internship. Remember: Your internship must be structured, monitored, and evaluated somehow.

Recommendations for the Community/Internship Supervisors

Professionals in the community benefit from having student interns. A successful internship benefits all involved, including the community. But in order to accomplish this, internships must be well directed and supervised. If the internship is not for course credit, than it is up to the internship supervisor to do this more carefully. Internship supervisors have the opportunity to mentor students. An internship contract serves all these purposes; thus, the internship supervisor should make sure that student interns create a contract as explained in this chapter. See Appendix A. Agency mentors or internship supervisors should:

1. Give interns significant, goal-focused assignments closely connected to students' fields of study/majors/minors or related to their career interests.
2. Have measurable outcomes for the internship and be clear about expectations.
3. If the internship is not connected to a specific course or an instructor, develop a plan for a structured internship experience; this should include monitoring the internship.
4. Provide feedback and have student interns report their progress.
5. Provide all the necessary tools, sources, space, training, orientation, etc. for student interns to be able to complete their internship tasks, assignments, and projects.
6. Help student interns describe their experience, particularly on a résumé and/or application letter.
7. Provide student interns a platform to demonstrate their learning.
8. Evaluate student interns' work and performance, and likewise, request feedback from student interns to help improve the internship experience.
9. Treat student interns professionally and respectfully.

These recommendations contribute to the success of internships for both the student and the internship supervisor/agency mentor.

Conclusion

Internships are a high-impact practice in higher education. They allow students to explore career interests and/or to apply what they have learned in their studies. Internships contribute to students' professional development and help them acquire skills not learned in the classroom. According to Pierson and Troppe (2010), "Internships embedded within a curricular pathway that facilitates students' integration of academic knowledge and professional knowledge are what is called for today." The urgency for students to be given the opportunity to intern in a real workplace setting is there. Students, faculty, employers, and the community benefit from internships if these are structured, monitored, and evaluated effectively. Internships engage students in learning and with their community. As a high-impact practice, internships do as Benjamin Franklin said, "Tell me and I forget, teach me and I may remember, involve me and I learn." Internships involve students in meaningful ways.

Recommended Readings

The following list provides suggested readings on internships. These readings can assist you in selecting an internship and knowing what to expect from internships, including the legalities connected to student internships:

- Berger, L. (2012). *All work, no pay: Finding an internship, Building your résumé, making connections, and gaining job experience.* Berkeley, CA: Ten Speed Press.

- What is an internship: A brief overview. (March 2017). Retrieved from https://www.thebalance.com/what-is-an-internship-1986729
- What are internships for? (March 2013). Retrieved from http://aley.me/internships
- Why are internships so important? (April 2010). Retrieved from http://www.cnn.com/2010/LIVING/worklife/04/14/cb.why.internships.important/
- Let's get legal: Guidelines for paid and unpaid internships. (March 2017). Retrieved from http://www.fastweb.com/career-planning/articles/let-s-get-legal-guidelines-for-paid-or-unpaid-internships

References

Internships.com. (2017). Retrieved from http://www.internships.com/student/resources/basics/what-is-an-internship

Kuh, G. D. (2008). *High-impact educational practices: What they are, who has access to them, and why they matter.* Washington, DC: AACU.

New Research on Internships and Experiential Learning Programs. (2010, Fall). Retrieved from https://www.aacu.org/publications-research/periodicals/new-research-internships-and-experiential-learning-programs

O'Neill, N. (2010). Internships as a high-impact practice: Some reflections on quality. *Peer Review, 12*(4), 4–8.

Pierson, M., & Troppe, M. (2010). Curriculum to career. *Peer Review, 12*(4), 12-14.

APPENDIX A

Sample Internship Contract

Community Literacy Internship Contract

The University of Texas at El Paso

This contract must be signed by the student and the agency mentor, then reviewed and approved by the instructor. All three parties must have a copy.

Organization:	AVANCE El Paso
Mailing Address:	616 N. Virginia Ste. B El Paso, TX 79902
Agency Mentor:	Juan Martinez Telephone: (915) 555-5555 Email: jmartinez@nonprofit.org
Student:	Patricia Carbonell Telephone: (915) 444-4444 Email: pcarbonell@university.edu
Instructor:	Dr. Isabel Baca Telephone: (915) 333-3333 Email: ibaca@university.edu
Course:	RWS 5318—Community Literacy Internship
Semester:	Spring 2017

The project will consist of creating quick reference procedural manuals for AVANCE departments as specified below with the purpose of facilitating the work processes within and between departments.

Specific duties will include

- Interviewing the directors of the following departments in order to identify the departments' work procedures: <add a list of departments.
- Collecting materials that the departments use in their work procedures.
- Writing follow-up, confirmation, and thank you letters to departments.
- Collaborating with agency mentor in order to discuss any potential redundancies and/or necessities in the workflow.
- Composing quick reference procedural manuals for the aforementioned departments that will include: objectives, job descriptions, an outline of the required or suggested work procedures, and documents used in the workflow.
- Creating digital versions of the manuals, including links for easy access to appropriate documents.
- Preparing a presentation for AVANCE personnel to showcase the accessibility and usability of the manuals.

Other considerations

- Student and agency mentor are also aware that some additional tasks not specifically mentioned in this contract will arise during the course of the project, and they agree that if both parties deem the task necessary to the project, if it requires only a reasonable time commitment from the student, and if the student feels that it is within the realm of her experience and abilities, then the student will take on that task as well.
- All work by the student will be unpaid.
- Student and mentor will meet once a week in person, via email, or by phone to discuss progress.

- Mentor will provide feedback to student within five (5) days of draft submission.
- A final evaluation will be completed by the mentor at the completion of the internship.
- Student's work will begin on Monday, February 1, 2017, and must be completed by May 1, 2017.

Student

Signature: _____   Date: _____

Agency Mentor

Signature: _____   Date: _____

Instructor

Signature: _____   Date: _____

APPENDIX B

Student Self-Evaluation Of Internship

Evaluation of Agency, Agency Mentor, and Internship

RWS 5318—Community Literacy Internship

As the semester comes to an end as does your internship, please evaluate your agency and agency mentor. Your honest answers and feedback will help improve the course as well as the community literacy internship experience. Your responses will not be shared with the agency. Submit this evaluation in your portfolio.

Your Name: _____   Semester: _____

Agency Name: _____

Agency Mentor's Name(s): _____

1. How satisfied are you with your agency selection?

    A. Very satisfied   **B.** Satisfied   **C.** Somewhat   **D.** Unsatisfied   **E.** Very unsatisfied

2. How would you describe your internship experience with this agency?

    A. Excellent   **B.** Good   **C.** Fine   **D.** Poor

3. How would you describe the communication between your agency mentor and you?

    A. Excellent   **B.** Good   **C.** Fine   **D.** Poor

4. How would you describe your relationship with your agency mentor?

    A. Excellent   **B.** Good   **C.** Fine   **D.** Poor   **E.** No relationship

5. How useful/beneficial (to the agency) are the writing tasks/projects you completed?

   A. Extremely useful   **B.** Very useful   **C.** Useful   **D.** Not useful   **E.** Not sure

6. How useful/beneficial (to the community) are the writing tasks/projects you completed?

   A. Extremely useful   **B.** Very useful   **C.** Useful   **D.** Not useful   **E.** Not sure

7. How helpful/beneficial was this internship experience to you?

   A. Extremely useful   **B.** Very useful   **C.** Useful   **D.** Not useful   **E.** Not sure

8. How would you rate your overall RWS 5318 Community Literacy Internship experience?

   A. Excellent   **B.** Good   **C.** Fine   **D.** Poor

9. Will you continue working at this agency?   Yes   No   Not sure

Please answer the following questions completely and specifically. Your input is important.

1. What did you like best about working with this agency?
2. What did you like least about working with this agency?
3. What did you like best about your community literacy internship?
4. What did you like least about your community literacy internship?
5. What have you learned from your community literacy internship?
6. How would you recommend this course and internship experience be improved?
7. What recommendations do you have for your agency and/or agency mentor?
8. What recommendations do you have for your RWS 5318 instructor?
9. What advice would you give to an incoming RWS 5318 student?
10. Please write any additional comments you may have:

APPENDIX C

Agency Mentor Evaluation of Student Intern

Evaluation of Student Writer

The University of Texas at El Paso

Department of English

RWS 5318: Community Literacy Internship

Dr. Isabel Baca

Thank you for participating and working as an agency mentor for the course RWS 5318, *Community Literacy Internship*, at the UTEP, Department of English. Please complete the following evaluation so that the course may be improved, and student interns can better assist your agency in future semesters. Your input is very important, and your honesty and cooperation are appreciated.

Be sure to complete both sides of the form. Please return this evaluation form to Dr. Isabel Baca by May 5, 2017. You may mail it in to the following address or you may have the student writer turn it in in a sealed envelope with your signature across the seal. You may also email it to ibaca@university.edu. Thank You.

Mailing Address: UTEP – Department of English
Dr. Isabel Baca
500 W. University Ave.
El Paso, TX 79968

Student Name: _____   Date: _____

Agency Name: _____   Phone: _____

Your Name: _____   Email: _____

1. The student completed all the assigned tasks as specified in the contract.   Yes   No

2. The student met all deadlines.   Yes   No

3. The quality of the student writer's/intern's work is

   A. Excellent   **B.** Above Average   **C.** Good   **D.** Fair   **E.** Poor

4. What were the strengths of this student writer/intern in his/her work for your agency?

5. What were the weaknesses of this student writer/intern in his/her work for your agency?

Agency Evaluation of Student Intern

6. How would you recommend this course/work experience be improved?

7. What are/were your concerns, if any, about working with a student writer/intern? Have these concerns been resolved? If not, how can they be?

8. What requirements and/or conditions, if any, do you have for placement of student writers/interns in your agency?

9. How would you describe your communication and working relationship with the student?

10. Are you willing to work with other student writers/interns?   Yes   No

11. Would you like to meet with me to discuss internship possibilities/concerns?   Yes   No

12. Do you have any additional comments or feedback?

Your signature: _____   **Thank you!**

English

Chapter 9

Critical Incident Interviews: Cultivating Dialogue Across Difference

Jennifer Clifton

DIVERSITY/GLOBAL LEARNING

UNDERGRADUATE RESEARCH

Use these questions to guide your reflection prior to reading the chapter. Use the notes/follow-up section to write your thoughts after you have read the chapter. Your notes can include thoughts in reference to the reflection questions, or general observations about the chapter.

1) Think of a time that you realized that your initial perception or opinion about something was wrong. How did you come to realize this? Did you like this realization? Why or why not?

2) How important is it for those around you to think the way that you do about issues of importance to you?

3) How do you feel about dialogue, conflict and debates? How do you approach challenging conversations? Do you feel skilled to do this? Why or why not?

Notes/Follow-up:

_____

_____

_____

_____

_____

Introduction

One of the most pressing issues of contemporary public life is how to deal with the volatile presence of diversity. Open up your university's homepage and you'll see what we tend to know to do with difference: celebrate identity politics and "diversity" or "inclusion" (i.e., an afterschool program with Latin@s or a computer hacking group for African American girls); celebrate outreach and a common humanity that whitewashes difference; and brand entrepreneurial efforts to or on behalf of "exotic" international sites (i.e., sending mosquito nets or vaccinations to Africa) (c.f. Clifton, 2016). And yet, these instantiations sustain the notion of a normative homogenous "center," with difference—however that shows up—as an anomaly that is relatively static, knowable, and something to be folded into the center or cast, even on celebratory terms, to the margins (cf. Spivak, 1994), often somehow marked as "in need" or "undesirable" or even "criminal."

The ways we think about and represent difference to ourselves and others matters because we *act* on these representations. This is especially significant for university–community partnerships, both because there are lots of ways that we need to work across difference in universities and in community settings, often with both resources and dignity at stake, and because, as knowledge-building enterprises and publicly responsive institutions, universities have a unique responsibility and are uniquely poised to inquire into the most pressing concerns of democratic public life. Further, the logic underlying these representations and practices can threaten the ideal of a deep democracy where the goal is not to bring people from the margins to the center but instead to "destabilize" the hegemonic core (Dhaliwal, 1996, p. 44).

The Role of Difference in Public Life

With regard to difference, political philosopher Iris Marion Young (1997) challenges us to take a different tack: rather than thinking about difference as enclaved, a communicative democracy would use a whole range of repertoires to elicit and value difference in the service of taking up concerns people didn't know they shared as members of a polity—as people who find themselves, for one reason or another, interdependently "stuck" with one another (Young, 1997). That is, a communicative democracy would make difference and how to productively navigate and call on volatile differences central to the values and practices of interdependence. This is especially relevant for universities and community partners because engaging in class and in community settings involves being up close and personal with people who might be very different from us, and yet, we find ourselves engaging with people who have different upbringings and worldviews. The question, then, becomes how might we engage with others across difference in ways that support joint thriving that is not dependent on homogeneity or conformity?

In recent decades, in rhetoric and composition, this concern has informed research in community literacy (Flower, 2008; Higgins, Long, & Flower, 2006); technical communication (Scott, Longo, & Wills, 2006; Simmons, 2007); and teaching argument (Clifton, 2017). This chapter moves beyond typical accounts of diversity in terms of identity politics or multiculturalism, which attempt to *describe* difference primarily around race, nationality, language, gender, sexuality, or class, to instead address the very difficult question of how people might learn to *attend to* rhetorically constructed differences and *negotiate* and *use* difference to further joint inquiry and to solve problems. In particular, this chapter considers how a concern moves from a personal or private concern to a concern that others—even people with quite different experiences, backgrounds, interests, and values—might share in some way, to some degree with others for the purposes of shared inquiry into the complexities of that concern and what might address that concern in ways that move toward shared thriving. For example, how does a person's experience with learning disabilities, domestic abuse, financial aid, or immigration become something that others also care about, are invested in thinking about, and will problem-solve with people who might reasonably disagree about what the problem is and how to address it? (cf., Flower, 2008; Higgins and Brush, 2006).

In writing courses, community literacy scholars have adapted critical incident interview questions to focus students' attention on what precisely goes wrong in moments when policies and practices are operationalized in ways that disrupt someone's life-world and that warrant more public attention and dialogue (Clifton & Sigoloff, 2013; Flower, 2008; Higgins, Long, & Flower, 2006). According to Jurgen Habermas (1996), when a person's values, beliefs, and attitudes align with those normalized in society and institutions, a person's life-world and the system world are "coupled," and everyday practices and rituals are carried out relatively seamlessly. However, when a single incident or a pattern of behaviors or series of similar behaviors are frustrating, ineffective, or even harmful, they may disrupt the life-world—a person's attitudes, beliefs, and values—in such a way that she calls the system world of society and institutions and the values underlying them into question. These life-world disturbances may indicate a site for further joint inquiry and shared dialogue, and yet unless they happen to us or directly affect us (i.e., Black youth being killed by police or contaminated water in Flint, Michigan), we may not recognize these disturbances as concerns others of us do or should share. Critical incident interviews are a deliberate attempt to jointly inquire into relationships of interdependence across deep differences by eliciting people's experiences of the ways broader societal and institutional practices are out-of-sync (Long, 2018) with the ways people hope and expect their communities and institutions to construct interdependence and operationalize the experiment in cooperation that is at the heart of deep democracy.

Life-world disturbances often play out in relatively mundane ways—a nurse keeps showing up late and her co-workers have to cover for her, for example—and as one-off occurrences may not rise to the level of disrupting attitudes, values, and beliefs. However, if an occurrence is disturbing enough or if mundane disturbances become chronic, they erode beliefs, attitudes, and practices of cooperation. Life-world disturbances are, thus, often emotionally charged and contested, marking a need for further dialogue even as the rising conflict makes the possibility of engaging in productive dialogue across difference more challenging and remote.

That impasses and stand-offs characterize the ways many people think about navigating disagreement—whether this plays out in avoiding conflict altogether, "agreeing to disagree," or vocally shouting past each other—indicates that we are facing a deep crisis of imagination in the ways we think about difference and public life. Our (in)ability to imagine, to take seriously, and to some degree share and navigate the interests and experiences of others across deep differences limits not only how we understand domestic and global citizenship but also how we enact that citizenship with others. In talk and in practice, the inability to take seriously the interests and experiences of others leads Americans—in university classrooms and in public life—to cast those who disagree as deeply flawed in character. As we've seen on the Senate floor or in presidential campaigns, casting disagreement as morally wrong brings democratic deliberation to a screeching halt. More disturbing, the suicides of gay youth across the nation (Erdely, 2012), the criminalization of black bodies (Alexander, 2010), and the proposed expulsion of immigrants (Leopold, 2015) remind us that casting disagreement as immoral is a kind of annihilation that makes difference—and anyone who embodies difference—an enemy to be squashed.

This is troubling for the everyday enactment of public life. People with quite different histories, cultures, backgrounds, and perspectives need public resources like schools, roads, infrastructure for water and sanitation, open spaces and parks, equitable laws, and so on to work for them. Making public resources and institutions work for them or changing them when they don't work are not things an individual can do on his or her own. Neither, however, are these merely concerns of government; they are, instead, primarily the concerns of everyday people whose lives depend on such systems working for them. Of course, when there is a gap between government and people, community organizations, non-profits, and community partners often emerge to address these needs. Across these complex networks, the lives of strangers are, thus, inter-dependently intertwined.

Attending to Life-World Disturbances

When these institutions, networks, and relationships work for people, they may not give them much thought. Indeed, people tend to become more aware of this interdependence when systems don't work for them or when new needs or conditions emerge. However, the stability of a practice or policy isn't necessarily an indicator of justice or effectiveness or equality. A practice or policy that one person gives no thought to may completely up-end another person's life-world.

In response to life-world disturbances, we suddenly sit upright and pay attention; what had previously gone mostly unnoticed is suddenly an object of inquiry and action. As literacy scholar Bob Fecho (2011) explains, "When something wobbles—a wheel on a car, a glass of wine on a waiter's tray, a child's top, the Earth on its axis—we notice. It causes us to stare and consider. Wobble taps us on the shoulder and *induces us to ask why. It nudges us toward action. It suggests we get out of our chair and do something*" (p. 53). Life-world disturbances prompt us not only "to ask why" but also to *explain why*. These explanatory accounts are "shaped at the point of utterance" (Britton, 1980, p. 147), *before* a person has a sense of understanding what has happened to them, or why, or what to do to remedy the situation.

Importantly, this sense-making and problem-solving is a collaborative process. We often recognize this kind of provisional knowledge building in our private lives. A person might call a mom, a partner, a friend, or a colleague, for example, after something strange and unexpected happened at work. Maybe a person followed procedures as best she knew how and somehow a supervisor or colleague corrected or reprimanded her for what she thought was the right thing to do. If the experience was troubling enough and confusing enough, she would likely tell someone what happened and begin to tell him why she thought it happened, what was really going on. Perhaps, she'd say something like, "I followed all the directions on the document. I got their permission ahead of time. Then, after I turn things in, they say it's all wrong. I have no idea why they would do that. The only thing I can think is that . . ." and then offer an explanation. She is generating and shaping accounts as she utters them. She does this to consider as best she can what might have been reasonable to others, to try to access the otherwise hidden logics informing people's actions or structuring an institution's practices. She likely does this in large part, initially, to gain a more full understanding of the situation. In trying to account for and understand deep differences, she is starting a dialogue across difference.

In attending to life-world disturbances and in venturing explanations, people are also often testing and constructing the possibility of public life. In tentative explanations, they engage in a "moment by moment interpretative process by which [they] make sense of what is happening around [them]," (Britton, 1980, p. 149), recognize and construct patterns (Leonardo, 2005), and in *sharing* these explanations, raise implicit questions that set up a demand for further shaping and justification (Britton, 1980, p.149):

- Is this just me?
- Is this something to work out with my boss?
- Does this concern other people here, too?
- Is this a broader concern for people—workers, bosses, African Americans, people of color, women, mothers—in other workplaces too?
- *Should* this concern others, if it doesn't yet?
- Who else should this concern?
- What relationships should I reasonably be able to rely on in making sense of and rectifying this life-world disturbance?

These are questions of what Iris Marion Young (1997) calls polity: "people who live together, who are stuck with one another" through proximity and/or economic and political interdependence (p. 126). This idea of polity is at the heart of public life. Even so, the "*stuck* part" can be troubling, the implication being, as Fecho reflects, that there's "nothing voluntary about it, nor does it suggest movement of any kind. Instead I see tires stuck in the mud, cars stuck in snow, gum stuck in a toddler's hair, keys stuck in a lock, windows stuck in the frame, fingers stuck in my face" (Fecho & Clifton, 2017 sidebar 2.1). What is perhaps most lovely and troubling about Fecho's reflection is that he has precisely grasped a central conundrum of deliberative publics: what will we do with the volatile presence of difference? To be sure, people do not always want to be *stuck* with the people they're stuck with. As Fecho recognizes, being stuck with others is not always a pleasant affair, and often not of our choosing. And yet, if a policy informing, say, quality control of water in Flint, Michigan, is not working for some people, those folks need to be able to get others in Flint or beyond Flint to share that concern if anything is going to change. This is also true in relation to some of our most private experiences, like domestic abuse or child abuse or which bodies can use which bathrooms at school or at McDonald's.

Sometimes, talking with an elder or friend or co-worker is enough to make sense of a situation and what to do next. We may realize that a situation doesn't necessarily need more public attention or dialogue. However, as a person experiences a life-world disturbance as more urgent or more chronic, more confusing, and more complex, more extended dialogue among strangers might be needed to gain a more full understanding of what's going on. In this iterative process of attending to life-world disturbances and of offering, eliciting, and considering differing explanatory accounts, people construct polity as they search for and construct patterns by making claims about what happened and why as well as why it matters and who should care. This is the being of public life. And yet simply "going public" is not enough. Response is required.

Of course, this is also precisely where difference is so charged. When people anticipate others responding, they often anticipate something adversarial. Explanatory accounts of life-world disturbances are often tentative, conflicting, and perspectival (Young, 1997). The account a mother in Flint, Michigan, offers will be different than that of the mayor or a city council member or a worker at a water treatment plant or a scientist or environmentalist or doctor or a water meter reader. And yet, these varying perspectives are necessary for a more full understanding of a complex situation. The likely fact is that others around us—in our towns, in our schools, in our churches and mosques and synagogues, in our economies, in our mayor's office—do not share our experiences or our perspectives, and perhaps don't agree with us or necessarily think they have any reason on their own to pay attention to someone like us. They haven't necessarily *chosen* us; we are strangers—strange and unknown to each other. But clean water, safe buses, school funding, and more all depend on people being able to construct what Warner (2005) calls *stranger relationality*—ways of relating with strangers—that relies on far more than mere tolerance. Relating across differences is, then, a primary condition and essential aspect of public life. After all, we deliberate not simply because we disagree but rather because some experience has disrupted our sense of stability to such a degree that we are compelled into inquiry and action (Crick & Gabriel, 2010, p. 209). There's something we've got to figure out, something in our experiences that's got to change, and we need others to help us do both.

We need ways, then, of learning to attend to life-world disturbances that others name, disturbances that might warrant more public attention—like suicides of gay youth across the country, school policies for dealing with bullies, or harmful water in Flint, Michigan. We especially need practices for doing this in ways that elicit differences in experiences, expertise, and perspectives as valuable resources for public deliberation and pragmatic problem-solving. Deliberation is not about universal reasoning about all possible scenarios but about situated reasoning about this particular scenario that we are facing now. To do the work of situated reasoning together—of argument as dialogue across difference—we need the grounded details of lived experiences "if we are going to deliberate with the fullest range of facts available to us" (Lauritzen, 2004, p. 24). After all, it is within the actual lives of citizens that the impacts of life-world disturbances can be perceived most sensitively (Habermas, 1996, p. 307–308). One method for attending to life-world disturbances and drawing on differences as a resource is the critical incident interview (Flanagan, 1954)—a technique often used to better understand problems in high-order performances like landing an airplane or making a medical diagnosis.

Cultivating Dialogue Across Difference: A Case Study

In a First-Year Composition class, students read essays and articles, viewed documentaries and films, and listened to radio interviews where people around the world discussed their experiences of different kinds of institutions not coming through for them. Students also discussed and wrote about their own and others' experiences with ineffective, harmful, confusing, or frustrating policies or practices in El Paso. Some focused on difficulties applying for financial aid, lack of accessible water in colonias, being labeled "disabled," racial profiling, difficulties of students crossing the U.S–Mexico border, people who drive drunk even though they know they shouldn't, to name a few.

One pair of students who are the focus of this case study made an inquiry into bullying at a large, predominantly Hispanic local middle school and high school. Because of their siblings' experiences, they were particularly concerned about what administrators do about bullying once they learn of it. To better understanding what happens once bullying is reported, the students conducted *critical incident interviews* (Clifton, 2017; Clifton, Long, & Roen, 2012; Flanagan, 1954; Flower, 2008; Higgins, Long, & Flower, 2006) of several students, parents, and a school administrator.

In critical incident interviews, they asked a range of stakeholders to tell them about what they observed about school practices and policies related to bullying—"Think back about a time when someone reported bullying at this school. Tell me what happened." They also prompted for specifics that would elicit differences of experience, perspective, and expertise. First, they prompted for differences in fine-grained details of behavior: "What was the setting or situation? What happened? What did you or X or Y say? How did people respond to each other? What was the outcome of that? What were you thinking when you said xyz? What did you think that X and Y were thinking?" Then, they prompted for differences of interpretation: "Looking back, why do you think this happened the way it did? What do you think made this an example of good (or bad) decision-making? Can you imagine what someone else might say, or how he or she might interpret this particular incident? "

In an early critical incident interview the students conducted, a principal noted that the administrators take bullying very seriously and follow a specific protocol outlined by the district. The principal told the students, "Every incident of bullying we come across, we deal with it" (interview date 02 Mar 2015). In interviews with students, there was a very different refrain: "It didn't help to tell anyone. I just kind of got used to it," as one student put it (interview date 11 Mar 2015).

These interviews elicited details that were useful for recognizing a range of documents, processes, and stakeholders, indicated in italics below, who might need to be part of these deliberations—people and processes they hadn't previously considered. A high-school principal told the students: ". . . we actually have *records* on it. We have to fill out an *incident report*. The *district* and the *state* have *guidelines* on how to handle bullying. It may involve *police reports* as well if they get involved, if there's a physical aspect, damage to property, *threats* made. That's a big one: threats, especially on *social media*." In these early interviews, accessing stakeholders' conflicting experiences and perspectives was valuable for better understanding a complex situation and recognizing a need for careful and informed responses that would be attentive to people's different needs and experiences. One student noted, "In this case, I don't think the 'one side is entirely right' type of argument works because one side is not entirely right."

As they learned more about how distributed, difficult, and complex the processes for dealing with bullying were, they also realized they might need to engage in further inquiry. Importantly, it is the inquiry itself—asking students, parents, teachers, and administrators to describe their interactions around reports and guidelines—that begins to mark how bullying is dealt with in these schools as a public concern for some stakeholders and to create it as a public and shared concern for others, requiring further inquiry and dialogue to determine what might be done differently.

The students looked up district and state guidelines; interviewed other students and parents about specific experiences of bullying; and conducted a voluntary survey of 80 ($n = 80$) students across the middle and high school about their experiences of bullying:

- 71% of the students surveyed said that they had been bullied in the past.
- 22% percent of students who said they'd been bullied reported that the school did nothing at all to help their situation.
- Only seven of the 57 students who reported being bullied said the school resolved the problem.

Subsequent critical incident interviews with middle and high-school students described what happened, from a student perspective, when they reported bullying to administrators. One student said, "At first I talked to the vice principal, but she didn't do anything. She said she would talk to them but she didn't. And now I'm dealing with the counselor. And the vice principal again." Because they felt the school did little to protect their safety or improve their circumstances, many students reported that they stopped telling school officials about their own or others' experiences of bullying. One student, in response to questions about her interpretation of administrators' responses, said she felt like "they only care about their reputation."

The students took these results to school administrators to see how they might react to the results. The high-school principal was visibly startled: "71%. Wow. That's a little bit of a surprise. I wouldn't have thought that it would have been that high." It's worth pausing here to note that the students' and the principal's stance toward difference and data. The students are valuing data to mark a significant difference in experiences and understanding as an important site for further inquiry, dialogue, and problem-solving. They do not leverage this difference to prove the principal wrong, per se. Nor does the principal rely on his authority as principal to refute the different perspectives he's encountering. Instead, it is precisely their differences that provide valuable information to begin to better address bullying in the school.

The critical incident interviews drew on difference as a resource to indicate specific responses, actions, and decisions that stakeholders needed to problem-solve together to create practices and policies that worked better for everyone involved.

The students compiled this data designing a combination of textual documents and filmed interview excerpts to cultivate additional and ongoing dialogue as they came to realize that particular instances of bullying and addressing bullying are always different, requiring different judgments in each situation and different judgments or possible actions by different stakeholders.

Students later called together previously interviewed stakeholders to deliberate over this concern. Students used their texts and multimedia creations to invite and scaffold a collaborative problem-solving dialogue in which differences are prized rather than feared, ignored, or quashed. The interviews not only created the data necessary for these dialogues but also created the trust among stakeholders that their different experiences would be valued and useful.

This process led to changed practices—a student advisory committee at the school specifically focused on bullying and changes in counseling interventions within the school, for example—the critical incident interviews also impacted students' stances toward differences. One said, "One thing I am also taking away . . . is that I want to be more self-aware when it comes to treating my own opinions like they're the norm or expected view. I think I have done myself a disservice at times by not speaking less and listening more! While I consider myself to be thoughtful of others' feelings, I think we all have blind spots."

What Made this High-Impact Practice Successful?

With an impasse as a starting point, students set out to construct a *shared concern* around a school's practices related to addressing bullying, despite deep differences in experiences and perspectives among administrators, students, and parents. The students did this, not by ignoring or oversimplifying differences, but by highlighting differences as sites of shared inquiry and as valuable resources for productive dialogue. In particular, the students started their inquiry with critical incident interviews that sought: 1) to understand individual instances of addressing bullying as they played out in relation to near and distant stakeholders; 2) to consider a range of perspectives informing and shaping a given incident; 3) to understand how different stakeholders responded in a given instance as well as the hidden logics that informed what actions seemed available and reasonable to them at the time; 4) to shift the ways different stakeholders understood this concern and to invite alternative and more productive ways of relating; 5) to analyze and contextualize larger patterns across these instances; and 6) to recognize a range of systems, policies, practices, and people connected to this incident. Learning to conduct critical incident interviews involved students in looking simultaneously at this one incident *and* at the systems, policies, practices, and claims it contributes to and is produced by—and in critically re-imagining public life—seeing again through dialogue across difference possibilities for producing what's not present or has not yet been experienced both in terms of pragmatic aims and in terms of ways of relating and talking together.

What Were Some of the Challenges?

Students are accustomed to thinking about their own experiences but may be less familiar with thinking about the experiences of others. If things are going smoothly in their own lives, and especially if students inhabit dominant or privileged identities, particular instances of life-world disturbances that need more public attention may be a bit elusive. In this case, compelling readings and films that explore grounded, data-driven accounts of everyday encounters—of immigration policies or eviction notices, for example—that are in some way difficult, confusing, or harmful can help students pay attention to their own and others' experiences that may warrant more public dialogue. Interactions with strangers or systems (and their people, policies, and practices) in which students have found themselves asking, "What the heck just happened there?" or saying, "That's not right!" or "I can't believe that just happened [to me or to someone else]!" or "That doesn't really make any sense. Why do we do it that way?" often indicate wobble experiences that might also point to concerns others share, or should share. Teachers will know students are on to a rich problem space when students share concerns—or urgently need others to share their concerns—and ask, *So, what do we do?!*

Recommendations For Faculty

Attending to public or yet-to-be-public concerns asks students to consider the ways they and others are affected by the world around them. This high-impact practice asks students to approach differences with an inquiry stance and offers a method for engaging students in multi-dimensional, purposeful research aimed at creating more complex understandings of shared concerns that need people's differences of perspectives, of experiences, of institutional positions in order to approach life-world disturbances as sites of shared knowledge building. For faculty interested in employing critical incident interviews, it can be helpful to first read or view examples of others from a variety of perspectives and backgrounds documenting or "going public" about life-world disturbances. Doing critical incident interviews in class first, before engaging community residents, can also help students get used to interviewing and can open up conversations about the kinds of data they might need to attend to or elicit in the interviews—details that will help foster productive dialogue among multiple stakeholders later.

Recommendations For Students

When systems aren't working, it can be easy to think of people as obstacles, as problems, or as victims. This high-impact practice instead invites students to consider what a person—even someone they disagree with—is up to on their own terms and how that person's experiences and perspectives might be valuable and helpful. Questions about different stakeholders' goals and desires; struggles, problems, concerns, or limitations; tools, strategies, logics, stances, or actions; potential gains or losses can be useful for re-seeing people in particular situations as they navigate systems.

Recommendations For Community

As world renowned literacy scholar James Gee has noted about the work I describe in this chapter, the stakes couldn't be higher. Gee writes, "I can think of no more timely, moral, and smart approach to literacies in or out of school. . . . Unless we humans learn to discuss critical issues with one another across differences in a joint journey, not to conversion, but to a better shared world there may soon be no world left for us" (Gee qtd. in Clifton, 2017). In particular, community organizations might employ critical incident interviews to determine how institutions might be more responsive to local residents (Dodson, 2011; Long et al., 2016). Lisa Dodson, for example, employs a similar method in educational settings, hospitals, and with middle managers in local businesses. Critical incident interviews might also point to the need for coalitions and collaborative problem-solving across institutions, for example, related to refugee education (cf., Clifton, 2016; Long, 2018).

The Critical Incident Interview

The critical incident interview is essentially a procedure for gathering important facts based on direct observations of human behavior in defined situations (Flanagan, 1954) as a way to facilitate their potential usefulness in solving practical problems. The critical incident interview does not consist of a single rigid set of rules governing data collection/production. Instead, it is a flexible method that must be modified and adapted to the specific situation at hand. In an early study (Finkle, 1949), for example, critical incidents were gathered from foremen, general foremen, and staff personnel of the Westinghouse Electric Corporation in East Pittsburgh. Some examples of these questions are:

1. Think of a time when a foreman has done something that you felt should be encouraged because it seemed to be in your opinion an example of good foremanship. (Effective—slight deviation from norm.)
2. Think of a time when a foreman did something that you thought was not up to par. (Ineffective—slight deviation from norm.)
3. Think of a time when a foreman has, in your opinion, shown definitely good foremanship—the type of action that points out the superior foreman. (Effective—substantial deviation from the norm.)
4. Think of a time when a foreman has, in your opinion, shown poor foremanship—the sort of action which if repeated would indicate that the man was not an effective foreman. (Ineffective—substantial deviation from norm.) (qtd in Flanagan, 1954).

Questions, like these, however, might be easily adapted to other domains—nursing, education, community police work, social services, or water resource management, for example. The case study earlier in this chapter points to questions students asked to access a range of experiences with bullying in local schools.

Critical incident interviews are tools to support pragmatic, collaborative problem-solving. This chapter provides a method for determining incidents that warrant more public attention and public dialogue. In documenting critical incidents, it is precisely the differences across a range of perspectives, experiences, and expertise that will support greater and more nuanced understandings as well as more grounded and viable pragmatic problem-solving. To explore suspension policies at a particular school, for example, it would be important to interview principals, vice-principals, school counselors, students, and parents. It's likely that in accounting for particular behaviors and decisions, each person interviewed offers a different observation of what happened as well as a different rationale for those behaviors and decisions—their own and others'. Lorraine Higgins, Elenore Long, and Linda Flower (2006) describe the critical incident interview as a resource for subsequent joint inquiry and deliberation among people who otherwise have few occasions to listen and to learn from one another: "Yet personal stories alone don't necessarily support intercultural inquiry. The challenge is harnessing narrative's capacity to dramatize the reasons behind the teller's values and priorities (Young, 1997, p. 72) and to illustrate the rich contextual background and social conditions in which problems play themselves out" (p.21).

Conclusion

In conducting critical incident interviews students are attempting to hear where the private, localized knowledge of an individual or group might be reflective of or indicative of a more public issue of shared concern. Rather than avoiding each other's differences and difficulties in the name of "safety," critical incident interviews offer a research-oriented way of calling on differences as resources for public dialogue.

References

Alexander, M. (2010). *The new jim crow*. New York, NY: The New Press.

Britton, J. (1980). Shaping at the point of utterance. In R. Young & Y. Liu (Eds.), *Landmark essays on rhetorical invention in writing* (pp. 147–152). New York, NY: Routledge.

Clifton, J. (2016). Feminist collaboratives and intercultural inquiry: Constructing an alternative to the (Not So) hidden logics and practices of university outreach and micro-lending. *Feminist Campus-Community Partnerships: Intersections and Interruptions* Special Issue of *Feminist Teacher*, 24(1): 110–137.

Clifton, J. (2017). *Argument as dialogue across difference: Engaging youth in public literacies*. New York, NY: Routledge.

Clifton, J., Long, E., & Roen, D. (2012). Accessing private knowledge for public conversations: Attending to shared, yet-to-be-public concerns in the deaf and hard-of-hearing DALN interviews. In S. L. DeWitt, H. L. Ulman, & C. L. Selfe (Eds.), *Stories that speak to Us: Exhibits from the digital archive of literacy narratives*. Logan, UT: Computers and Composition Digital Press.

Clifton, J., & Sigoloff, J. (2013). Writing as dialogue across difference: inventing genres to support deliberative democracy. *Choices and Voices: Teaching English in a Democratic Society*. Special Issue of *English Journal*. Nov 2013. Print. [Note: Publication co-authored with doctoral student]

Crick, N., & Gabriel, J. (2010). The conduit between lifeworld and system: Habermas and the rhetoric of public scientific controversies. *Rhetoric Society Quarterly*, 40(3), 201–223.

Dodson, L. (2011). *The moral underground: How ordinary Americans subvert an unfair economy*. New York, NY: The New Press.

Erdely, S. (2012). One town's war on gay teens. *Rolling Stone*. Retrieved from http://www.rollingstone.com/politics/news/one-towns-war-on-gay-teens-20120202

Fecho, B. (2011). *Teaching for the students: Habits of heart, mind, and practice in the engaged classroom*. New York, NY: Teachers College Press.

Fecho, B. & Clifton, J. (2017). *Dialoguing across cultures, identities, and learning: Crosscurrents and complexities in literacy classrooms*. New York, NY: Routledge.

Flanagan, J. C. (1954). The critical incident technique. *Psychological Bulletin*, 51(4), 327–358.

Flower, L. (2006). Intercultural knowledge building: The literate action of a community think tank. In C. Bazerman & D. Russell (Eds.), *Writing selves/Writing societies: Research from activity perspectives* (pp. 239–79). Fort Collins, CO: The WAC Cleaninghouse and Mind, Culture, and Activity.

Flower, L. (2008). *Community literacy and the rhetoric of public engagement*. Carbondale, IL: SIU Press.

Habermas, J. (1996). *Between facts and norms* (W. Rehg, Trans.).Cambridge: Polity Press.

Higgins, L. & Brush, L. (2006). Personal writing and public debate: Writing the wrongs of welfare. *College Composition and Communication*, 57(4), 694–729.

Higgins, L., Long, E., & Flower, L. (2006). Community literacy: A rhetorical model for personal and public inquiry. *Community Literacy*, 1(1), 9–43.

Lauritzen, P. (2004). Arguing with life stories: The case of Rigoberta Menchu. In P. J. Eakin (Ed.), *The ethics of life writing* (pp. 19–39). Ithaca, IL: Cornell University Press.

Leopold, D. (2015). The shocking reality of Donald Trump's plan to deport millions. Retrieved from http://www.msnbc.com/msnbc/donald-trump-shocking-reality-deportation-plan

Long, E. (2018). *A responsive rhetorical art: Artistic methods for contemporary public life.* Pittsburgh, PA: University of Pittsburgh Press.

Scott, B., Longo, B., & Wills, K. (2006). *Critical power tools: Technical communication and cultural studies.* Albany, NY: SUNY Press.

Simmons, M. (2007). *Participation and power: Civil discourse in environmental policy decisions.* Albany, NY: SUNY Press.

Spivak, G. (1994). Can the subaltern speak? In P. Williams & L. Chrisman (Eds.), *Colonial discourse and postcolonial theory.* New York, NY: Columbia University Press.

Young, I. M. (1997). *Intersecting voices.* Princeton, NJ: Princeton University Press.

Chapter 10

Community and Academic Public Health Perspectives in Pharmacy Education: Linking the Learning Outcomes of Service-Learning and Community-based Participatory Research

Eufemia (Pema) B. Garcia and Jeri Sias

SERVICE LEARNING,
COMMUNITY-BASED LEARNING

UNDERGRADUATE RESEARCH

DIVERSITY/GLOBAL LEARNING

Use these questions to guide your reflection prior to reading the chapter. Use the notes/follow-up section to write your thoughts after you have read the chapter. Your notes can include thoughts in reference to the reflection questions, or general observations about the chapter.

1) Based on your understanding of service-learning, how do you think the experience may or may not be different if it is held in the U.S. Mexico-Border? Please explain.

2) How do you think that the public health sector may or may not benefit from students engaging with community organizations instead of or in addition to hospitals or pharmacies?

3) What do you think is meant when statements about the need for diversity in the public health sector are made? What role do universities have in addressing this issue?

Notes/Follow-up:

_____

_____

_____

_____

_____

Introduction

This chapter provides perspectives on linking service-learning and community-based participatory research from the viewpoints of a community leader and a pharmacist–educator partnership. To understand our approach to education, we start by describing the social context of the border community of El Paso, Texas. The authors encourage students, community, and faculty learners to engage in dialogue as you develop a working definition of service-learning and community-based participatory research. As we identify elements of civic responsibility in service-learning, we invite you to learn from our own community–university partnership experiences to better understand rationale for linking service-learning and community-based participatory research. We conclude by identifying practice tips for students, community members, and faculty when working together.

Throughout the chapter, we invite readers to reflect and explore the following questions: What has been your experience with volunteering? With service-learning? How is volunteering different from service-learning? What are elements of student civic learning in service-learning? What should students consider before, during, and after engaging in service-learning?

Our Community Context

El Paso, Texas rests on the Texas–Mexico border at the intersection of two countries (United States of America and Mexico) and three states (Texas, New Mexico, and Chihuahua). According to US census data, El Paso County is a predominantly Mexican-American community with nearly 800,000 people where two-thirds of households speak Spanish in the home. The overall household income and educational attainment are below the state and national averages. Access to health care is often limited, as it is an area with a health professional shortage and need to nearly double the pharmacist workforce.

Some unique assets to the community include recognizing that El Paso is an international community where students experience global living on a daily basis. When health care and medications are not available or affordable, patients can seek service in the sister city of Ciudad Juárez, Mexico. As one of the largest international border communities in the world, people move back and forth across the border where exchanges in higher education, shopping, family, and work. The University of Texas at El Paso (UTEP) is a rising research-intensive university seeking to provide access and excellence for a student population that reflects the region's demographic make-up. For those living in El Paso, we enjoy a family friendly and generally safe community.

Contributed by Eufemia B. Garcia and Jeri J. Sias. © Kendall Hunt Publishing Company.

Our Approach

Service-learning (see definitions section) provides students and faculty a way to learn about the community from the community perspective and to allow questions about these settings to emerge more organically. Having students then use these basic questions to develop small Community-based participatory research (CBPR) projects (see definitions section) with faculty is a natural "next step" in the student's professional development. Service-learning in pharmacy education in the context of living and working on the US–Mexico border has provided a canvas for exploring and enhancing student learning while exposing them to opportunities for student research with faculty. Depending on the length of the service-learning experience, some students complete a shorter project using CBPR principles (1 semester) and others actually conduct a small research project (2–4 semesters).

What Are the Elements of Service-Learning in our Pharmacy Education Experience?

We view service-learning as an educational vehicle for pharmacy students to reflect on their personal and community values while advancing their knowledge and skills related to the following goals:

1. Develop an understanding of healthcare issues, disparities, and cultural health beliefs found in the Texas–Mexico border regions.
2. Be engaged in community as civic-minded healthcare professional students.
3. Gain experience in community-based project development.
4. Improve community-based communication, teamwork, and project evaluation skills.

Definitions and Civic Responsibility

What is Service-Learning and its Role in Health Professional Education?

Service-learning (S-L) is a structured educational practice using preparation and reflection to integrate classroom learning with hands-on experience in communities (Seifer, 1998) encouraged via national organizations such as the Community-Campus Partnerships for Health and Campus Compact. S-L has been an educational mechanism that has been well-described in health professional education to develop professionalism and student citizenship, understand public health, engage with diverse cultures, as well work in interprofessional teams.

Since as early as 1999, the role of service-learning has been explored in pharmacy education journals (Kearney, 2004; Murawski, Murawski, & Wilson, 1999). Through service-learning courses, pharmacy students develop foundational skills to address and resolve medication-related issues based on understanding social issues facing patients and reflecting on the real-world context that affects the patients and communities around them.

What is CBPR?

CBPR is an approach to research that engages the community as equitable collaborators with academic researchers to conceptualize the research question and then develop, implement, evaluate, and disseminate the research while participating in each step of the process. CBPR values the community and academic perspectives, knowledge, and abilities that together contribute to positive social changes such as creating health equity and improving health outcomes (Minkler & Wallerstein, 2003). Minkler and Wallerstein describe CBPR as an "orientation to research" not just a method. This orientation relies on basic principles of "trust, power, dialogue, community capacity building, and collaborative inquiry" that builds on strengths and assets of communities.

For pharmacy education in a health professional shortage area (HPSA), the link between service-learning and CBPR provides foundational skill development for pharmacy students to involve the community in proactively identifying and solving its own concerns. Further, skills used in service-learning align well with CBPR. Note the similarities in characteristics of service-learning and CBPR (Table 1).

Table 1 Comparing Service-Learning and CBPR Characteristics in Health

Characteristics1	S-L	CBPR
Uses participatory methods of inclusion	✓	✓
Develops relationships that are cooperative & equitable (Community members & researchers/educators)	✓	✓
Encourages co-learning	✓	✓
Builds the capacity of the community	✓	✓
Values diverse cultures	✓	✓
Seeks to understand cause of health disparities and create health equity	✓	✓
Is "Praxis" based (transformative action based on critical reflection) (Freire, 1970)	✓	✓

Source: Minkler and Wallerstein (2003).

Where is the Civic Responsibility in Service-Learning?

Service-learning equips students to evaluate their civic responsibility moving through the following life-learning elements of development (Eyler & Giles, 1999): Values, Knowledge, Skills, Efficacy, and Commitment.

To apply Eyler and Giles elements of civic responsibility to pharmacy education on the US–Mexico border, I have found that students in pharmacy often intrinsically have the **value** of wanting to "help people." It is out of genuine care that they have entered a health professions career path. UTEP students will feel a natural connection to the region because they come from the community, and often represent the socioeconomic and ethnic demographic of the border. They recognize a social need for change because they have seen and lived this experience through their families and friends.

While naming and identifying values of students, the service-learning course also recognizes that students should enter communities understanding their own strengths and beliefs from a cultural perspective. One of the first reflections student complete in the course is to name their cultural attributes and social norms. For example, what do students value as individuals, in their families, and in their communities? What do students believe they can contribute to their communities?

Students will also generally have the **knowledge** that broader social problems exist in their communities such as lower educational attainment, health disparities, and sometimes fear of immigration laws. They have

Table 2 Elements of Civic Responsibility

Elements of Civic Responsibility	Reflective Statement	Cognitive and Affective Domains
Values	"I ought to do"	Develop a sense of social responsibility and need for change
Knowledge	"I know what I ought to do and why"	Develop increased understanding of social problems Begin to function as a problem solver
Skills	"I know how to do"	Develop knowledge on how to strategically engage in communities
Efficacy	"I can do, and it makes a difference"	Develop confidence in personal skills and in ways able to engage with communities
Commitment	"I must and will do"	Develop commitment to social change

Source: Eyler and Giles (1999).

the capacity to expand this knowledge via homework assignments using census data, public health reports (regional, national, and international), literature reviews, and news reports.

To build a balanced perspective on strengths and opportunities of the community, we invite students on a community walking tour in the heart of El Paso to identify the strengths and needs in neighborhoods (Kretzmann & McKnight, 1993). For example, we can explore the relationship among schools, clinics, libraries, grocery stores, and other community entities (nonprofit, government, and for-profit) and the built infrastructures that support healthy communities such as good sidewalks, clean parks, and access to healthy foods. Through this process of focusing on the assets of a community first, we (students and instructor) can develop a more balanced perspective of the community. This dual approach (public health/literature statistics and community background) to knowledge development encourages students to balance facts and realities while not making assumptions about what constitutes a healthy community.

During the service-learning course, students develop basic communication and relationship-building **skills** when they interact with their service sites. In the community, they engage with youth, patients with diabetes or other chronic diseases, persons facing food insecurity, or the elderly. Through reflections, students begin to understand what is important to community members; students may be surprised that sometimes people do not worry about their health and medications all the time! On the contrary, sometimes community members seek connections and experiences that are simply enjoyable and fun.

During actual class time, students develop skills related to how to conduct a community-based research question, write objectives, and develop strategies appropriate for interacting within different communities. For example, we have explored literacy levels (English and Spanish) of informed consent and documents, how to build trust for recruitment, and whether focus groups or surveys will even work in the populations they are serving. By linking service-learning with CBPR, pharmacy students have the opportunity to gain basic skills to respectfully interact and understand the community agencies as well as to find relevant and realistic methods to examine community questions.

Through the process of reflection, engagement, study, and project development using a CBPR orientation, students explore challenges faced by patients and demonstrate that they can make a difference in a person's life **(efficacy)**. They learn from the experience as well (reciprocal learning). This awareness can add another dimension to their development as a pharmacist who has greater self-confidence and can empathize and problem-solve with their patients.

It is difficult to assess the students' final **commitment** to social change. However, one way to guide students through this learning journey is through the "praxis." Paulo Freire's writings, Brazilian educator and philosopher, has highly influenced "praxis" as found in education and social change theory and practice (Freire, 1970). Praxis is an iterative process of critical reflection and action through dialogue (genuine shared experiences) that can lead to transformation in individuals, communities, and structures, particularly in marginalized communities (Freire, 1970). In service-learning, through "praxis," educators can challenge students to explore their personal commitment to change.

Case Study

Why Do We Link Service-Learning and CBPR?

We select sites that have a connection to public health, but purposely do not place students in pharmacies. We have not designed our service-learning experience to replicate real-pharmacy experiences (note: would be required to have a pharmacist present for experiences where students provide medication information). Rather, to complement the pharmacy educational experience, we have focused on the sociocultural aspects of health at sites such as food banks, after school programs, health education classes, or senior recreation centers. We recognize that the sociocultural aspects of access to medication may include understanding patients' financial priorities, work limitations, literacy levels, and perceptions of traditional and western medicine. Service-learning brings the community members' realities and barriers to the forefront of the pharmacy student education.

In the spirit of CBPR, we do not permit pharmacy students to come up with their projects on their own. They are expected to spend at least a few weeks at their service site prior to working with the site on a project (unless the site already knows a project at the beginning). This element of engagement and relationship building before research is stressed. Too often, professionals and researchers perceive that they have the "expertise" to give and serve. However in service-learning and CBPR, our communities are the co-educators and co-researchers. Our community liaisons provided valuable and needed insight into selecting the projects.

The course/experiences have been developed sequentially so that ideas and concepts build on each other and lead to the final product (project or research findings). Examples of this linked sequential process are outlined in Table 3.

Alongside the experience students complete reflections. Reflections are designed using Kolb's iterative process of learning summarized as "What happened?" "So what happened and why?" and "Now what?" (Eyler, Reflection: Linking Service and Learning—Linking Students and Communities, 2002) **Case: Applying Kolb's Cycle (Figure 1):** One example that often resurfaces in class as a **"What happened?"** question is that nonprofit agencies can experience an often high turnover rate. This change could occur in the middle of a semester and with a perceived "break" in the continuity for student learning. However, in class we discuss **"So what happened and why?"** and include reflections as to root causes of high turnover. The first myth we discuss is that high turnover does not necessarily mean poor quality of a site. Students learn to name several reasons for potential changes in leadership including 1) we are an underserved population and there are often job opportunities at another site; 2) funding for non-profits is

Table 3 Linking S-L Activities with CBPR Outcomes

Service-Learning Activities	CBPR Outcomes
Conduct reviews of census data, public health, and literature based on population served. Conduct mini-interviews with site personnel, and newspaper/television reports.	Gain background Understanding.
Engage in service site. Observe, reflect, and read.	Form community-based research question.
Work with community liaisons and faculty to identify project.	Develop community-based research question.
Work with community liaisons and faculty on culturally-, linguistically-, and literacy level-appropriate methods to complete project and gather information on research question.	Develop methods/approach to CBPR.
Engage in project (e.g., health education project, brochure, intervention, and quality of service survey).	Collect and analyze data.
Reflect on project or data collection process.	Recognize discussion points.
Present a final report/summarize findings.	Present project/results to sites.

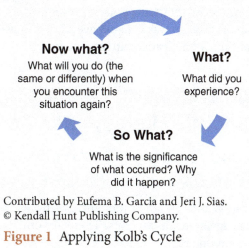

Now what?
What will you do (the same or differently) when you encounter this situation again?

What?
What did you experience?

So What?
What is the significance of what occurred? Why did it happen?

Contributed by Eufema B. Garcia and Jeri J. Sias.
© Kendall Hunt Publishing Company.

Figure 1 Applying Kolb's Cycle

often dependent upon fund-raising and/or government funding cycles; and/or 3) personal or professional reasons not related to quality of the site. We also deliberate on the high turnover from the patient/client perspective. I urge students to remember that they are training in a HPSA. I follow up with questions to pharmacy students and online discussion groups, "How do you think a patient feels if they have a new community pharmacist or primary care provider every 6 months?" and "What are barriers to care for patients when patients experience constant changes in their healthcare?"

These reflective dialogues lead up to the **"Now what?"** part of the iterative Kolb's cycle of questions. Pharmacy students then identify how they must re-enter their service site with a more realistic outlook and identify ways that they can contribute to the site. Students can avoid feeling disappointed if and when changes take place in the community and use these site challenges as opportunities to increase skills to be more pro-active in the educational process and have increased empathy for their patients.

Lessons Learned

What Made this High-Impact Practice Successful?

When first introducing the course in Fall 2001, in pharmacist education we realized that our graduates would provide patients with medication while expecting patients could afford the regimen, be adherent, and to be able to read and interpret information about their medications. Service-learning provides a venue for "real-world" problems to be explored by connecting students with service organizations prior to graduation.

What Were Some of the Challenges?

Sometimes, pharmacy students from the community are resistant to learn about their community. They may feel that they already know their region. However, through an iterative process of reflection and action students combine learning to conduct research (e.g., census data, literature review, news reports, and public health statistics) with community engagement (e.g., getting to know people at their sites, individual and group reflection, and projects).

In CBPR, communities contribute to identifying the questions. This process has worked with a fairly small number of students (~5–15 students), and students have been able to individualize their mini-projects when they conduct research and gather some pilot data for community sites. However, with larger cohorts of students, it is important to provide more longevity to the projects for the benefit of the community. We can prepare students, by first understanding the community via reviewing census and public health data, conducting community tours, and inviting community speakers into the class. As students interact in their service sites and conclude their experiences, they continue to learn about their community and reflect on their experiences. Some students have been able to pass on their project to a student (or group of students) in a subsequent year. For example, one student started a poison prevention education project in local elementary schools and the second group of students was able to have a larger outreach in a subsequent year. This passing of the baton also build continuity and leadership for students.

Community Perspectives and Tips for Students and Faculty to Apply this High-Impact Practice

What Should Students and Faculty Do When Engaging in Service-Learning and/or Community-Based Projects?

Based on our community organization and research experience, we have identified that there are four main keys for successful community engagement for students. There are other tips to consider as well and we maintain that flexibility is a vital component.

1. **Integrate.** When collaborating with a community organization, look for opportunities to integrate into the regular operations and activities of that organization by becoming a volunteer. Adapt to the organizations culture (e.g., pot lucks, special dress day, and participate in in-service training) and practices when possible. Align your own learning objectives to fall in line with that of the organizations' mission and purpose that serves community members.

2. **Eliminate prejudgment. Challenge your own assumptions and biased beliefs.** It is easy to walk into a community with a set of preconceived ideas of the community sector and the population that resides there or receives services from that site. Remember that we are not all alike in our habits, beliefs, and actions although we are part of a larger group (e.g., Hispanic, Spanish speakers, rural/urban residents, age groups, and gender). Treat each community member as an individual with their own set of values, traditions, beliefs, preferences, needs, and assets, although there may be similarities across a sector. It can also be helpful to find something personal that you can identify with that helps you embrace the community members or families as part of your own.

3. **Practice "dual" learning.** Be ready to share your knowledge with the host organization as well as the community members you will be serving. This sharing can be in the forms of presentations, workshops, skills building, or developing specific products such as data collection/analysis, a report, budget, proposal, or a poster presentation. Make sure that the community partners have feedback on how their organization is described in any reports. As you are sharing your skills and knowledge, be cognizant that you will <u>also</u> be learning from members of that community organization as well as from community members. Be open to that learning and respectful that learning is done in many types of settings. We all have something to contribute as well as a great deal to learn from others. This shared learning can lead to authentic questions for projects and CBPR.

4. **Seek alternative yet complementary roles.** Look for opportunities to contribute to your organization and or host community beyond your academic role. Explore the ways your organization assists its community members and try to engage in a complementary activity. For example, you may be placed at an organization that provides health and nutrition education where you will be helping with a research project. You could participate in a variety of activities such as assisting with the community garden, food distributions, recipe development, cooking demonstration, photo/video documenting a project, writing a report or newsletter that captures the project, and promotion via social media. These activities help to create trust.

What Are Pitfalls of Students and Faculty When Engaging in the Community?

As students and faculty approach engaging with community organizations, some suggestions of behaviors to avoid.

1. Avoid thinking and acting as you are there to do a job and leave. Rather . . . fit in as if you were planning to stay.

2. Avoid behaving in a manner that is disrespectful to the organization and the community members by demonstrating or acting as if you are the asset and they are the liability. Conversely . . . be respectful recognizing the organization and community members have opened their doors for you. Be gracious and seek the learning in each part of your experience.

3. Do not forget your humility. On the contrary . . . be humble and keep an open-mind. You are learning. The community is your teacher.

When Engaging with Organizations, What Community Resources Should Students and Faculty Seek?

Look for the gatekeepers. Many times they are the quiet individuals who work behind the scenes or do not have a professional title. They can be people such as the front desk personnel, volunteers, or community health workers/promoters.

Academic Perspectives for Community and Faculty Engaging in Partnership

To Community: First, thank you for sharing your site to be part of the education of our future pharmacists and healthcare providers. A few tips in working with faculty and students follow.

1. **Set clear expectations.** Meet with faculty early to develop mutually beneficial outcomes for the service-learning experience and/or CBPR project.
2. **Share your story.** Students are eager to learn and are inspired by your stories of why you are committed to your community. Your words mean a lot as students identify their own life goals.
3. **Be assertive.** It is ok to say "no" if the timing is not right to host a student or a project. Because the academic calendar often works on semester cycles, it is helpful to know if you cannot be a service-learning site with about one month's notice. Once a project has started, it is more challenging to stop. However, with adequate advanced notice, faculty can still often change gears and adjust the course!

To Faculty: Some tips for faculty seeking ways to connect service-learning with developing basic CBPR skills for students.

1. **Take time to build trust.** For your service-learning sites to flourish, you will need to be committed to this educational process and also take time to build trust in the partnership with your community sites.
2. **Be practical.** Evaluate how much time you have to for the course develop the skills. If you have a one-semester course, two-semesters, or two years, your outcomes will be different. In one semester, the student will not necessarily complete a research project, but they can complete a small project using CBPR principles and they may gain interest to participate in an actual research project.
3. **Develop team learning models for students**. Provide room (if possible) for students to meet in smaller groups (2-5). They can learn from each other and often build richer projects with the community.

Guiding Reflective Questions

As you explore service-learning and CBPR in health professions and other fields, consider the following questions.

• What are qualities in service-learning that are similar to CBPR? What approaches can students and faculty take when developing rapport and trust with community agencies and leaders?
• Reflect on a volunteer or service experience that may not have gone well. Use the Kolb's reflective process to evaluate how the experience could have ended with a more positive learning outcome.

Summary/Conclusion

By linking service-learning and CBPR, faculty, students, and community can all benefit in mutual learning and outcomes. In pharmacy and health professions, we have employed a model that allows students to build foundational skills for connecting with communities, develop civic responsibility, reflect on their professional roles in society, and engage in mini-projects and research.

Selected Readings

The following readings and activities may be helpful background for linking service-learning and CBPR.

1. **Community-Campus Partnership for Health (CCPH) website.** This website includes a number of tools for developing service-learning experiences in health professional education. (https://ccph.memberclicks.net/)
2. **Building Communities from the Inside Out.** This workbook provides ideas on how to explore the assets of a community. (Kretzmann & McKnight, 1993)
3. **Census Data.** When students access census data at a neighborhood/zip code level and compare socio-economic variables to the larger city, state, and nation, they begin to realize that their communities are unique. (www.census.gov)

Sample Census Data Collection and Comparison Table

	Zip Code #1	Zip Code #2	Zip Code #3	City	State	Nation
Population						
Racial & ethnic comparison						
Median household income						
Educational attainment						
Percentage of veterans						
Percentage unemployed						
Percentage of grandparents taking care of grandchildren						
Percentage of language other than English spoken in home						

4. **City/County/State Health Reports and Healthy People 2020.** By accessing these reports and initiatives online, students can gain insight to the high priority health issues facing their immediate communities and how these priorities compare to national health goals. (https://www.healthypeople.gov/)
5. **CBPR in Health.** This textbook includes definitions and examples of CBPR from leaders in this field of research. (Minkler & Wallerstein, 2003)

References

Eyler, J. (2002). Reflection: linking service and learning—Linking students and communities. *Journal of Social Issues, 58*(3), 517–534.

Eyler, J., & Giles, J. D. (1999). *Where's the learning in service-learning?* San Francisco, CA: Jossey-Bass, Inc.

Freire, P. (1970). *Pedagogy of the oppressed.* New York, NY: Seabury Press.

Kearney, K. R. (2004). Service-learning in pharmacy education. *American Journal of Pharmaceutical Education, 68*(1), 26. doi:10.5688/aj680126

Kretzmann, J. P., & McKnight, J. L. (1993). *Building communities from the inside out: A path toward finding and mobilizing a community's assets.* Chicago, IL: ACTA Publications.

Minkler, M., & Wallerstein, N. (2003). Introduction to community based participatory research. In M. Minkler, N. Wallerstein, M. Minkler, & N. Wallerstein (Eds.), *Community based participatory research in health.* San Francisco, CA: John Wiley & Sons, Inc. Jossey-Bass.

Murawski, M. M., Murawski, D. & Wilson, M. (1999). Service-learning and pharmaceutical education: an exploratory sruvey. *American Journal of Pharmaceutical Education, 63*(2), 160–164.

Seifer, S. D. (1998). Service-learning: Community-campus partnerships for health professions education. *Academic Medicine, 73*(3), 273–277.

Health Science

Chapter 11

Using Capstone Course Fieldwork to Serve the Older Adult Community

Sandor Dorgo

CAPSTONE COURSES

Use these questions to guide your reflection prior to reading the chapter. Use the notes/follow-up section to write your thoughts after you have read the chapter. Your notes can include thoughts in reference to the reflection questions, or general observations about the chapter.

1) What is your understanding of capstone courses and the role they play in students' academic experience?

2) What would be the ideal capstone experience you would like to have connected to your field of study? What would make it ideal and how would it benefit you?

3) Based on your own knowledge, what kind of service would be of most benefit to older adults? How do you know this?

Notes/Follow-up:

_____

_____

_____

_____

_____

Introduction

Physical activity is essential for good general health and wellness all throughout the lifespan. During the aging process, however, regular physical activity or well-structured exercise programming becomes even more important. As an individual ages, a number of physical and physiological functions decline. Lack of physical activity has a causal relationship to coronary heart disease (Murphy et al., 2002; Williams, 2001; Jolliffe et al., 2001), hypertension (U.S. Department of Health and Human Services, 2004), elevated blood lipids (Halbert et al., 1999), obesity (Wing, 1999), type 2 diabetes (Willey & Singh, 2003), osteoporosis in men (Kelley, Kelley, & Tran, 2000) and women (Howe, 2011), osteoarthritis of lower limbs and rheumatoid arthritis (Hurkmans et al., 2009), lower back problems (Vuori, 2001), chronic obstructive pulmonary disease (Montgomery & Dennis, 2003), diminished mental health (Fox, 1999), and sleeping disorders (Kubitz, Landers, Petruzzello, & Han, 1996). Furthermore, the deficiencies in physical function associated with a lack of physical activity are highly correlated with the greater prevalence of falling (Melzer, Benjuya, & Kaplanski, 2003; Schoenfelder & Rubenstein, 2004).

These declines eventually lead to health deterioration and an acceleration of the aging process, which in turn leads to premature death. The negative effects of aging on the various physiological functions can be mitigated and substantially slowed down by regular and structured exercising. Frequent physical activity provides great benefits for older adults through a marked impact on the function of muscles, joints, and bones, the regulation of hormones, neural stimulation, metabolism, and circulation. Regular physical activity is the single most effective method for the maintenance of functional capacity and achieving health benefits such as reduced risk of coronary heart disease and stroke (Wannamethee, 1998), reduced all-cause mortality (Jolliffe et al., 2001), controlled high blood pressure (Young, 1999), and reduced risk of type 2 diabetes (Evans, 1999). Furthermore, cardiovascular fitness may reduce stress and anxiety (Stewart et al., 1998), and enhance sleep quality in the elderly (Alessi, Yoon, Schnelle, Al-Samarrai, & Cruise, 1999). Muscular strength training programs lead to increases in strength (Whitehurst, Johnson, Parker, Brown, & Ford, 2005), muscle mass (Trappe et al., 2000), bone density (Englund, Littbrand, Sondell, Pettersson, & Bucht, 2005), and positive changes in body composition (Ibanez et al., 2005). Furthermore, lower body strength and balance interventions can lower the number of fall incidents and the fear of falling among elderly (Li et al., 2005; Melzer et al., 2003; Schoenfelder & Rubenstein, 2004).

Our undergraduate curriculum in the Department of Kinesiology is structured to guide students to a comprehensive understanding of the anatomical, physiological, and biomechanical basis of exercise, a clear understanding of the various benefits of exercise, and the ability to design and implement well-structured client-centered exercise programs. It is critical that graduating students who are to become advocates and experts of exercise training achieve a clear understanding of the above listed concepts and research findings. Moreover, they must possess practical, hands-on experiences to have the skills necessary for program implementation. To achieve this, our undergraduate curriculum culminates in a capstone course, where all previously learned concepts are used comprehensively through a multicomponent capstone project and a capstone fieldwork. The Physical Fitness in the Golden Age program is a carefully designed intervention for older adults to positively impact chronic disease risk, functional capacity, cardiovascular fitness, muscular strength and endurance, and injury prevention through well-developed physical and educational activities in a supervised, comfortable, and highly social environment. This program is connected to our undergraduate curriculum to involve students in a capstone course fieldwork setting, thereby provide critical capstone experiences to senior-level undergraduate students while serving and positively impacting the community. This chapter aims to introduce this unique capstone course fieldwork experience that is currently used to prepare the future generation of trainers and exercise experts.

Case Study

A Description of the Capstone Course Experience

The Association of American Colleges determined that successful career preparation of college students must include a "study in depth" experience in the students' major field (1985). Successful education of college students typically include a sequential curriculum starting with introductory courses, leading to basic (lower-division) and then to advanced (upper-division) courses, and finally culminate in one or more capstone courses. Capstone courses generally aim at integrating the learned concepts and various elements of the student's coursework into a coherent experience in the given field. Capstone courses can be broadly defined as a culminating experience at the very end of the course sequence with the objective of making connections between knowledge pieces and integrating fragmented knowledge into a unified whole (Durel, 1993). Such crowning course experience typically allows senior-level students to reflect on their entire undergraduate curriculum in an effort to make sense of the capstone experience. Moreover, this experience also has forward looking effects, as students can build on such experience for their professional development (Durel, 1993). Through such intense capstone experience, senior-level students begin their separation from the undergraduate student status and transition toward becoming graduates of the program, prepared for the critical thinking and assessment skills needed in their professional career.

The capstone course experience connected to the Physical Fitness in the Golden Age program aims at achieving these goals for the Kinesiology undergraduate senior students, who are close to graduation and to start their careers in the health and physical activity fields. The Physical Fitness in the Golden Age program is a community-based exercise program for older adults 60 years of age and older, which offers a comprehensive fitness approach that aims to improve overall health and functional ability, and maintain independent living and mobility. This approach simultaneously improves fitness and fosters healthy living habits for program participants with training sessions that focus on the improvement of muscular strength, cardiovascular fitness, mobility, coordination, speed, agility, flexibility, and balance. The program provides a comfortable environment for individuals of the same age working together for a common goal: to achieve successful aging and improving quality of life. Program participants are trained with the help of Kinesiology undergraduate students from a capstone course titled Geriatric Fitness Programming (KIN 4442).

Exercise sessions are supervised by trained and experienced Kinesiology graduates, typically holding a Bachelor's degree and a relevant certification from a leading professional organization. These paid program supervisors are responsible not only for supervising the day-to-day operation of the program and the design of the daily program sessions, but also hold the responsibility to supervise and grade the undergraduate students completing their capstone fieldwork experience. Students provide individualized attention to program participants and follow the general program design with individualized modifications for older adult participants.

The program initially started out as a collaborative project with the Department of Recreational Sports and used the university's student recreation center. Later, as the program gained traction and membership increased, an abandoned facility was provided for the program with a modest renovation budget as in-kind support from the university. A few years later, building on the program's success, a collaborative agreement was signed with the city's Parks and Recreation Department to expand the program to one of the local recreation centers. Further success of the program brought additional opportunities for expansion through a collaborative agreement with the YWCA El Paso del Norte. With that, the program was now offered at several locations, allowing some variety in program delivery and also student capstone experiences.

The Success of a Capstone Course Experience

The success of the Physical Fitness in the Golden Age program and the associated capstone student experience is heavily dependent on the strong ties developed with the local community and our partners at the city's Parks and Recreation Department, as well as the YWCA. Altogether this capstone experience prepares students for the multitude of professional challenges they face following their graduation. For many students, this is their first real-life professional challenge, or the first time their professional practices and skills are put to the test outside of a controlled classroom environment. Typically, this is their first experience where they professionally communicate and connect with real-life members of the local community, analyze and attempt to solve real-life problems of real-life clients, and truly collaborate with other students in a concentrated effort toward problem solving. The capstone experience aims to further enhance student learning while cultivating essential professional and life skills.

This capstone course experience has been very successful for all parties involved. The greatest beneficiaries are the older adults from the local community, who are participating in the program and see a substantial positive change in their personal health and fitness. A myriad of personal testimonials have been shared with us in both writing and face-to-face conversations, along with positive comments from family members or physicians treating these older adults. This collaborative project is also a success for the city's Parks and Recreation Department and the YWCA, as their fitness centers are now heavily used during the program session times and their services are now provided for a unique segment of the local community that otherwise would unlikely to join these centers.

Finally, the project is an immense success for the undergraduate students participating in the capstone course. These students are getting valuable hands-on skills and real-life professional experiences that they otherwise would not attain from their undergraduate program. Many students point out these obtained professional skills in their resumes and highlight their fieldwork experiences in their job interviews, which generally make them more marketable compared to their peers without any capstone course fieldwork experience. Interestingly, many students join the capstone course fieldwork experience with some level of apprehension when they learn that their task will include working with older adults. Working with this population appears to be a difficult challenge for many students. This proves to be an incorrect assumption in most cases, and the vast majority of students become not only well-prepared trainers, but also dedicated supporters and cheerleaders for their clients. In a number of cases, students moved on to successful professional careers working with older adults in various training or rehabilitation settings, despite their initial apprehensions of working with this population.

The Challenges of the Capstone Course Experience

Organizing this capstone course fieldwork experience is clearly not a light task. Elaborating on the Physical Fitness in the Golden Age program took years of practice, as many nuances had to be worked out that were not considered initially. The fieldwork was well-set from the very beginning, but it took several semesters if not years to precisely define fieldwork expectations and exact student practices. The integration of the fieldwork into the course, combining coursework and fieldwork, elaborating on the scheduling and other logistics, and precisely defining the fieldwork value in the overall course grade scheme took repeated adjustments over several years. Also, sometimes students appear to be apprehensive of new educational experiences, so students who were involved in the early phases of the capstone course fieldwork experience were more reluctant than later generations of students. It took years for this fieldwork to become the "norm" in the undergraduate program, so by now all students come to the capstone course already aware of the challenges of the fieldwork. As acceptance of the capstone course fieldwork experience grew among students, the program functioned more seamlessly, and both the students and the participating older adults benefited from it increasingly. Therefore, as the fieldwork experience became a known integral part of the undergraduate curriculum, student apprehension about fieldwork completely disappeared for the later generations of students.

There have been and continue to be challenges about the overall management and logistics of the program. Older adult program participants come and go, some stay only for a semester or two in the program, while others may become program members for many years. Nevertheless, life events affect the older adult population just as much as others, including serious health issues, changes in employment or retirement status, death in the family, or moving out of town. Such events result in fluctuations in program enrollment, which makes it challenging to provide the same fieldwork experience to all students across multiple semesters. Other program management issues, such as facility access and maintenance, or equipment maintenance and budget for new equipment purchases are also to be considered as challenges. To overcome all of these challenges, a dedicated faculty member who oversees the entire capstone course fieldwork and the related community program needs to be in place, and must be willing to spend time and effort with the various management tasks. Alternatively, if budget allows and the size of the program affords it, a full-time program director can be hired with the exclusive task of program management, substantially mitigating the listed challenges.

Integrating Other Types of Capstone Course Experiences

The Physical Fitness in the Golden Age program—and the related capstone course fieldwork experience—is just one example of how capstone courses can be used to better prepare undergraduate students for their professional career. Capstone course experiences can be integrated into any undergraduate curriculum, if the end goal in mind is the professional preparation of students. Even within a single major or single undergraduate program, many different type of capstone course experiences can be implemented, depending purely on the program needs and the creativity of the faculty. In the Kinesiology field, for example, similar fieldwork programs could be implemented with a different client population, whether children, adolescents, a specific patient population, or a group of professionals with specific physical activity needs (occupational fitness). In fact, our program has experimented with a variety of different capstone course fieldwork ideas before the Physical Fitness in the Golden Age program was established and designated as the uniformed capstone course experience for all Kinesiology undergraduate students. A single capstone course fieldwork experience can hardly encompass the broad variety of career options and professional scenarios students will likely have, but such fieldwork experience can be designed to be comprehensive and draw upon knowledge and scientific concepts students obtained throughout their undergraduate studies. If a capstone course fieldwork experience achieves that, it serves the curriculum well.

Recommendations for Faculty

Before investing any time and effort, faculty considering the development of a capstone course or a related fieldwork experience must first consult with their departmental or college administration. Faculty may want to make sure that administration supports the idea of such curriculum revision, and that perhaps can devote administrative and financial resources toward the development of such student experience. Importantly, it must be clear upfront that time and effort invested by the faculty member will count toward productivity, perhaps be included in the annual evaluation reports or in the tenure/promotion portfolios. Faculty may want to also discuss upfront if such work will be aligned with the mission of the program or the institution, and whether efforts invested in this endeavor will be counted toward instruction, scholarship, service, or perhaps of a combination of each. As developing a capstone course or a related fieldwork experience is no small task, faculty would want to make sure that they are properly compensated for such effort, either financially or by credit toward workload and work accomplishments.

Faculty who are new to teaching capstone courses may want to consult with other experienced faculty on their past work and approaches to teaching the given course. Faculty should not be afraid to experiment and adventure into uncharted territories if such capstone course experiences are not yet established at their institution. In some cases, as in curriculum redesigns and new program developments, it is possible that faculty are designing the capstone courses from scratch, including the related fieldwork experiences. If that's the case, capstone course-related projects should start small, perhaps initially lacking comprehensiveness. It is important to test an idea or concept first, before dedicating substantial time, effort, or resources to fully developing the given capstone course experience. A small project, perhaps something that students can complete in a few weeks may be a good start. Faculty should build the project gradually, learning from the experiences of one semester and further refining the project for the next semester. Understanding that building a comprehensive capstone course fieldwork may take many semesters or even years, faculty should be under no pressure to get it right the first time.

If no capstone course fieldwork is yet established in a program, faculty in charge may also seek out collaborative projects with colleagues from other disciplines. A multidisciplinary project approach may also be beneficial for small programs, for those with low budget, few faculty, or low student enrollment. If the resources are limited, partnering with other programs that already have capstone course experiences established may allow an easier start. At the same time, faculty who have capstone course experiences established may want to think of it as a dynamic and ever-evolving entity, instead of being stagnant. Inviting or incorporating project aspects from other disciplines may provide students a more comprehensive experience. For example, although the Physical Fitness in the Golden Age program focuses on the physical activity (fitness) aspect of health, a multidisciplinary approach would include collaboration with other undergraduate programs that can reasonably connect to the older adult population. Nutrition and food science, for example, can easily connect to a physical activity program, or any disciplines of rehabilitation sciences, perhaps even psychology. A current effort, for example, is to introduce a healthy eating nutritional component to the Physical Fitness in the Golden Age program, within which undergraduate students majoring in Nutrition Sciences and completing their capstone courses will be involved in the program to educate program participants on healthy eating and food preparation choices.

Nevertheless, long-term success of a capstone course fieldwork experience will heavily depend on the overseeing faculty member's sensitivity to feedback. Faculty must seek out and strongly consider feedback from program participants, students, as well as all other stakeholders of the established enterprise. Students and program participants should all feel comfortable with reflecting on the program and perceive that their feedback are welcome and are to be taken into consideration for future decision making. Faculty should discuss ideas for fieldwork experience refinement with all stakeholders involved and should regularly consider modification and program expansion ideas. At the same time, making mistakes will likely be part of the development process, so faculty must not be discouraged and abandon the project. Gradual, small adjustment and tweaks on the program application will yield strong results in the long run.

Recommendations for Students

Student buy-in is crucial to a successful capstone course fieldwork experience. Students must understand that such fieldwork is established for their own professional development and to help them achieve their career goals more easily. A clear communication is vital, and communication must go both ways. Faculty should take the time and effort to clearly communicate with the students the purpose and overarching themes of the capstone course fieldwork experience, and if possible highlight what specific knowledge, skills, and experience students will gain through this fieldwork. Students must keep an open mind and faith in the faculty's effort and the aligned fieldwork experience. Students must become devoted to the fieldwork and perform an honest job with full effort. In the meantime, students also bear the responsibility to provide feedback to faculty and share their views on the fieldwork experience. They must understand that modifications to the fieldwork will likely come from information and situations that the supervising faculty knows about. Thus students should consider themselves as the front line of information sources for the faculty, and should be diligent with sharing their views.

From the students' perspective, the capstone course fieldwork experience should be viewed with the eventual benefits in mind. It is clear that a capstone course fieldwork experience may not only be stressful and time consuming, but may require some sacrifices from students (schedule adjustment, cutting short on leisure time, transportation changes, deviations from commute routine, etc.). However, students should not be overwhelmed with these temporary inconveniences, but see the full picture. The benefits of capstone course fieldwork experiences may not be immediate; sometimes students may not even realize these benefits until after graduating from the program and starting their careers in the given field. Therefore, students must keep an open mind and good faith that the faculty are putting such capstone course fieldwork experiences in place for the students' best interest. With such acceptance of the fieldwork experience, students may complete the requirements with an upbeat attitude and positive approach to challenges. The overall fieldwork experience should be perceived as fun, as the enjoyable experience should lead to an enjoyable career path.

Recommendations for Community Partners

In case of the Physical Fitness in the Golden Age program, direct community partners include the older adult program participants, the city's Parks and Recreation Department staff, and the YWCA administration. The older adult program participants may be considered beneficiaries of the program, rather than partners, although that does not take away their opportunities to shape the program and influence decision making. Nevertheless, the true collaborative partners for the program are those at the city's Parks and Recreation Department and the YWCA, who contribute to the successful implementation of the program. In general, community partners must be sympathetic to the educational efforts and supportive of the idea of enhancing students' professional development through the capstone course fieldwork experience. Yet, community partners also have their own agenda in mind and must meet their own institutional goals. Accordingly, it is acceptable for community partners to participate in such collaborative efforts while making sure that their institutional benefits are also achieved. An open line of communication is essential, informing the supervising faculty or other university staff about the special problems, unique challenges, or program needs to take into consideration for continued future collaboration. Problems must be solved together through frequent discussions. The collaborative enterprise is a learning process for all and successful collaboration may lead to new ideas.

Additional Resources

The following video links provide an illustration of the University of Texas at El Paso's Kinesiology students' involvement in fieldwork and their hands-on experiences working with the older adult program members:

- http://cbs4local.com/news/local/a-fitness-program-specialized-for-55-and-older-may-be-coming-to-your-neighborhood
- http://kfoxtv.com/archive/the-golden-age-program
- http://kfoxtv.com/archive/using-rubber-bands-for-resistance-exercises
- http://kfoxtv.com/community/carpe-diem/the-use-of-ropes-for-physical-agility
- http://kfoxtv.com/community/carpe-diem/agility-drills
- http://kfoxtv.com/community/carpe-diem/gear-friday-swiss-balls

Additional description and thorough explanation of the Physical Fitness in the Golden Age program can be accessed through the below links:

- http://goldenagefitness.utep.edu/
- https://www.facebook.com/goldenagefitnesselpaso/
- https://www.youtube.com/watch?v=Uq5goJ1IhcU&t=381s
- https://www.youtube.com/watch?v=VhhMfugOymA&t=11s
- http://ktep.org/post/focus-campus-golden-age-fitness

Various news items describing the program:

- https://www.utep.edu/newsfeed/campus/golden-age-fitness-program-celebrates-10-years.html
- http://news.utep.edu/utep-offers-courses-to-keep-older-adults-engaged-educated/
- http://news.utep.edu/older-adults-eager-to-join-utep-led-fitness-program/
- http://www.elpasoinc.com/elpasoplus/utep-s-golden-age-fitness-opens-in-east-el-paso/article_47381de4-4d8c-11e4-a5b7-0017a43b2370.html
- https://ia.utep.edu/Default.aspx?tabid=47642
- http://news.utep.edu/utep-partners-with-city-of-el-paso-to-pump-up-seniors/

Conclusion

This chapter offered a unique example for a capstone course fieldwork experience. The Physical Fitness in the Golden Age program has been time tested and it has been proven that benefits can be delivered simultaneously to community members and undergraduate students. The program started from a small project and a brief idea for a capstone course fieldwork experience, and grew to a program highly recognized in the region. Over the years, several generations of students benefited from this capstone course fieldwork experience and moved on to a successful career often based on the skills and knowledge obtained during the fieldwork. Similarly, the program has positively impacted the lives of many older adults from the community, who not only improved their general health and physical function, but perhaps expanded their lifespan by participating in this exercise program. The successful implementation of a project of this magnitude would not be possible for a single faculty member or course instructor. It is a joint effort among several entities, but all of whom believe in the positive effects for the community and the students. Faculty responsible for teaching capstone courses or those who have an opportunity to establish a capstone course in their undergraduate curriculum should consider developing a comprehensive fieldwork experience for students, with student professional development in mind as a first priority. This should be in alignment with the mission of their institution or their program, and effort invested in developing such capstone course experience should count as credit toward the faculty member's evaluation, or the tenure/promotion decisions. It is a noble effort and an investment into our future.

References

Alessi, C., Yoon, E., Schnelle, J., Al-Samarrai, N., & Cruise, P. (1999). A randomized trial of combined physical activity and environmental intervention in nursing home residents: Do sleep and agitation improve? *Journal of the American Geriatrics Society, 47*(7), 784–791.

Association of American Colleges (1985). *Integrity in the college curriculum*. Washington, DC: Association of American Colleges.

Durel, R. J. (1993). The capstone course: A rite of passage. *Teaching Sociology, 21*(3), 223–225.

Englund, U., Littbrand, H., Sondell, A., Pettersson, U., & Bucht, G. (2005). A 1-year combined weight-bearing training program is beneficial for bone mineral density and neuromuscular function in older women. *Osteoporosis International, 16*, 1117–1123.

Evans, W. (1999). Exercise training guidelines for the elderly. *Medicine and Science in Sports and Exercise, 31*(1), 12–17.

Fox, K. R. (1999). The influence of physical activity on mental well-being. *Public Health Nutrition, 2*(3A), 411–418.

Halbert, J. A., Silagy, C. A., Finucane, P., Withers, R. T., Hamdorf, P. A., & Andrews, G. R. (1999). Exercise training and blood lipids in hyperlipidemic and normolipidemic adults: A meta-analysis of randomized, controlled trials. *European Journal of Clinical Nutrition, 53*(7), 514–522.

Howe, T. E., Shea, B., Dawson, L. J., Downie, F., Murray, A., Ross, C., . . . Creed G. (2011). Exercise for preventing and treating osteoporosis in postmenopausal women. *Cochrane Database of Systematic Reviews*, (7), CD000333. doi:10.1002/14651858.CD000333.pub2

Hurkmans, E., van der Giesen, F. J., Vliet Vlieland, T. P. M., Schoones, J., & Van den Ende, E. C. (2009). Dynamic exercise programs (aerobic capacity and/or muscle strength training) in patients with rheumatoid arthritis. *Cochrane Database of Systematic Reviews*, (4), CD006853. doi:10.1002/14651858.CD006853.pub2

Ibanez, J., Izquierdo, M., Arguelles, I., Forga, L., Larrion, J. L., Garcia-Unciti, M., . . . Gorostiaga, E. M. (2005). Twice-weekly progressive resistance training decreases abdominal fat and improves insulin sensitivity in older men with type 2 diabetes. *Diabetes Care, 28*(3), 662–667.

Jolliffe, J., Rees, K., Taylor, R. R., Thompson, D. R., Oldridge, N., & Ebrahim, S. (2001). Exercise-based rehabilitation for coronary heart disease. *Cochrane Database of Systematic Reviews*, (1), CD001800. doi:10.1002/14651858.CD001800

Kelley, G. A., Kelley, K. S., & Tran, Z. V. (2000). Exercise and bone mineral density in men: A meta-analysis. *Journal of Applied Physiology, 88*(5), 1730–1736.

Kubitz, K. A., Landers, D. M., Petruzzello, S. J., & Han, M. (1996). The effects of acute and chronic exercise on sleep. A meta-analytic review. *Sports Medicine, 21*(4), 277–291.

Li, F., Harmer, P., Fisher, K. J., McAuley, E., Chaumeton, N., Eckstrom, E., & Wilson, N. L. (2005). Tai chiand fall reductions in older adults: A randomized controlled trial. *Journal of Gerontology: Medical Sciences, 60A*(2), 187–194.

Melzer, I., Benjuya, N., & Kaplanski, J. (2003). Effects of regular walking on postural stability in the elderly. *Gerontology, 49*(1), 240–245.

Montgomery, P., & Dennis, J. A. (2002). Physical exercise for sleep problems in adults aged 60+. *Cochrane Database of Systematic Reviews*, (4), CD003404. doi:10.1002/14651858.CD003404

Murphy, M., Foster, C., Sudlow, C., Nicholas, J., Mulrow, C., Ness, A., & Pignone, M. (2002). Cardiovascular disorders: Primary prevention. *Clinical Evidence, 7*, 91–123.

Schoenfelder, D. P., & Rubenstein, L. M. (2004). An exercise program to improve fall-related outcomes in elderly nursing home residents. *Applied Nursing Research, 17*(1), 21–31.

Stewart, A., Mills, K., Sepsis, P., King, A., McLellan, B., Roitz, K., & Ritter, P. (1998). Evaluation of CHAMPS, a physical activity promotion program for older adults. *Annals of Behavioral Medicine, 19*(4), 353–361.

Trappe, S., Williamson, D., Godard, M., Porter, D. Rowden, G., & Costill, D. (2000). Effect of resistance training on single muscle fiber contractile in older men. *Journal of Applied Physiology, 89*, 143–152.

U.S. Department of Health and Human Services. (2004). *Physical activity and health: A report of the Surgeon General*. Atlanta, GA: U.S. Department of Health and Human Services, Centers for Disease Control and Prevention, Nation Center for Chronic Disease Prevention and Health Promotion.

Vuori, I. M. (2001). Dose-responses of physical activity and low back pain, osteoarthritis and osteoporosis. *Medicine and Science in Sports and Exercise, 33*(6 Suppl.), S551–S586; discussion 609–611.

Wannamethee, S., Shaper, A., Walker A., & Ebrahim, S. (1998). Lifestyle and 15 survival years free of heart attack, stroke and diabetes in middle aged British men. *Archives of Internal Medicine, 158*(22), 2433–2440.

Whitehurst, M. A., Johnson, B. L., Parker, C. M., Brown, L. E., & Ford, A. M. (2005). The benefits of a functional exercise circuit for older adults. *Journal of Strength and Conditioning Research, 19*(3), 647–651.

Williams, P. T. (2001). Health effects resulting from exercise versus those from body fat loss. *Medicine and Science in Sports and Exercise, 33*(6 Suppl.), S611–S621; discussion S640.

Willey, K. A., & Singh, M. A. (2003). Batting insulin resistance in elderly obese people with type 2 diabetes: Bring on the heavy weights. *Diabetes Care, 26*(5), 1580–1588.

Wing, R. R. (1999). Physical activity in the treatment of the adulthood overweight and obesity: Current evidence and research issues. *Medicine and Science in Sports and Exercise, 31*(11 Suppl.), S547–S552.

Young, D., Appel, L., Jee, S., & Miller, E. (1999). The effects of aerobic exercise and Tai Chi on blood pressure in older people: Results of a randomized trial. *Journal of American Geriatric Society, 47*(3), 277–284.

Chapter 12

Building Latinx Solidarity Through Global Learning Communities in the 21st Century

Irma Victoria Montelongo and Isabel Martinez

UNDERGRADUATE RESEARCH

FIRST-YEAR SEMINARS AND
EXPERIENCES

COLLABORATIVE
ASSIGNMENTS AND PROJECTS

Use these questions to guide your reflection prior to reading the chapter. Use the notes/follow-up section to write your thoughts after you have read the chapter. Your notes can include thoughts in reference to the reflection questions, or general observations about the chapter.

1) What elements must be present in an experience in order for it to be impactful in the realm of "diversity" and "global learning experience" as the High Impact Practice suggests?

2) What elements of experiences meant to expand upon "diversity" and "global learning" are of most importance to you?

3) Have you ever found yourself in a situation when someone else had a different understanding of where you live and how it impacts residents' lives? How did you feel about the difference in perspective? How did you clarify your own understanding and experience?

Notes/Follow-up:

_____

_____

_____

_____

_____

Introduction

Fried eggs, mashed plantains otherwise known as mangu, fried cheese, and fried salami. These are not from a late-night plate of *tres golpes* (three blows) at one of the crowded 24-hour diners located some one hundred blocks north in Washington Heights; instead, this is a typical weekday breakfast fare in John Jay College's school cafeteria. Lured in by the smells, a diversity of students, including many Dominicans, but also Russian, African-American, Mexican, Puerto Rican, native-born White, and others, can be seen gulping down these dishes before running off to their first classes. Prepared by a mostly Mexican and South American staff, these dishes reflect the majority Latinx population at the largest Hispanic Serving Institution in the United States northeast. A thousand miles away at University of Texas at El Paso (UTEP), another group of Latinx students rouse themselves from sleep to prepare for morning classes. Their first stop is often the lively food court located at the center of campus where the smell of huevo con chorizo (eggs with spicy sausage) and frijoles guisados (refried beans) emanate from *El Cazo*, the Mexican restaurant where the sounds of Mexican rock, sharing time with American Top 40, fill one's auditory senses. To say that the staff at the food court is mostly Mexican is an understatement. Approximately, 81.1% of the inhabitants of the El Paso region are ethnic Mexicans, and these demographics are further reflected in UTEP's student profile.

As the current administration enters its first term under the mantle of "building walls," both metaphorically between people and specifically on the US–Mexico border, ***convivencia (cohabitation) as resistance*** in and across these institutional spaces has become more imperative. For all students, but especially for students who have been historically underrepresented on college campuses and who may have less access to enriching activities and curriculum, high-impact practices, or pedagogies that result in higher levels of student learning, student engagement, and retention in college curricula and programming, are necessary to ensure academic success. Grounded in coursework that goes beyond credits toward graduation, high-impact practices empower students to learn outside of their classrooms, to develop deeper, more significant, working relationships with faculty mentors and students, and to participate in collaboration between diverse individuals (Kuh, 2008; Schneider, 2008). The following study discusses the development of global learning communities taught across two Hispanic Serving Institutes, John Jay College of Criminal Justice in New York City and the UTEP, located squarely on the US–Mexico border.

What Do Students Learn?

In a world that is technologically, economically, and politically more interconnected today than ever before, employers have identified high-impact skills essential for 21st century employment (Banks, 2004; Clark &

Contributed by Irma Victoria Montelongo and Isabel Martinez. © Kendall Hunt Publishing Company.

Drudy, 2006). One of those skills is Diversity and Global Learning, which is growing in prominence across college and university campuses. Students who engage in global learning are taught to collaborate with diverse individuals, explore different cultures and worldviews, and delve more deeply into pronounced racial, ethnic, and gender inequalities. Over the last 15 years, more and more colleges and universities have revised their mission and vision statements to reflect their interest in Diversity and Global Learning. Mission and vision statements, however, are as unique as the institutions they represent.

Some institutions define their global objectives as social, political, and moral imperatives that allow students to better understand cultures and worldviews different from their own. Others emphasize new expectations for professional and business careers. How each institution views itself within a global context will determine how global learning takes place (Hovland, 2014). With that in mind, the meaning of a "global" student becomes more complex. Although global competency is a rising expectation in higher education, few students will have the opportunity to study abroad for academic enrichment. The global classroom provides an alternative, a critical space for teaching and learning about ourselves as global citizens without incurring the expense of Study Abroad Programs. Otherwise, the global learning experience would be out of reach for many students, especially those coming from working-class Latinx backgrounds.

Why Is It Important?

Aside from living in an increasingly interdependent world, our students are also coming of age in a decreasingly White United States that is projected to become more diverse in the years to come. In fact, demographers predict that by 2055, there will be no racial or ethnic majority (Cohn & Caumont, 2016). Although we see modest increases in diversity on college campuses and in graduates, most college campuses still rely on traditional means such as Study Abroad Programs to develop global competencies (USDOE, 2016). However, only 1.55% of all US college students, of which the overwhelming majority, or 73%, are White, participate in such programs (National Association of Foreign Student Advisers, 2015). The global classroom, then, can easily be used to provide *all* students with Diversity and Global Learning experiences. The UTEP–John Jay Global Learning Communities (GLCs) illustrate how underrepresented students, on opposite ends of the nation, used collaborative projects, writing intensive assignments, e-portfolios, and overall development of digital literacies to construct and represent a vast body of knowledge about race, ethnicity, and space.

About the Authors' Experiences

When the authors first met in Spring of 2011, UTEP was already theorizing cultural diversity as a member of an international GLC with Victoria University in Melbourne, Australia. The partnership proved to be a great success for both UTEP and Victoria University, but more importantly it served as an observable template for the possibility of creating a collaborative learning environment within the United States, which would provide a unique opportunity to both deconstruct and reconstruct notions about race and space within national borders. Focusing on the stereotypes and discrimination that exist about and within groups, and in particular the Latinx population, UTEP and John Jay College created a GLC that addressed these particular issues. The course intended to dismantle the archetypes that often determine region-based teachings of Latinx identities, in favor of perspectives that extend beyond regions and create a better understanding and teaching of the entire Latinx population.

Separated by distance and migration histories, UTEP and John Jay College of Criminal Justice, just like other universities located in different regions, teach Latinx and Chicanx Studies in ways that reflect and remain bounded by the regional and ethnic contexts that they are found in. In spite of calls to simultaneously honor and transcend national-origin approaches to Latinx and Chicanx Studies, the fact remains that professors in these departments and programs have largely remained in regional silos: Southwest Chicanx Studies departments and programs teach about ethnic Mexicans while East Coast Latinx Studies departments teach about Puerto Ricans and Dominicans with limited mention of the other hybrid cultures that are created through the mixing and meshing of Latinx identities. As heterogeneous Latinx populations continue to grow, both demographically and politically across the United States, yet continue to be subject to neocolonial practices, this adherence to regionalization is becoming more and more tenuous, and the time has come to challenge and dismantle this regional myopia.

This approach does very little to generate broader understandings of the Latinx population across the United States nor of relationships between regional Latinx groups and the far-reaching network of Latinx groups across the United States. The intent of the UTEP–John Jay GLCs was to move away from these approaches and broaden the foci in an effort to share knowledge and discourse about Latinx identities and experiences that have emerged in these two most oft-researched and studied geographic areas in the United States. By bringing together faculty and students across regions and backgrounds, we began to bridge the differences and commonalities experienced in two unique cultural spaces.

Case Study

As diverse Latinx students comprise larger percentages of the university student body, as well as move through increasingly globalized worlds that are simultaneously shaped and reshaped by borders, both internal and external to the United States, it is imperative that they understand the meanings of borders, spaces, and discourses especially as they shape the experiences of U.S. Latinx and Latin Americans. With this in mind, we initiated our ongoing collaboration during the academic year 2011–2012. We set out to create what Chicana historian Emma Pérez refers to as a *sitio and a lengua* (a site and a language). Pérez argues that when people of color speak, their voices emerge from specific spaces that reject colonial ideology. Both the space and the language, according to Pérez, are rooted in both the words and the silences of people of color who create a place apart from traditional, imperialistic, and patriarchal sites (Pérez, 1991). We designed two *sitios*, in-between spaces, in the form of global classrooms, made up of young Latinx and Chicanx located on opposite ends of the country. We delivered the first iteration in Fall 2011 and the second in Spring 2012.

The courses linked two First-Year Experience Seminars that examined Ethnic Studies in general with an emphasis on Latinx communities. They were delivered in both synchronous and asynchronous time where students met, studied, shared, and debated race relations in the U.S. as well as the heterogeneity that exists among Latinx. Speaking from the margins, students grappled with the geopolitical and metaphorical borders that shape Latinx communities in the U.S. They examined how Latinx identities and experiences have been constructed not only across racial, ethnic, gendered, and sexual landscapes, but also across an East Coast-Southwest paradigm as well. Our *sitio* (global learning space) provided students with the tools to subvert their own regional myopia by bridging Latinx cultures across a national landscape. We maintain that because of these courses, students at both campuses not only developed more holistic understandings of Latinx cultures and borders, but also that through authentic interactions, their understandings of each other's spaces were more genuinely transformed. But, not without a hitch.

What Were the Challenges?

We experienced a number of challenges beginning in Fall 2011 when the students from both institutions entered the collaboration with the notion that their global classroom would be a happy, safe space where everyone would get along by virtue of being "Hispanic." We quickly learned otherwise. The UTEP students envisioned the New York setting as a glamorous location underscored by the glitz of Broadway, home to world-class museums, art galleries, and the famous restaurants highlighted on the Food Network. In their imagination, their John Jay counterparts were Latinx, who, unlike them, resided in the most cosmopolitan city in the world; therefore, it stood to reason that they were Latinx immersed in the progressive political, social, and economic cultures that New York City offered. In the case of the John Jay students, their responses to what they knew about the US–Mexico border mirrored the steady diet of drugs, undocumented immigrants, and militarization that is disseminated across news sources. In spite of El Paso being one of the safest cities in the U.S., John Jay students overwhelmingly characterized the US–Mexico border as "dangerous," "very scary," or "full of criminals."

What Made This High-Impact Practice Successful?

Within weeks of the start of the collaboration, the initial excitement gave way to tribalism. To say that the rapid descent of our much-anticipated GLC caught us by surprise is an understatement. We knew that we would have to turn this situation into a creative teaching moment, but how? We decided to reintroduce what had caused the problem to begin with: 21st century digital media and its construction of Latinx as well our student's overdependence on it. When we reconvened as a borderless, digital classroom, what developed was a fruitful discussion on how media outlets create misconceptions, stereotypes, and divisions between and among racial and ethnic communities. Students began to argue evidence-based ideas based out of their readings and personal experiences, and what was most clear, was how essential the *dialogue* between the students, both not only through the web platform but also through videoconferencing, was decolonizing the student's attitudes about each other's spaces, and Latinx realities in those spaces. These learning outcomes provided the foundation for our next attempt at bridging Latinx identity formation and cultural expression in the United States.

How to Move Forward and Skills Learned

During the academic year 2015–2016, we once again created a cross-campus global classroom, but this time we designed the course for upper-division Juniors and Seniors. Entitled *Brown Tide Rising: Interrogating Latinx Identity in the 21st Century*, the course was delivered in Fall 2016 and focused squarely on Latinx identity/ies and its/their constructions nationally, as well as in New York City and El Paso, Texas. We designed the course in a way that facilitated student learning about "cultures, life experiences, and worldviews that might be similar yet different than their own," as well as exploration of "'difficult differences' such as racial, ethnic and gender inequalities." Our learning objectives encouraged students to develop and demonstrate an understanding of heterogeneity among Latinxs; to identify how historical and contemporary social, economic, and political conditions shape contemporary Latinx identity formation across the United States; and to analyze and articulate how intersectionality, or race, class, gender, sexuality, etc. shape Latinx identity formation in the United States. Our ultimate objective was to encourage students to effectively share diverse viewpoints, develop new knowledge, and collaborate with people of diverse backgrounds.

Methodology

We met our learning objectives by having students produce individual as well as cross-campus collaborative projects. The semester-long projects included individual e-portfolios, as well as a final group e-portfolio, that contained developed "think pieces," including written reflection papers, digital stories, and images that reflected their understandings and mastery of the theories guiding the course. Additionally, students verbally discussed the materials, both not only within but also across our classrooms. Utilizing videoconferencing, we held cross-campus discussions with both groups of students no less than six times during the semester. In these discussions, students interrogated not only the assigned texts, but also each other's lives as sites of lived theory defined by commonalities and differences and shaped by the built environments that the students lived in, the US–Mexico border and New York City. Moreover, by utilizing e-portfolios and collaborative assignments, students learned to not only develop and design web content, but also how to successfully collaborate on group projects by effectively manipulating other existing technologies, software, and apps including WhatsApp, Rabb.it, Skype, Google Drive, etc. They learned that various digital tools could be utilized for professional, as well as social, purposes. This was especially important to the course as we aimed to simulate future professional situations in which our students could be engaging in professional projects with peers around the country and world.

Collaborative Assignments and E-Portfolios

To complete collaborative projects, students were placed on teams with their peers, both in their brick and mortar classrooms as well as across digital space. Students were asked to review each other's work as well as assign roles, communicate, plan, and execute all of the tasks needed to create group digital stories to share with each other and with the students from the other campus. For our most recent global classroom, delivered in Fall 2016, we added the use of cross-campus teams on which students learned how to plan and then execute the components of one shared collaborative e-portfolio. All of our GLCs were designed to be writing intensive. Students produced and revised original writings that took on a myriad of positions, drew from a variety of disciplines and readings, and were also the foundations for subsequent digital assignments like digital stories. These writings included short, simple biographies, and pointed critical response papers, to more complex scripts used in digital storytelling.

Evidence of Student Learning

Across all assignments, students revised their own and peer's writings before, during, and after they posted in their individual and shared digital tools. In this way, they partook in the shared development and revision of their own, shared written "theories in the flesh," or what Cherie Moraga refers to as theories of Latinidad that draw from the "physical realities of (their) lives . . . to create a politic borne of necessity" (Moraga, 1981). Additionally, students expanded their digital literacies. Although our students have grown up with technology, there are "participation gaps" or inequalities in "(digital) opportunities, experiences, skills, and knowledge" that youths need in order to be active, conscientious citizens in an increasingly "complex global society" (Brown et al., 2016; Jenkins et al., 2006; Rehn, 2017; Watkins, 2012). By mandating the individual and shared uses of a multimedia web platform and e-portfolios, our students were taught how to represent their ideas in both written and visual forms as well as to digitally collaborate with peers and professors. Students were moved closer to full digital participation, and were taught to actively, adequately, and multi-modally resist dominant attempts to create, reinforce, and exploit complicated differences among racial and ethnic groups and between Latinxs living in different US geographic regions. As the courses unfolded, the positive learning outcomes became obvious and so did the need for careful, well-crafted assessment pieces.

Assessments

For all GLCs, we administered two surveys at the start and end of the semester. A pre-and post-assessment included questions matched to each of the course's learning objectives as well as to our broader objectives of developing digital literacies and bridging participation gaps. Student responses about whether or not and how they met learning objectives provided us a better understanding of the strengths and weaknesses of the readings and pedagogies we utilized in the course. Additionally, we triangulated the students' responses with the course artifacts, including the final group e-portfolios, to develop conclusions about whether or not students mastered the stated course outcomes. Wherever possible, we noted the ways in which students built upon the knowledges they constructed in the class as they continued coursework as well as engaged in cocurricular and extracurricular activities including internships and employment that utilize their learning. We witnessed, first-hand, that students who participate in GLCs acquire critical thinking skills that benefit them in local, state, national, and international settings.

How Does This Practice Contribute to Deep Life Learning?

The unique experience of sharing a classroom with a cohort that is half way around the globe or at opposite ends of the nation produces students that are informed, responsible, and open-minded people conscientious of diversity. They develop a personal sense of ethics and civic responsibility that informs their views of social and global issues. They seek to understand how their actions affect both local and global communities, and they learn to acknowledge the exclusion of marginalized populations in public-policy setting. For example, in response to the large numbers of unaccompanied Central American minors who arrived at the Texas–Mexico border in recent years, five GLC John Jay students, who were students in our GLC, *Brown Tide Rising* course, participated in the Unaccompanied Latin American Project (U-LAMP), a research and service project focused on providing academic, social, and legal support to recently arrived immigrant minors, or newcomers, who are presently in removal/deportation proceedings.

Reaching Students Intellectually and Emotionally

Through our course assessments of the student's learning outcomes, we were able to more deeply examine the impact that the GLCs had on students' understandings of commonalities and differences, particularly intraethnic and regional ones within and across the often-homogenized U.S. Latinx community. This became quite evident in the case of one John Jay student, who recently completed a summer internship in Texas during which she related that she drew upon her understandings of Chicanx identity, developed in dialogue with the UTEP students and through course readings and films. These and other examples of successful learning outcomes from our GLCs are now coming to fruition, and we have begun sharing this information at academic conferences alongside our students. Seeing our students presenting at academic conference testifies to their scholarly and professional growth and to the importance of Diversity and Global Learning. There is, however, an additional element to further develop authentic, intraethnic understandings.

In May 2017, at the Sixth Biennial Inter-University Program on Latino Research Conference, nine students, six from John Jay and three from UTEP from the Fall 2016 GLC, met in person for the first time and developed presentations that focused on their general experiences in the global classroom, the relevance and meaning of the course during a U.S. presidential election in which discussions of Latinxs were reductionist and overwhelmingly negative, and lastly, the development of digital literacies through the creation of final e-portfolios. From their presentations, it was evident that students continued to benefit intellectually from the exchange of ideas that were rooted in their disparate geographic locations and ethnic identifications as well as shared racialization. The strength derived from their casual interactions, their everyday experiences as Latinxs and mostly first-generation college students, their shared stories about growing up in their respective spaces as Latinxs, about their families and partners, and their plans to stay in touch and visit, all provided proof of the emotional impact a course like this has on students, and that should be replicated at all levels of higher education.

How to Replicate This Project

The key to a successful global classroom is effective and synchronized collaboration and communication between the faculty members. This includes developing and establishing shared visions and objectives for the course, aligning syllabi, readings, and assignments, scheduling synchronous meeting days and times, and creating thoughtful and academically enriching class discussions. In our experience, we found that if students sensed the slightest asynchronicity, the rhythm of the course and even cross-campus discussions could be disrupted. Faculty must ensure that they are expressing the same instructions and messages to both sets of students so that misunderstandings do not arise, especially where successful completion is dependent on the students' shared understandings of the tasks as well as the timing for conclusion. Additionally, faculty must ensure that they have adequate access to technology as well as technical support.

Technical details such as the alignment of videoconference equipment between the two institutions must be finalized before the course begins. Faculty must also make sure that students have access to technology. In our case, some students encountered difficulties in accessing computers to complete digital assignments and/or were unable to access campus technical support. Additionally, only John Jay possessed an e-portfolio support specialist, which could have made course completion more difficult. Fortunately, synchronized videoconferencing capabilities made it possible for John Jay's e-portfolio specialist to train and support the UTEP students. And yet, in spite of increasing technology and globalization, 21st-century college students carry limited notions of Latinx community and identity formation.

Perspectives and Recommendations for Faculty

As Chicanx and Latinx Studies professors reimagine their classrooms as incubators of the next generation of U.S. Latinx scholars, we must *teach* in ways that bring about authentic understandings of how Latinx exist and are constructed both regionally and nationally. In a nativist moment, where attacks against Latinxs are constant and ubiquitous, fostering and strengthening relationships among Latinxs across long distances is but one tool in combatting the trauma inflicted on our communities and against our young people. Global classrooms provide intellectual weapons, a psychic *herramienta* (tool), to combat the resurgence of nativism by purposefully creating an intercultural, inter-Latinx classroom across regions. They provide heterogeneous Latinx students with the spaces to interact, confront, and discuss both their shared and distinct histories of colonization that differ by region, first and foremost, but also by nativity, generation, and citizenship. Through active and guided learning across multiple texts and spaces, global classrooms have the potential to not only name the fractures that exist in the U.S. Latinx community and in U.S. Latinx Studies but more importantly to overcome them.

Selected Readings, Sources, and Tools

Banks, J. A. (2004). Teaching for social justice, diversity, and citizenship in a global world. *The Educational Forum, 68*(4), 296–305.

Braskamp, L. A., & Engberg, M. E. (2011). How colleges can influence the development of a global perspective. *Liberal Education*, Summer/Fall, *97*(3–4), 34–39.

Brown, A., López, G., & Lopez, M. H. (2016). *Digital divide narrows for Latinos as more Spanish speakers and immigrants go online.* Washington, DC: Pew Research Center: Hispanic Trends.

Clarke, M., & Drudy, S. (2006). Teaching for diversity, social justice and global awareness. *European Journal of Teacher Education, 29*(3), 371–386.

Fluker, W. (2011). Preparing students for ethical complexity at the intersection where worlds collide: The quest for character, civility, and community. *Liberal Education*, Summer/Fall, *97*(3–4), 14–21.

Hoveland, K. (2014). Global learning: Defining, designing, demonstrating. Washington, DC: A Joint Publication of NAFSA: Association of International Educators and The Association of Colleges and Universities.

Jenkins, H., Clinton, K., Puruhotma, R., Robison, A. J., & Weigel, M. (2006). *Confronting the challenges of participatory culture: Media Education for the 21st Century.* Cambridge, MA: MIT Press.

Kuh, G. (2008). *High-Impact educational practices, what they are, who has access to them, and why they matter.* Washington, DC: Association of American Colleges and Universities.

National Association of Foreign Student Advisers. (2015). *Trends in US study abroad.* Washington, DC: National Association of Foreign Student Advisers

Schneider, C. G. (2008). *The dangerous assault on disciplines basic to democracy.* Washington, DC: Association of American Colleges and Universities.

United States Department of Education. (2012) Succeeding Globally through International Education and Engagement: US Department of Education International Strategy 2012-2016. Retrieved from https://www2 .ed.gov/about/inits/ed/internationaled/international-strategy-2012-16.pdf

Watkins, S. C. (2012). Digital divide: Navigating the digital edge, *International Journal of Learning and Media, 3*(2), 1–12.

Additional Readings, Sources, and Tools

Braskamp, L.A. and Engberg, M.E., (2011). "How Colleges Can Influence the Development of a Global Perspective," L.E.A.P., Summer/Fall, Vol. 97, No. 3-4.

Fluker, W. (2011). "Preparing Students for Ethical Complexity at the Intersection Where Worlds Collide: The Quest for Character, Civility, and Community," L.E.A.P., Summer/Fall, Vol. 97, No. 3-4.

John Jay College of Criminal Justice, Department of Latin American and Latina/o Studies. https://www.jjay .cuny.edu/department-latin-american-and-latinao-studies

Merryfield, M. M. (1998). "Pedagogy for global perspectives in education: Studies of teachers' thinking and practice." *Theory & Research in Social Education*, 26(3), 342-379.

Ortiz, A.M. and Santos, S. (2009) *Ethnicity in College: Advancing Theory and Improving Diversity Practices on Campus.* Sterling: Stylus Publishing.

Ramirez, T.L. and Blay, Z. "Why People Are Using The Term 'Latinx,'" *Huffington Post* updated April 7, 2017

Salinas, Jr. C. and A. Lozano. (2017) Mapping and Recontextualizing the evolution of the term Latinx: An environmental scanning in higher education, Journal of Latinos and Education, http://www.tandfonline .com/doi/full/10.1080/15348431.2017.1390464

The University of Texas at El Paso, Chicana/o Studies Program. https://www.utep.edu/liberalarts/chicano/

The SUNY Center for Collaborative Online International Learning (COIL). www.coil.suny.edu

Nonprofit and Border Studies

Chapter 13

Scaling Up: Mini-Internships in Nonprofit Management

Kathleen Staudt, PhD

INTERNSHIPS

Use these questions to guide your reflection prior to reading the chapter. Use the notes/follow-up section to write your thoughts after you have read the chapter. Your notes can include thoughts in reference to the reflection questions, or general observations about the chapter.

1) How many nonprofit organizations are you familiar with? What attributes do they have in common?

2) What aspects about nonprofit organizations are you most interested in? If you are not familiar with non-profit organizations, what questions do you have about them?

3) What is your understanding about grant writing in relation to community organizations?

Notes/Follow-up:

_____

_____

_____

_____

_____

Introduction

The pedagogical and research movement to engage campus and community began several decades ago with the late former President of the Carnegie Foundation for the Advancement of Teaching Ernest Boyer, his many publications on its value and assessment strategies, and on the Campus Compact as a nonprofit organization with state affiliates that offer guidance, conferences, and membership affiliations, now numbering over 1,000 higher-education institutions.[i] Internships have an even longer history in higher education, especially for professional training as future nurses, teachers, and doctors. Many universities offer courses, programs, majors, and graduate certificates in nonprofit management which would, ideally, be connected to a campus center for engagement and experiential/service-learning opportunities.

The University of Texas at El Paso's (UTEP) Center for Civic Engagement, begun in the late 1990s and a pioneering leader in the University of Texas system, actively participated in national Campus Compact efforts, including the former Texas Campus Compact. In Texas, like many other regions, government downsizing spawned the creation of many nonprofit public service and advocacy organizations that focus on social service, education, social justice, and civil rights, including women's empowerment, among other organizations. If faculty members are to prepare students for asset building in community organizations and the opportunities for leadership therein, it is important to provide rigorous content and training in the strengths necessary for effective nonprofit organizations.

As a service-learning practitioner, I took heed from Center for Civic Engagement Director Azuri González's remarks in a university-wide committee and subcommittee on which I served to move toward developing more complex skills in students' upper-division courses.[ii] I believe it is valid to scale up my usual offer to students to choose between the more typical 20 hours of service-learning in a community organization or a research paper (worth 25% of the course grade) to a more advanced experience of a thirty-hour mini-internship in one of the hundreds of nonprofit (NP) organizations in the metropolitan central transborder region for the Nonprofit Management course. In the course, students learned about nonprofit programs and funding needs. They then turned that growing knowledge into a complex, staggered set of assignments of multiple parts toward a final writing project over the semester: a grant proposal written for the best funding foundation for the program and our region based on a list of ten likely funders that students identified after grant-searching training in the huge Foundation Center database of over 700,000 funders, accessible through keyword searches by geography, funding history, and content interests.[iii]

This essay makes the case for "scaling up" from the basic service-learning high-impact practice to internships, another high-impact practice, as a way to advance and consolidate community-based learning and practical skills for students' futures. Students that came to the course with some experience in service-learning were able to hit the ground running and better prepare a draft grant proposal for and with their community partner. I believe that the key way students can truly imbibe the needs of the nonprofit organization is through

---

[i] See Boyer's (1996) publication, among others. On the Campus Compact, see https://compact.org.

[ii] González, coeditor of this volume and Director of the Center for Civic Engagement who chaired a subcommittee during the lengthy 'reaffirmation' (formerly called reaccreditation) process of 2015–2016, spoke about levels of increasing challenge and complexity in course offerings at the lower and upper division, culminating perhaps in a senior project.

[iii] http://foundationcenter.org.

experience inside the organization where they develop relationships with the staff. All of this, in turn, leads to life-long learning with mutual benefits to students, soon-to-be professionals, and community organizations.

Case Study

Course and Author Background

With a PhD in political science, and both feet situated solidly in the subfield of public administration/policy and the interdisciplinary field of women/gender studies, I have long sought to impart practical skills to and with students that have action components to make a better world and better community. The word "better" is, of course, subjective, but what I mean by that is a commitment to social justice, equality, a decent wage and standard of living, and the political capacity to work with others and sustain those commitments toward a more equitable world and community.

In political science, another of my subfields was and is comparative politics in so-called developing countries. I had been a 2-year Peace Corps Volunteer in the Philippines, a one-year dissertation researcher in Kenya, and thankfully, a borderlander (*fronteriza*), situated next door to Mexico since 1977. In the calendar year 1979, under the Intergovernmental Personnel Act, I worked in the Women in Development office of the U.S. Agency for International Development, attended project proposal meetings, and wrote a proposal that eventually joined the Government of Kenya, over twenty Peace Corps Volunteers, and $200,000 worth of vehicles and bicycles to widen equitable access to agricultural services to men and women farmers (the topic of my dissertation in 1976).

At UTEP, before there was a Center for Civic Engagement, I initially taught the course called Development Management. Students acquired knowledge about a country of their choice and its development needs in health, education, and small business (among other fields) and then wrote development project proposals just like what Non-Government Organizations and government agencies write in the real world. Eventually, I wrote a book, *Managing Development . . . .*, that was adopted in upper-division and graduate seminars in other universities (Staudt, 1990). It gave me great satisfaction when colleagues from other parts of the U.S. had read or reviewed the book. The publisher reissued the book in four printings.

During the 1990s, thanks to mentorship from Former UTEP Dean of Education Arturo Pacheco, I became very interested in and commitment to regional education, community development, and community organizing and leadership development with the Industrial Areas Foundation.[iv] As a border studies scholar, my binational region included both El Paso and Ciudad Juárez. When the political science department housed the Masters in Public Administration program, I taught a graduate seminar in Nonprofit Management; there, I pilot-tested the transformation of the Development Management course to our border region with a project proposal/internship for the undergraduate, upper-division course, now retitled Nonprofit Management. In both the graduate and undergraduate classes, several of the nonprofit organizations, with the elated consent of "their" students, submitted the proposals to funders. During the last 30 years, I also had lots of experience not only serving on multiple nonprofit boards of directors but also serving as a reviewer for grant proposals (the latter sometimes requiring a week's stint in Washington, DC with other reviewers from around the country).

From all of this professional background and experience, I learned a lot and formulated the syllabus for POLS 4356, Nonprofit Management. In the forthcoming paragraphs, I move on to discuss what made the course successful and what challenges it posed for all the stakeholders involved: students, the nonprofit organizations, and myself.

[iv] IAF (Industrial Areas Foundation) leaders work at state and local levels to develop leaders and policy changes in response to small-group meetings in the member institutions, many of them affiliated with churches and synagogues. In El Paso, the two IAF groups, connected to approximately a dozen IAF groups in other Texas cities, are called EPISO and Border Interfaith. Big organizations like these supply the numerical power base to push for policy changes that, alas, many nonprofit organizations try to address but cannot do more than serve as bandaids. See www.swiaf.org for more details on many of the groups in the US southwest and nationwide. The first big grant from the Kellogg Foundation to the CCE involved a partnership with EPISO. On the challenges of doing what has become known as "community-based participatory research," see Staudt, Dane'el, and Márquez-Velarde (2013).

What Made the Nonprofit Management Course Successful?

From the outset, students realized that the course intended to develop practical skills that they could use after graduation in various work settings. Within 3–4 weeks, students had to choose "their" nonprofit organization from among a long list at the Center for Civic Engagement (CCE). Before solidifying the internship, however, they needed to present themselves for interviews with their possible supervisors at the organizations. First students went through exercises to reflect on their skills with such instruments as the Myers-Briggs. Then I asked them to send me their curriculum vitae (CV)/resume and an introduction letter, so that I could provide feedback to strengthen their presentations of themselves. All students, whatever their skills levels, got tips from me on ways to strengthen their CVs and resumes.[v] Though most of my students are bilingual in Spanish and English, I noticed that many students did not highlight this asset on their CV; indeed, many were surprised to hear that employers (especially in other parts of the U.S.) view bilingual capacity as a premium, sometimes awarding additional stipends to such employees.

In class, we evaluated the websites of various nonprofit organizations based on assignments in which the students had been asked to complete information about for two nonprofits on forms that I developed. The syllabus contained scores of NP options, and the CCE's Community University Engagement website contained information on more than a hundred. Needless to say, I always invited a student assistant from the CCE to explain the CUE, how to log in and post their hours, and to be verified by a NP supervisor. I also invited former student "veterans" of this class to come in and make a pitch for them to recruit in the nonprofit organizations in which they—the former students, now staff members—worked. The presenters included staff from Girl Scouts, Las Americas Immigrant Advocacy Center, and the offices of public officials. My current students, then, see a great value in doing good work as an intern and grant writer, for they too might be invited to apply and ultimately gain employment from this experience.

Students and I evaluate nonprofit websites based on various topics they will read about in their textbook, *Nonprofit Management: Principles and Practices*.[vi] We assess layout, clarity, colors, logos, pictures, and board members with their affiliations (along with why they might have been selected as board members). These assessments relate to text chapters on marketing, board governance, and mission statements. On nonprofit missions and visions, which should always be on websites, together we evaluated the statements that ranged from the concise statements to pedantic, wordy, and confusing statements. We even check multiple university mission and vision statements, finding some of them wanting.

In the next phase of the course, students set up interviews with potential intern supervisors. We share stories in class about how things went during an interview or how to get busy supervisors to return phone calls or respond to emails. At this stage, students learn about "their" nonprofits, the needs, the invariable budget shortfalls within them, and deep website and annual report readings. This is the ideal time for me to invite the CCE professional staff to give a workshop to students on grant-searching in the UTEP Library in its computer room containing electronic access to the Foundation Center data base of 700,000+ foundations. Students are expected to learn how to do keyword searches in order to develop a list of ten possible funders whose missions resonate with that of "their" nonprofit and/or the nonprofit program proposal students will draft. A month into the course, this is a major turning point for students. They see the relevance of developing good, creative ideas to generate external funding to better the lives of people in our region.

---

[v] UTEP, like many universities, offers a Career Advising Center with services such as 'how to improve CVs, yet many students do not avail themselves of this benefit. It behooves us all, as faculty members, to integrate this exercise—another high-impact subpractice—into courses.

[vi] By Michael J. Worth, now in its fourth edition (Thousand Oaks, CA: Sage, 2017), available in 2016. [For content about justice and inequity in the US–Mexico borderlands, see chapter selections in both Lusk, Kathleen, and Moya (2012) and Vélez-Ibáñez and Heyman (2017)]. While Worth's focus is national, the material is up to date and contains case studies at the end of each of the chapters. I often break the class into 'teams,' where they discuss the case, how problems were resolved, and what they would have done differently. Sometimes we do role plays from the cases, like my student roleplaying a boss trying to turn-around a lazy worker, roleplayed by me. We have lots of fun with these! The textbook contains a wealth of detail and is worth keeping, I tell students, if they want to work in nonprofits after graduation.

Once students have invested about half of their thirty internship hours, and completed about half the textbook chapters, I provide the Peer Evaluation form that their student peers and I will use, ultimately, to score their grant proposal on multiple criteria and decide whether, "bottom line," the proposal should be funded. The form, appended to this essay, is based on my experiences in writing and reviewing proposals.[vii] Again, the real world became obvious to students. In class, we spent a good deal of time brainstorming and talking specifics about "goals" and "objectives" for the grant along with the format of the fifteen-page proposal. A particular challenge for students involved a collective "thinking through" the costs of the proposal for the budget page (also appended), along with the nonprofit's "in-kind" contributions which would enhance the value of the overall effort.

Several weeks before the end of the semester, students were asked to send their draft proposals to two peers for feedback, tracked in the draft document (for the especially attentive peers) and in the Peer Evaluation form (appended, as noted). As in the real world, I expect constructive comments for each criterion, not a comment like "great!" or "LOL!" Then students could use feedback, verbal and written, to strengthen their final copy. Students submitted and presented their final proposals the last week of class. Students are asked to invite their nonprofit supervisor or community partner to hear their presentations, though generally only a few attend, if any (such as fall 2016).

In sum, the class became a series of staggered assignments and workshops with participation from all to write the best proposals possible for the ultimate goal of making a better community. Nevertheless, we all encountered challenges, in addition to successes, which I discuss generally in the following paragraphs and then unpack for the three major stakeholders: students, community partners (the nonprofits), and faculty members.

What Challenges Were Encountered in the Course?

Students entered the course with a variety of skill sets and preparation, contributing to a major challenge. I found students with previous service-learning experiences to be among the best able to move forward with some confidence about the mini-internship. Some of these students came from the Museum Studies Program, a UTEP minor, and one that conveys that revenue-generating challenges of public and private museums through experiences and field trips. They were a delightful addition to the class.

Another typical preparation issue in upper-division classes involves the extent to which students have confidence and experience in writing papers. Alas, standardized testing through multiple-choice questions, as practiced in public schools and even in large, lower-division classes in the university, does little to prepare students for writing papers, whether they are grant proposals or research papers. Even grammar, spelling, and punctuation issues may be an issue for some students, although I always recommend Purdue University's Online Writing Center ("OWL") and its free modules. UTEP offers feedback for students at the Library Writing Center, but students who wait until the last minute to prepare their assignment cannot available themselves of such assistance. Discipline is required for students to complete assignments several days ahead of time during busy times at the Writing Center.

I have encountered some of these challenges in my other courses. And, just as challenges are constant in other settings, so also are the assignments and successes of this course possible in other settings.

[vii] Through experience, I learned about RFPs/Requests for Proposals, when on leave at USAID and at week-long reviewer experiences in Washington, DC. I have written various research grant proposals, the biggest award from the National Science Foundation in the early 1990s. When I became CCE Director in the late 1990s and for ten years thereafter, we at the center wrote many proposals to private foundations and federal agencies. We enjoyed many successes, (but also losses), especially successes with two large grants from the Kellogg Foundation and one large grant from HUD; the resources allowed us to partner with, even create new nonprofit organizations in El Paso. In 2008, under the able leadership of CCE Director Azuri González, UTEP began to invest routine budget funding into institutionalizing the Center. We wrote about this in *Metropolitan Communities*, 2011.

How to Move High-Impact Practices Forward and Make Them Work in Other Settings

As noted earlier, I typically offer students the final project choice of service-learning or a research paper for a good portion of their overall grade. I believe in choice, for our students' lives are complicated. However, in this Nonprofit Management internship, I had to make it clear from the outset that an off-campus experience was required. If students had personal challenges with travel, I could have accommodated them with an on-campus internship. However, no students ever approached me about that option. I am a strong believer in experiential learning. As should be clear from my own background, as aforementioned, I learned how to teach this material based on my experiences in government and the nonprofit world as well as the grant-writing world so common in academia now. I am not aware of any political science program that teaches material like this. Should they? Absolutely yes! However, one can find these courses in business, public administration, and communication/leadership programs.

The idea of staggered assignments is a worthy one that can be adapted to other settings. I have used this idea in other courses partly for my own sanity. Few faculty members are not disappointed when students attempt to write a final paper based on slapping material together an evening before the due date.

It is also very useful to provide forms that clarify what students might use to analyze material, whether evaluating websites or preparing a budget, such as in this Nonprofit Management course. Moreover, I am a great believer in peer evaluation and "second chances" to improve and polish a draft into more final form. When students know they are writing, not only for a professor, but also for their peers AND a community partner AND a potential funder, it raises expectations and a sense of accountability to a wider audience and community. While grant-writing will not be part of many other courses, peer evaluation can be used in many settings. After all, in the real word, little writing escapes from large institutions without prior reading by peers (committee members) or supervisors.

Major Takeaways for the Primary Stakeholders in High-Impact Practice Courses Like NP Management

Faculty

Nonprofit Management contains numerous assignments that offer the opportunity to get to know about and care about students in more in-depth ways. From the Myers-Briggs test to the CV/resume and multiple writing assignments, I get to know students' assets along with the capacities that they need to develop to be successful in the course and the real world. Sometimes I feel a little like a surrogate mom, reminding them about various issues to put their best feet forward, but, hey, I think we could all use more supportive surrogate parents!

I would encourage more faculty members to be involved off campus in the community. They might even consider accepting appointments on a Board of Directors, hopefully with full knowledge of the huge time commitments involved. We all learn from experience, including people with advanced degrees.

Students

Students come into the Nonprofit Management course and its mini-internships with incredible passion and commitment for their community. They come from many majors, minors, and besides the College of Liberal Arts and its scores of programs, even the College of Business. I welcome and enjoy people from multiple fields working together. Yet many students work part-time or full-time, so time management becomes an issue. I have been impressed when students had to withdraw from the class, yet promised they would complete their thirty hours with the nonprofit partner because, as a student said to me, he promised "his" nonprofit.

Nevertheless, a course like this with multiple assignments and due dates must be taken seriously. The syllabus makes assignment due dates very clear, so the students who missed opportunities for feedback or turned assignments in late, dealt with consequences. As I shared with students over and over, if grant writers get their proposals in a day, or even a minute late, the lateness becomes an excuse for the funder to avoid the work of even reading the proposal, much less funding the proposal. Despite all the incentives to be present in class, some students are absent too many times and their skill levels suffer, given the workshop-like setting. There is no substitute for being there and learning from the experiences.

Community Partners, That is, the "Nonprofits"

By agreeing to supervise an intern, nonprofit staff have the opportunity to groom our community's future leaders and perhaps identify potential employees for future positions they advertise. They also may be able to get a draft grant proposal written by a student who cares and who is in turn supervised by a faculty member. Every time I teach this course, about a quarter of the grant proposals are good enough to be submitted to the funder with a little tweaking and editing.

I know that our community partners are extremely busy, pressed for time with too few staff and budgets that are too small. However, if and when they do not answer phone call messages and/or respond to emails, even for appointment, it is discouraging for students. It is "ok" to pass on the opportunity to house a student in a semester, but they need to respond to the query quickly enough for students to identify another possible nonprofit.

I hope community partners take greater advantage of the Foundation Center's 700,000+ database in the UTEP Library. It is available to any and all in the community. The CCE worked hard to gain permission to get the database and undergo training. The annual fee was over $1,000, and the CCE was always writing grant proposals to pay for items like this, big and small. Thankfully, the UTEP Library took on the responsibility of paying for the annual fees as part of the institutionalization process.

Conclusion

The Nonprofit Management course, with its mini-internship and grant-searching/grant-writing experiential learning, provides a complex and advance way to scale up and strengthen high-impact practices that students acquire in other high-impact practices like service-learning. For majors that require a high-impact senior capstone course, Nonprofit Management would be an excellent option. I look forward to the day when each type of high-impact practice can be offered in staggered ways, so that students can move upward on stepping-stones for success to senior capstone courses and full-fledged internships.

Selected Readings

Boyer, E. (1996). The scholarship of engagement. *Journal of Public Service and Outreach*, *1*(1), 11–20.

Campus Compact. Retrieved from https://compact.org

Foundation Center. Retrieved from http://foundationcenter.org

Lusk, M., Kathleen, S., & Moya, E. (Eds.). (2012). *Social justice in the U.S.-Mexican borderlands*. Netherlands: Springer Publishers.

Staudt, K. (1990). *Managing development: State, society, and international contexts*. Thousand Oaks, CA: Sage.

Staudt, K., Dane'el, M., & Márquez-Velarde, G. (2013). Stories, science and power in policy change: Environmental health, community-based research, and community organizing in a U.S.-Mexico border colonia. *Environmental Justice, 6*(6), 191–199.

Staudt, K., & González, A. R. (2011). Sustaining a university engagement center at borders: Taking risks in a risk-avoidant atmosphere. *Metropolitan Universities, 22*(2), 65–78.

Vélez-Ibáñez, C., & Heyman, J. (Eds.). (2017). *The U.S.-Mexico transborder region: Cultural dynamics and historical interactions*. Tucson, AZ: University of Arizona Press.

Worth, M. (2017). *Nonprofit management: Principles and practice* (4th ed.). Thousand Oaks, CA: Sage.

APPENDICES

Project Proposal Peer Review

Dr. Staudt

Insert Comments and Points in Each Column!
(Use Reverse Side If Necessary)

Title of the Proposal_____

Author_____

1	What are the project goals? How will the money be used for achieving goals? What measurable results can be achieved in the time period?	Up to 15 points
2	Is the 'need' for this project and money clear and documented? How?	Up to 15 points
3	HOW will the goal(s) be implemented? Is the plan thought through? What could go wrong?	Up to 15 Points
4	Is the budget realistic, exaggerated, and/or underestimated? Will the nonprofit contribute 'in-kind' contributions (examples)?	Up to 15 points
5	Nonprofit track record: What is the nonprofit mission? Do the goals fit? Is this a safe investment?	Up to 15 points
6	Evaluation: How will the nonprofit and funder determine if the project is successful?	Up to 15 points
7	Is the proposal well written?	Up to 10 points

TOTAL_____

Bottom Line! Should this proposal be funded?   Yes   No
Other comments:

Signed by _____

Funding Review Committee

Budget Worksheet

Name of the Project Proposal _____

	YEAR ONE		YEAR TWO	
	Requested	In-Kind	Requested	In-Kind

Personnel Salaries

_____
_____
_____

Personnel Benefits (Health Insurance)

_____
_____

Equipment and Supplies

_____
_____

Transportation

_____
_____

Space/Rent, Utilities

_____
_____

Incentives for Participants

_____
_____

Contingency

_____
_____

Indirect Costs (federal, for higher ed)
TOTALS

Philosophy

Chapter 14

Wondering with Others:
Philosophy for Children and Place-Based
Community Engagement

Amy Reed-Sandoval

SERVICE LEARNING,
COMMUNITY-BASED LEARNING

DIVERSITY/GLOBAL LEARNING

Use these questions to guide your reflection prior to reading the chapter. Use the notes/follow-up section to write your thoughts after you have read the chapter. Your notes can include thoughts in reference to the reflection questions, or general observations about the chapter.

1) What are your thoughts about philosophy and its use or benefit in society?

2) If you were tasked with teaching school-age children about philosophy, how would you go about doing that?

3) If someone asked you about your personal philosophy on life, what would the answer be? What about your philosophy about community engagement?

Notes/Follow-up:

_____

_____

_____

_____

_____

Introduction[1]

I have been a Philosophy for Children practitioner for 8 years. I have a special interest in the complex ethical, pedagogical, and philosophical issues that stem from the practice of facilitating P4C classes with comparatively underprivileged and epistemically marginalized children and youth. After receiving my P4C pedagogical training from the University of Washington Center for Philosophy for Children, I went on to found two Philosophy for Children outreach programs: The Oaxaca Philosophy for Children Initiative in Oaxaca City, Mexico, and the Philosophy for Children in the Borderlands program in El Paso, Texas, and Ciudad Juárez, Mexico. I also serve on the American Philosophical Association Committee on Pre-College Philosophy.

While humans of all ages have been philosophizing for thousands upon thousands of years, Philosophy for Children has only existed as a recognized academic subdiscipline since the 1970s, when Matthew Lipman, then a Professor of Philosophy at Columbia University, founded the Institute for the Advancement of Philosophy for Children at Montclair College. Since then, Philosophy for Children (P4C) has steadily grown both as a philosophical subfield and a community-outreach method, with Philosophy for Children centers and Service-learning courses becoming established at universities and other learning centers across the globe.

All Philosophy for Children classes begin with an understanding that children, including very young children, are inherently philosophical. Constantly bearing in mind the philosophical capabilities of children, P4C facilitators employ a variety of pedagogical techniques as they seek to provide young people with opportunities to raise and explore the philosophical questions that are most meaningful in collaborative, open dialogues with their peers. For instance, a facilitator may read children a philosophically suggestive children's book and then ask the children to articulate the philosophical "why questions" that the book inspires for them. The ensuing philosophical conversation will feature students working collaboratively to address the "why questions" they found most interesting. These open dialogues are sometimes called "Communities of Inquiry" (Lipman, 1980).

Undergraduate and graduate students who facilitate Philosophy for Children sessions at local schools and community centers quickly gain appreciation of the philosophical capabilities of children and youth. They also learn about the sorts of political, epistemological, esthetic, and metaphysical questions that are salient and of greatest concern to the young people and families with whom they are working. This undoubtedly contributes to life-long learning, as P4C facilitators frequently come to see that philosophical dialogue is not confined to the university classroom. Rather, they find that it is a core feature of our everyday social and interpersonal interactions in our communities. This can render P4C outreach valuable and potentially transformative for the individuals and communities who practice it.

---

[1] I am grateful to Aleksandar Pjevalica for his helpful commentary on a previous draft of this chapter.

The goals of this chapter are twofold. First, I aim to provide general advice for those who are interested in starting a new P4C outreach Service-learning program. Second, I shall explore what it means to engage in what I call a "place-based" P4C practice, as my P4C outreach in Oaxaca and at the Mexico U.S. border has often required that my students and I adopt such a pedagogical approach in order to achieve success.

Case Study

Before the Oaxaca Philosophy for Children Initiative could get started, the community partners of the Centro de Esperanza Infantil (CEI) in Oaxaca City, Mexico needed some convincing.

It's not that they weren't motivated to seek out great opportunities for the children and youth they serve. In fact, the Centro de Esperanza Infantil is a nonprofit organization devoted to providing some of Oaxaca's poorest children and youth with the resources they need to achieve a K-12 and university education. Through acquiring financial support from donors, the organization provides qualifying Oaxacan families with the money they need to pay for school fees (which, in Mexico, even public school students must pay), school uniforms, and essential school supplies like backpacks and notebooks. They also provide students with after-school tutoring and a warm lunch 6 days a week.

Why would an organization like this—devoted as it is to providing such basic and essential resources to some of Oaxaca's poorest children and families—want to offer Philosophy classes to the children and youth they serve? Isn't the study of Philosophy a luxury? It seemed that Philosophy classes should be reserved for those blessed with the time, social status, comfort, and privilege that tends to be associated with musing about life's supposedly unanswerable questions. At first blush, the idea of doing philosophy with the children of the Centro de Esperanza Infantil seemed comical at best, and a wasteful distraction at worst.

As a PhD student in Philosophy who was still learning the "ropes" of Philosophy for Children teaching and outreach, I struggled at the time to articulate to the CEI the value of philosophy to people of all ages, backgrounds, and perspectives. Still, I had done enough reading and was sufficiently inspired to fumblingly make my case.

I pointed out that in addition to what we might call the value of doing philosophy "in and of itself," or the intrinsic value of leading what Socrates called an "examined life," there are many "practical" reasons why children and youth of the Centro de Esperanza Infantil should do philosophy. First, it enhances self-confidence. When young people see that their deepest and most difficult questions are deserving of serious attention in the classroom, they come to see themselves as philosophical "knowers." For students dealing with the harsh realities of poverty, racism, sexism, and epistemic injustice (or the injustice that occurs when one is denied the status of a "knower," and/or when one's knowledge system is not given uptake in one's society; for more on this, see Fricker, 2009), then, the value of pre-college Philosophy can be quite significant. Second, P4C teaches children and youth to engage in open, respectful dialogue with their peers, thus empowering them to become engaged citizens in their society. A thriving democracy needs empowered citizens who are able and willing to engage in open discourse about controversial questions pertaining to our lives. Pre-college Philosophy can contribute to the process of preparing such citizens—not only in Oaxaca, but in the U.S. and across the globe. Third, Philosophy for Children classes inspire in students an intellectual curiosity that can help them thrive in other academic classes, such as reading and math. This has been confirmed, I pointed out, in recent studies demonstrating wide-ranging academic benefits of Philosophy for Children (see, for instance, Topping & Trickey, 2007).I was delighted, and unexpectedly nervous, when the Centro de Esperanza Infantil authorized me to teach my first P4C class to 12 children during the summer of 2010. I worked with a diverse group of Oaxacan Indigenous children whose parents agreed to sign them up for a full month of P4C classes. Each day, the 13 of us sat and dialogued around a wooden table in a cramped but tidy classroom space. Despite my already-existing understanding of children's philosophical abilities, I was astonished by my students' openness to exploring all sorts of philosophical questions, from the nature of friendship to the composition of the universe to the timeless worry about whether we truly are "free." Importantly, I also found that the students taught me a great deal about philosophy, as they regularly drew from different traditions of Oaxacan Indigenous knowledge. We dialogued, for instance, about the Zapotec theories of tequio, Guelaguezta, and cooperación (for more on this, see Reed-Sandoval, 2014a); all of these theories are part of a comprehensive Zapotec sociopolitical framework of political egalitarianism. My "students" taught me about ongoing political conflicts with which Triqui children and families are currently contending, and this inspired philosophical exploration of the nature of social justice as applied to the Triqui and Oaxacan political context.

Today, after years of summer pre-college Philosophy at the CEI, the Oaxaca Philosophy for Children Initiative continues to flourish. Many of the children and youth who were involved in the inaugural summer course are now studying at university. One alumna of the program went on to specialize in Philosophy as part of her high-school "bachillerato," and she is now studying law in college in Oaxaca City. Many students who subsequently signed up to participate in the program aspire to be writers, artists, and photographers; they see pre-college Philosophy as a space in which they can engage the sorts of questions, curiosity, and wonderment that motivates them to do creative work under difficult circumstances. Most importantly, in my opinion, the Oaxaca Philosophy for Children Initiative demonstrates that children and youth of all backgrounds are themselves philosophers. Life's most important questions emerge everywhere and from everyone, and we, as humans, deserve to be able to carefully explore them.

Lessons learned from the Oaxaca Philosophy for Children Initiative, some of which I shall discuss in the upcoming sections, inspired aspects of the organizational framework of the Philosophy for Children in the Borderlands program, through which undergraduate and graduate students doing service-learning at the University of Texas at El Paso facilitate weekly pre-college Philosophy classes in the El Paso-Ciudad Juárez community. Like the Oaxaca Philosophy for Children Initiative, the Philosophy for Children in the Borderlands program aims to provide pre-college Philosophy courses for children and youth who face different forms of socioeconomic disadvantage. Furthermore, like the Oaxaca program, the Philosophy for Children in the Borderlands program aims to honor and engage the local linguistic, sociopolitical, and philosophical context in which it operates through a "place-based" P4C practice.

For instance, UTEP students teach bilingual P4C classes that frequently address issues of concern to children and families of the Mexico–U.S. borderlands. To date, UTEP students and faculty participating in the program have led P4C sessions at Rayito de Sol Daycare and Learning Center (run by La Mujer Obrera), Aliviane, Inc., Morehead Middle School, Austin High School, and the YWCA El Paso del Norte (all in El Paso), as well as the Biblioteca Independiente Ma'Juana in Ciudad Juárez.

What Made This High-Impact Practice Successful?

Both of these P4C outreach programs aim to honor the local linguistic, sociopolitical, and philosophical context in which the philosophical dialogues with children are taking place. This is one the most important reasons why this high-impact practice has been successful, with community partners, children, and families regularly requesting more P4C classes.

In the context of the Oaxaca Philosophy for Children Initiative, doing "place-based" Philosophy for Children (Reed-Sandoval, 2014a) entails two key things. First, it requires P4C facilitators to transcend the paradigms of the Western philosophical cannon in order to learn about Indigenous knowledge, all the while seeking ways to incorporate such knowledge into P4C lesson plans (for more on Indigenous knowledge, epistemic marginalization, and P4C, see Rainville, 2000). Second, it involves taking time to learn about the day-to-day lives of the children and youth with whom one is working. Without such background knowledge, it is significantly more difficult to demonstrate to children the connections between the philosophical questions they are exploring in class and their day-to-day lives. This is particularly important for P4C facilitators who are trying to demonstrate the value of philosophical dialogue to members of marginalized groups. As Darren Chetty points out (2014), it is inappropriate to expect children—particularly children of color dealing with everyday racism—to openly vocalize such connections in the P4C classroom. P4C facilitators working with underprivileged youth need to understand the challenges faced by the children and youth they serve if they want to lead truly impactful philosophical dialogues.

At the Mexico–U.S. border, students and faculty involved in the Philosophy for Children in the Borderlands program also engage in "place-based" philosophy. Whenever possible, pre-college Philosophy sessions in El Paso are conducted in Spanish *and* English, enabling children to access their full linguistic and conceptual "tool-kit" as they participate in philosophical dialogues. Lesson plans have been developed around and in response to important elements of Mexican-American and Chicanx histories, such as the annual dialogue on justice, fairness, and worker's rights that is held in El Paso on Cesar Chavez day (for further details see Chavez Leyva & Reed-Sandoval, 2016). Classroom dialogues frequently reflect local philosophical interest in questions pertaining to the ethics of borders, social identity, and group rights. Undergraduate and graduate students involved in the Philosophy for Children in the Borderlands program receive training in both cultural and "philosophical sensitivity" (Mohr Lone, 2013) prior to initiating their work in the community.

Such "place-based techniques" have contributed to the success of both programs. Once local children, families, and community leaders come to see that their histories, struggles, languages, and concerns are being respected and even philosophized *about* in Philosophy for Children classes, they often become even more motivated to participate in the program. Furthermore, at the University of Texas at El Paso, which is a Hispanic Serving Institution, undergraduate and graduate students who are involved in the program often appreciate the opportunity to give back to their communities through philosophy. As they come to see the connections between the philosophical dialogues they are facilitating and the concrete concerns of their communities, the value of their participation is greatly enhanced. The children and youth who are served by these programs, meanwhile, come to see philosophy as something that is "for them" and even part of them, which serves to accelerate their learning and philosophical development.

Some Challenges

Of course, there are challenges associated with all community-outreach projects, and these Philosophy for Children programs are not exceptions to this rule.

As explored in the case study, one of the main challenges that one faces in initiating such a program is that of building trust with community partners and families and (as part of this) dialoguing with them about the value of pre-college Philosophy. The study of Philosophy is sometimes regarded with some suspicion, with some people viewing it as hopelessly elitist, and others regarding it as inappropriate for children due to a widespread misconception (one that exists at all "levels" of society) about children's philosophical abilities. Indeed, dialoguing with community partners of the value of philosophy has been the most challenging aspect of both projects. I shall explore strategies for dealing with this challenge in the next section, and I include a list of additional resources (including visual resources that convey what P4C classes "look like") at the end of this chapter.

A second challenge—which is, as the saying goes, a "good problem to have"—is that of finding enough philosophical supply to meet local philosophical demands. Once communities come to see the value of P4C, which often happens quickly (following a period of initial suspicion), community partners may start to request more Philosophy for Children classes. Finding enough interested and qualified people to facilitate P4C classes in Oaxaca and at the Mexico–US border has been an ongoing challenge in the context of both outreach programs, and it is a challenge that P4C initiatives across the globe regularly face.

How to Start Your Own "Place-Based" Philosophy for Children Program

In this section I will cover two themes: 1) how to start a Philosophy for Children outreach program; and 2) how to adopt a "place-based" methodology for so doing. Allow me to begin with (1).

First, let me emphasize once again that dialoguing with community partners about the value of philosophy is, in my opinion, the most challenging aspect of starting one's own pre-college philosophy program. Community members may have trouble visualizing just what philosophy is—and they may even be inclined to regard it as a waste of valuable time. Thus, prior to meeting with a potential community partner to "pitch" the idea of facilitating a new P4C course in that community partner's space, one should spend a considerable amount of time preparing oneself to explain the value of Philosophy for Children to a potentially skeptical audience. I have included at the end of this chapter resources that one can consult in preparation for these early conversations.

On the bright side, however, one of the most "user-friendly" aspects of starting one's own Philosophy for Children course is the fact it is a relatively inexpensive undertaking; this fact can be emphasized in early conversations with potential community partners. As Sara Goering pointed out in a recent TEDX talk about P4C (the link to which I have included in the final section of this chapter), one does not require expensive technology or a functioning laboratory to do philosophy with young people. In fact, all one needs is a sufficiently quiet and peaceful space in which to engage in an open philosophical dialogue with the children and youth with whom one is working. If you are able to invest a small amount of money in your new course, it is a good idea—though it is by no means necessary—to purchase some philosophically suggestive children's books to use in the P4C classroom. To help you find the right books, there is a popular "wiki" you can consult that features readings lists and corresponding lesson plans. I have included a link to this wiki and other lesson plans at the end of this guide.

Once you have built trust with a community partner, such that your community partner has decided to allow you (or your students, if you are faculty member) to teach your own P4C class in their community space, you should address the question of how frequently and for how much time you ought to teach a particular pre-college Philosophy course. In this regard, there is widespread variation amongst P4C practitioners. Some facilitators teach classes every day, some hold weekly sessions, while others deliver monthly classes or only the occasional "teacher training." You should develop a schedule that suits you and your community partner. Be sure to avoid committing to more sessions than you can deliver, as this can damage your relationship with the community you hope to serve. Note that there is also variation in terms of how long individual P4C sessions tend to take; in general, very young (i.e., 3 to 5-year-old) children can stay engaged for a 20–30 minute session, while high-school classes tend to last for an hour.

With all these logistical matters sorted out, you can start your exciting new P4C class! As the course develops, conscientious practitioners will inevitably want to learn about new techniques, established areas of philosophical inquiry, and more. The bibliography at the end of this chapter is designed to guide you through this process.

Now let me address (2). That is, how can one develop a "place-based" method of Philosophy for Children outreach in one's community? I believe that the best way to approach this goal is by striving for a level of engagement that transcends the P4C classroom. If you are working at a local community center, then you should find ways to support and get involved with that center's activities outside of the context of your class. If you are working at K-12 school, then you might try to observe a couple of parent–teacher association meetings. Whenever possible and appropriate, get to know the families of the children with whom you are working. Ask questions about the obstacles and concerns confronted by the community you aim to serve, and do research to help you fully understand the answers.

After you have done sufficient background research, find time to develop Philosophy for Children lesson plans that reflect these community concerns. If the community you are serving is opposing, say, a concrete instance of environmental injustice (e.g., a private company is engaging in fracking and contaminating local groundwater despite widespread community opposition), then you might prepare a P4C class that addresses philosophical questions about the value of nature/the environment and the idea of justice. Of course, your job as a P4C facilitator is not simply to ascertain and endorse established viewpoints on particular issues. Rather, you should provide children and youth with opportunities to engage in open dialogue about the sorts of questions and concerns that they are both confronting and living on a daily basis. This, I believe, is the ideal route to achieving a "place-based" P4C.

Recommendations For Faculty

Faculty members who are interested in incorporating Philosophy for Children outreach in their classrooms most likely fall into two categories: 1) university Philosophy instructors who are intrigued by the idea of having their students dialogue philosophically with children; and 2) university instructors of other academic disciplines who feel that their students would benefit from such an opportunity. As P4C has become more "visible" in academic Philosophy, thereby making it easier for Philosophy instructors to access the resources they need to initiate a P4C project (see, for instance, the website of the APA Committee on Pre-College Philosophy), I will focus here on the possible needs of group (2).

I believe that faculty members who teach in disciplines such as education, anthropology, sociology, and psychology can enhance their courses by having their students teach pre-college Philosophy in the local community. In a recent article, I explored how teaching P4C classes provides opportunities for cross-cultural exploration (Reed-Sandoval, 2014b) and ethnographic research, rendering P4C outreach potentially appropriate for anthropology and sociology courses for which college students must perform fieldwork. Education courses can also be enhanced by incorporating a Philosophy for Children Service-learning component, as they enable future K-12 teachers to gain confidence in terms of deeply engaging, as opposed to shying away from, difficult and timeless philosophical questions in the classroom. In addition, given the ways in which P4C scholars have entered into dialogue with the subdiscipline of developmental psychology (Matthews, 1996), P4C teaching is frequently of interest to undergraduate and graduate students of psychology.

Faculty members who choose to incorporate into their classes a Philosophy for Children Service-learning component should be aware that it can be difficult to quantify precisely the sort of "philosophical sensitivity" that undergraduate and graduate students often gain through their P4C teaching. Nevertheless, there are a range of effective ways to evaluate student progress and learning. For instance, I ask undergraduate and graduate students in my Philosophy for Children Service-learning course to produce reflection essays and field notes after facilitating pre-college Philosophy lessons. In these notes, my students report the particular "why questions," core ideas, and points of contention that came up in the philosophical dialogues my students facilitated. This exercise requires students to evaluate the children with whom they work *as philosophers*—a task that requires careful listening, consideration, openness, and philosophical ability on the part of my students.

Recommendations For Students

If you are a student who wants to become a P4C teacher, you have many reasons to feel enthusiastic about your future work. Not only will you contribute to your community in unique ways through nurturing the philosophical impulse of local children and youth, you may also jump-start your own process of philosophical self-discovery as you explore a range of "why questions" in the Community of Inquiry of your co-creation. Why am I here? Why are we born, and why do we die? Why should I be good? Why do I have to do my homework? Your young students will undoubtedly get you thinking about these questions in your spare time.

Here are two concrete things you can do to prepare yourself for your upcoming experiences as a pre-college Philosophy instructor. First, to invoke a useful cliché, you should try to have an open mind. Try to let go, that is, of your preconceived notions of what philosophical dialogue must look like and sound like (note that if you are a Philosophy major, you may find this more challenging than your peers who have opted for different majors!). The children and youth with whom you are working will almost certainly demonstrate their philosophical contributions and abilities in a variety of unexpected ways. I have learned that the more open-minded and even relaxed you can become about what sorts of questions and statements are "valuable" and "philosophical" in the pre-college Philosophy classroom, the more effective you will be as a P4C facilitator.

Second, you should read as much as you can about P4C teaching techniques, existing P4C programs, and even the history of Philosophy. Even as you begin to teach, you should never stop educating yourself about these things. In the spirit of Paulo Freire's liberation pedagogy—which emphasizes a "bottom-up" pedagogy that transcends and displaces the "top–down" banking model of education—you should strive to regard *yourself* as a co-learner in the P4C classes that you will facilitate. This way, you will enjoy yourself more in your classroom, maintain a sense of excitement and curiosity, and also develop your own philosophical ideas and sensitivities. I believe that this can help you to become a better teacher in the classroom, a better listener in your personal life, and a more engaged citizen in your society.

Recommendations For Communities

Throughout this chapter I have been discussing, from the perspective of the Philosophy for Children instructor, the challenges of convincing community partners to "host" a pre-college Philosophy course. It probably strikes readers as unsurprising, then, that I will now encourage potential community partners to try to be open to the various ways in which pre-college Philosophy can be beneficial to your organization. If you are skeptical (as you have every right to be!), then you might consider allowing a new teacher to facilitate one ten-week course on a trial basis. That way, you can get a better sense of whether P4C is right for you and for the children and families you serve.

One of the best practices I have seen community partners engage in with respect to the P4C classes they host is that of requesting P4C training sessions for their staff. You might request that your would-be P4C teacher host a free all-day P4C "teacher training" for your employees, and even for the adult members of the families you serve. This way, you can experience P4C methodology for yourself to get a sense of what it entails. In addition, your staff members can use this training as part of an effort to keep the philosophical dialogues going throughout the week, long after the weekly P4C sessions have ended. Eventually, you might even consider starting a Philosophy for Children program of your own; you need not only practice pre-college Philosophy in collaboration with a university.

The following two documentaries, both of which can be accessed for free online, explore the value of Philosophy for Children classes from the perspective of community partners:

- *The Oaxaca Philosophy for Children Initiative* (Reihs & Reed-Sandoval, 2013): https://www.youtube.com/watch?v=Z3HEjPFf_20)
- *Philosophy for Children in the Borderlands* (Reihs, 2016): https://www.youtube.com/watch?v=mnt-XFg90Jk)

Conclusion

Philosophy for Children is a transformative undertaking. Through creating safe, inspiring spaces for children and youth to raise the philosophical "why questions" that are most important and meaningful for them, P4C impacts children and youth, P4C facilitators, communities, and university classrooms in numerous positive ways. Fortunately, P4C is now a recognized subdiscipline in academic Philosophy, with P4C Service-learning courses becoming more common in Philosophy departments across the globe. However, these methods can also be incorporated into broader education and social science Service-learning courses at universities across the globe. In this chapter, I have aimed to provide a basic framework for starting a new P4C class or outreach program. In addition, I have discussed the particular merits and challenges associated with doing "placed-based" Philosophy for Children.

Selected Readings, Resources, and Tools

Some Free Online Lesson Plans for P4C Teachers:

From Teaching Children Philosophy. Retrieved from https://www.teachingchildrenphilosophy.org/BookModule/BookModule

From the UW Center for Philosophy for Children. Retrieved from http://depts.washington.edu/nwcenter/resources/lesson-plans/

From Philosophy for Children in the Borderlands (includes lesson plans in Spanish). Retrieved from http://academics.utep.edu/Default.aspx?tabid=75331

Some Books That Contain Philosophy for Children Lesson Plans:

Mohr Lone, J., & Burroughs, M. (2016). *Philosophy in education: Questioning and dialogue in schools.* London: Rowman and Littlefield.

Shapiro, D. (2012). *Plato was wrong!: Footnotes on doing philosophy with young people.* Plymouth: Rowman and Littlefield Education.

Wartenburg, T, (2014). *Big ideas for little kids: Teaching philosophy through children's literature.* Plymouth: Rowman and Littlefield.

Some Articles Dealing With "Place" and Philosophy for Children:

Makaiau, A. S. (2017). A citizen's education: The Philosophy for Children Hawai'I approach to deliberative pedagogy. In M. R. Gregory, J. Haynes, & K. Murris (Eds.), *The Routledge international handbook on philosophy for children* (pp. 19–26). Ambingdon, Oxen: Routledge.

Phillip Ndofirepi, A. (2011). Philosophy for children: The quest for an African perspective. *The South African Journal of Education, 31*(2), 246–256.

Rainville, N. (2000). Philosophy for children in Native America: A post-colonial critique. *Analytic Teaching, 21*(1), 65–77.

Reed-Sandoval, A. (2014). The Oaxaca philosophy for children as place-based philosophy: Why context matters in philosophy for children. *APA Newsletter on Hispanic/Latino Issues in Philosophy, 14*(1), 9–12.

Some Videos about Philosophy for Children:

Picture Book Philosophy (Akeret, 2011). Retrieved from https://www.youtube.com/watch?v=x5wuHRyHez0

Philosophy for Children in the Borderlands (Reihs, 2016). Retrieved from https://www.youtube.com/watch?v=mnt-XFg90Jk

Dr. Sara Goering, TEDX talk, *Philosophy for Kids: Sparking a Love of Learning.* Retrieved from https://www.youtube.com/watch?v=7DLzXAjscXk

Some Blogs about Philosophy for Children:

The Philosophy Club (Michelle Sowey). Retrieved from https://thephilosophyclub.com.au/weblog/

Wondering Aloud (Jana Mohr Lone). Retrieved from http://philosophyforchildren.blogspot.com.au/

Imaginative Inquiry (Tim Taylor). Retrieved from http://www.imaginative-inquiry.co.uk/category/blog/

Exploring Philosophy in the Early Years (Kate Kennedy White). Retrieved from http://www.imaginative-inquiry.co.uk/category/blog/

Filosofia Crítica (Tomás Magalhães Carneiro). Retrieved from https://filosofiacritica.wordpress.com/

References

Chavez Leyva, Y., & Reed-Sandoval, A. (2016) Philosophy for children and the legacy of anti-Mexican racism in El Paso schools. *APA Newsletter on Hispanic/Latino Issues in Philosophy, 16*(1), 17–22.

Chetty, D. (2014). The elephant in the room: Picturebooks, philosophy for children, and racism. *Childhood & Philosophy, 10*(19), 11–31.

Fricker, M. (2009). *Epistemic injustice: Power and the ethics of knowing.* Oxford: Oxford University Press.

Lipman, M. (1980). *Philosophy in the classroom.* Philadelphia, PA: Temple University Press.

Matthews, G. (1996). *The philosophy of childhood.* Cambridge, MA: The President and Fellows of Harvard College.

Mohr Lone, J. (2013). Philosophical sensitivity. *Metaphilosophy, 44*(1–2), 171–186.

Rainville, N. (2000). Philosophy for children in Native America: A post-colonial critique. *Analytic Teaching, 21*(1), 65–77.

Reed-Sandoval, A. (2014a). The Oaxaca philosophy for children as place-based philosophy: Why context matters in philosophy for children. *APA Newsletter on Hispanic/Latino Issues in Philosophy, 14*(1), 9–12.

Reed-Sandoval, A. (2014b). Cross-cultural exploration: Reflections on doing philosophy with Triqui children in Oaxaca. *Teaching Ethics, 12*(1), 77–90.

Topping, K. J., & Trickey, S. (2007). Collaborative philosophical inquiry for young children: A two-year follow-up. *British Journal of Education Psychology, 77*, 787–796.

Chapter 15

A Standardized Service-Learning Structure: A Model for Partnering with Multiple Community Organizations in a Single Course

Gregory S. Schober, and Jennifer M. Lujan

SERVICE LEARNING,
COMMUNITY-BASED LEARNING

Use these questions to guide your reflection prior to reading the chapter. Use the notes/follow-up section to write your thoughts after you have read the chapter. Your notes can include thoughts in reference to the reflection questions, or general observations about the chapter.

1) Would you agree or disagree that in order for service-learning to be truly meaningful it must take place in a community context or setting? Why or why not? What makes it "meaningful"?

2) If you were given the option to select a service-learning site to complete 20 hours of service, what criteria would you personally utilize to select the site?

3) Under what circumstances, if any, should service-learning be mandated? What is the rationale for your thinking?

Notes/Follow-up:

_____

_____

_____

_____

_____

Introduction

In higher education courses, some students struggle to learn new course material through the required readings, lectures, and class discussions. Service-learning presents an opportunity for higher education students to take ownership of their own learning and overcome potential struggles with learning new course material. Following Bringle and Hatcher (1995), service-learning is defined as:

> a course-based, credit-bearing educational experience in which students (a) participate in an organized service activity that meets identified community needs and (b) reflect on the service activity in such a way as to gain further understanding of course content, a broader appreciation of the discipline, and an enhanced sense of civic responsibility. (p. 112)

Within this definition of service-learning, two key elements deserve more attention. First, the service-learning experience is a part of a specific course. The experience connects to the course content and objectives, and, by completing the experience, students fulfill a requirement for the course (or receive some form of course credit). Second, the service component of service-learning takes place outside of the classroom in a *community setting*. It is essential for the service component to take place in a community setting, so that students can directly observe and learn from 1) the community context; and 2) the knowledge and experiences of community members. Without a community setting, students will lose these valuable learning experiences, and they will miss the opportunity to identify, understand, and address community needs.

Although service-learning experiences vary in many ways, they typically take a general form. Instructors include the service-learning experience as an option or requirement for a particular course. Students perform service-learning as a part of the course and thus receive course credit. At least one community organization participates in the project and provides students with a specific opportunity to address a community need. Students engage in the service-learning experience outside of class and reflect on the experience inside and/or outside of class.

Service-learning, as one of the identified "high-impact educational practices," provides meaningful experiences for students (Kuh, 2008). Extensive research suggests that service-learning leads to several desirable educational outcomes, such as increases in retaining students, more engagement of students, and improvements in multiple learning outcomes (see Kuh, 2008; Kuh & O'Donnell, 2013). By allowing students to explore and reflect on their experience at their own pace, service-learning provides a self-directed pathway to learning. All students, including those who are struggling to learn new course material, have the opportunity to make their own connections to the course content and take more ownership of their own learning.

In the following chapter, we will describe one type of service-learning model: the Standardized Model for Partnering with Multiple Community Organizations in a Single Course. This model possesses a standardized

Contributed by Gregory S. Schober and Jennifer M. Lujan. © Kendall Hunt Publishing Company.

basic structure, because 1) each participating student is required to complete the full number of required service-learning hours at a single community organization site and also to reflect on their experiences; 2) each participating community organization is required to accept students at their site for the full number of required service-learning hours, and they must offer service-learning experiences for these students; 3) the participating faculty member must incorporate the service-leaning experience as a substantial and graded part of a single course and identify ways for the service-learning experience to meet the objectives of that course; and 4) the academic center coordinates, troubleshoots, and monitors the service-learning experiences. Given the standardized structure of the model, we refer to it as the "Standardized Model" throughout the paper.

In particular, we study the Standardized Model by examining its use in a specific course: the Leadership and Civic Participation course at The University of Texas at El Paso (UTEP). The Department of Political Science at UTEP offered this undergraduate course in spring 2017, and about 45 students enrolled in and completed the course. Dr. Gregory S. Schober, one of the authors of this chapter, was the instructor for this course, and Jennifer M. Lujan—the other author of this chapter—was the Assistant Director of the Center for Civic Engagement (CCE). The CCE is UTEP's academic center that connects community organizations and faculty, and it organizes, coordinates, and monitors service-learning experiences for students.

Case Study: The Standardized Model in the Leadership and Civic Participation Course

In the Standardized Model in the Leadership and Civic Participation course, an academic center first partnered with several local community organizations in order to create a standardized, recurring service-learning experience at each community organization site. Each service-learning experience followed the semester timeline, and it required each participating student to complete 20 hours of service-learning. Once these partnerships were established, a representative of the academic center (Jennifer M. Lujan) approached a faculty member (Dr. Gregory S. Schober) about offering the service-learning experiences as a part of his course. A menu of community organizations was presented to Schober for his review.

For the Leadership and Civic Participation course, Schober selected three community organizations or service-learning experiences: the YWCA El Paso del Norte, the Boys and Girls club, and Students Helping In the Naturalization of the Elderly (SHINE). The selected community organizations provided a range of service-learning experiences for students. At several YWCA sites, UTEP students taught and mentored elementary school children in the after-school program. Through the Boys and Girls club, UTEP students taught and mentored middle school children. In SHINE, UTEP students taught English-as-a-second-language (ESL) and citizenship classes to adults.

Schober selected these three community organizations or service-learning experiences, because they fit best with the content and objectives of his Leadership and Civic Engagement course. In particular, these three options allowed students to experience a form of civic participation, better understand the factors that influence civic participation, and recognize the role of civic engagement in American politics and society.

Throughout the service-learning experience for students in this course, the academic center at UTEP (CCE) played a critical role in presenting information about the community organizations to the students; registering and training the students; troubleshooting any potential challenges; monitoring and verifying the student hours; guiding reflection; and serving as the key contact for the faculty member, students, and community organizations.

To help facilitate the collection and organization of all the information that is needed for the service-learning experiences in this course, the CCE used a website called the CUE (cue.utep.edu). On the CUE, students were able to examine the community organization or service-learning options that were available in their participating class, register for a specific community organization or service-learning experience, and input their service-learning hours throughout the semester. Schober, as a faculty member, provided necessary information as well, including details about the Leadership and Civic Participation course and his preferences for in-class presentation and reflection session times. Prior to the CUE, faculty members were informed about potential community partners through verbal communication.

Of course, the participating community organizations also played an essential role in the Standardized Model in this course. The local community organizations provided a community setting for the service-learning experiences, which allowed the students to observe their sites and regularly interact with other community members. The community organizations helped to train and mentor the students. They also monitored and verified the service-learning hours that are reported by the students.

UTEP students, for their part, needed to complete several requirements in order to receive full credit in this course for their service-learning experience. Before starting service-learning, students needed to attend an orientation and training, contact a representative at the relevant community organization, and create a schedule that is acceptable for all parties. Students then needed to complete 20 hours of service-learning prior to the semester deadline, submit reflection comments through the CUE, and participate in an in-class reflection session at the end of the semester.

In this course, UTEP students were given the option of completing 20 hours of service-learning or completing a research paper that would require a similar number of hours from the student. Approximately 30 students, or about 67% of the numbered of enrolled students, selected the service-learning option and completed 20 hours of service-learning before the deadline.

What Made This High-Impact Practice Successful?

We believe that several key factors made the integration of the Standardized Model in the Leadership and Civic Participation course successful. The first factor is that students had the option of completing the service-learning experience or completing an alternative traditional assignment. By not requiring the service-learning experience, we avoided some scheduling challenges and did not attract students who did not want to participate in this experience. Thus, the option to complete service-learning likely created a more committed group of participating service-learning students, which in turn contributed to more successful service-learning experiences for the students and for the community organizations.

Second, the model was successful in this course, because it became clear that service-learning students were able to better meet some of the course learning objectives. In particular, I believe that service-learning students developed a deeper understanding of the factors that influence civic participation, were better able to explain how civic participation in the United States has changed, and became better at recognizing the role of civic engagement in American politics and society. By directly participating at a community organization site and continually reflecting on their own experiences, I believe that these students gained a greater perspective that contributed to the improved learning outcomes. Conversely, I think that non-service-learning students often had more trouble describing the relevance and importance of civic engagement.

A third factor that contributed to the success of the model in this course was the preparation stage when the faculty member (Schober) and the academic center representative (Lujan) met to specify our specific expectations for the service-learning experience. These meetings provide a structured opportunity to review successes and challenges from the previous semesters, thus allowing for reflection and discussion on how to improve the service-learning experience. The meetings also helped the CCE to communicate the faculty member's expectations to each of the participating community organizations.

Fourth, regular in-class opportunities for students to discuss and reflect on their service-learning experiences helped to make the integration of the Standardized Model in the Leadership and Civic Participation course more successful. These discussions revealed potential difficulties or challenges with the program, which allowed the faculty members and CCE to help address these problems. Also, when students shared positive learning experiences, the discussion served to motivate other students. Furthermore, the discussions allowed students to identify potential connections to the course material at their own pace, deepening their understanding of course content and allowing the students to take more ownership of their own learning.

Reflection was facilitated with the assistance of the CCE through a variety of methods during the beginning, middle, and end of the semester. At the beginning of the semester, the CCE staff visited with the class to help students prepare for their participation and provide step-by-step guidance on how to document their experiences. Students were asked to think about how they would make their experiences positive, phenomenal, and unforgettable. They also were asked to share ideas about what they could do before attending the community organization site. This type of reflection allows for students to gain a sense of ownership of their experience.

Throughout the semester, after each time that students participated in service-learning, students were asked to complete an open-ended questionnaire. Students were asked to answer these questions no more than a day after their participation and were able to submit their responses via the CUE webpage while inputting their hours. Having students respond to the questions after each participation day helped give them a sense and understanding of skills gained, personal growth, and professional development. In the Other Tools section in this chapter, a list of specific reflection questions are included. Questions 1–3 were asked to students after each service-learning day.

Another way that reflection was facilitated was through an end-of-semester reflection session. The CCE facilitated this session for 1 hour during a class session. The CCE used a variety of activities to engage students in discussions, to get them to share their learning experiences, and to help students make the connection between their participation in service-learning and the course content. For example, the CCE utilized Liberating Structure activities, such as the User Fishbowl Experience and 9 Why's Exercise, to engage students in open and lively group discussions and offer the opportunity for feedback and reflection (Lipmanowicz & McCandless, 2014). Please refer to the appendix for a detailed description of the activities utilized during the reflection session.

Challenges

In the Standardized Model that was integrated into the Leadership and Civic Participation course, we encountered several challenges. For example, a small number of students did not complete, or at least properly document, their service-learning hours before the deadline. When students did not complete their service-learning hours or the academic center was unable to verify the hours, it was difficult to grade these students on their participation in service-learning.

Also, some students procrastinated and completed almost all of their service-learning hours in the final weeks before the deadline. This procrastination may lead to inferior learning outcomes and jeopardize the interest of community organizations to partner and offer service-learning experiences in future semesters. In addition, not every service-learning student in the course had a great experience with service-learning. Negative student experiences are a challenge, because they may lead to worse learning outcomes. They also may create strained relationships with community organizations, as these organizations may question whether service-learning is worth the extra effort. Furthermore, the schedules of students at times created a challenge. Many students have additional responsibilities and time commitments outside of class, so their schedules sometimes did not match the schedules of the community agency.

To help address these challenges, students were given regular, in-class opportunities to reflect on their service-learning experiences throughout the semester. This allowed potentially negative experiences to be identified early on, reminded the students to contact the academic center if they were experiencing a problem, and showed the students that many of their classmates were learning from the service-learning experience. Also, the existence of multiple community organization sites in a single course helped to address student scheduling challenges, as students had several options to find a match with their schedules.

Utilizing the Standardized Model in Other Settings

We believe that our Standardized Model in a single course can be successfully implemented in other settings, but it may require some key modifications depending on the specific setting. For example, in settings where the academic center is not institutionalized or fully supported by the university administration, the responsibilities of the academic center will need to be significantly reduced. In these settings, the faculty members and/or community organizations will need to take on a larger share of the organization and coordination of the program.

In addition, the specific types of service-learning activities will depend on the faculty members, available courses, and community organizations in a particular setting. In our version of the Standardized Model, the activities reflect our community needs and course content areas. In an alternative setting, the specific activities likely will need to be changed, in order to match the community needs, the efforts of the community organizations, and courses of the faculty members. Even though the program structure is standardized in this model, the specific service-learning activities likely will vary across settings.

Furthermore, the overall size of the service-learning program will depend on the interest and commitment of the faculty members and community organizations. In the beginning stages of the model, it is likely that fewer faculty members and community organizations will participate, resulting in a smaller program. However, over time, more faculty members and organizations likely will become partners and the overall size of the program will grow.

Recommendations For Faculty

We offer the following recommendations for faculty members. At least at first, we suggest that faculty members utilize the academic center to build on existing community partnerships. One of the main advantages of the Standardized Model is that one entity (the academic center) can focus on developing strong relationships with many different community organizations. This arrangement avoids the duplication of efforts, which saves faculty members' time and is more convenient for the community organizations as well.

We also strongly believe that faculty members should provide in-class opportunities for discussion and reflection on the service-learning experiences. These opportunities allow students to consider and evaluate potential connections to the course content. In our experience, students will find interesting and insightful connections to the course if faculty members provide enough time for reflection. If possible, faculty members may even want to consider attending some of the service-learning sites and witnessing the experiences.

Even though faculty members are unable to guarantee meaningful experiences for all students, we still encourage the faculty members to be confident in the process. When students sense hesitation on the part of the faculty member, they too will become unsure about participating. It is difficult to expect students to have a positive attitude regarding service-learning if they sense that the faculty member has concerns.

Furthermore, we recommend that faculty members always have an alternative option for their students. Not all students will have the ability to participate due to work, family, and school schedules, and sometimes the community organization will not be able to accommodate all of the students that they initially envisioned. By having an alternative option ready for students, the faculty members will avoid unnecessary stress.

Lastly, faculty members should consider developing new research designs to analyze the effects of service-learning experiences. There are opportunities to publish the results of your analysis and advance our understanding of the effects of service-learning. Faculty members may want to work with the academic center to build on existing efforts.

Recommendations For Students

In our experience, students are more likely to have successful service-learning experiences if they follow three key recommendations. First, before you start service-learning, we recommend that you create a detailed schedule of your time commitments for the rest of the semester. Many conflicts, scheduling problems, and low grades can be avoided with a detailed and realistic assessment of your schedule during the semester.

Second, we suggest that you try to be comfortable outside of your comfort zone. Service-learning often puts students in new environments and social interactions. At first, you may feel uncomfortable. As long as you do not feel unsafe, we encourage you to continue on with the experience and embrace being outside of your comfort zone. By challenging yourself to remain outside of your comfort zone, you open new avenues for learning and growth.

Third, you should expect challenges with your service-learning experience. Service-learning is not perfect, but the imperfections often provide valuable learning experiences. Moreover, if you expect challenges, then you will have a more positive attitude and be better prepared to confront the challenges if they arise.

The fourth and perhaps most important recommendation for students is to take ownership of your service-learning experience. More than anyone, you control the quality of the learning experience. Please take the responsibility seriously. If there is a problem with your experience, try to work with the community agency and academic center to find a solution. Take time to reflect on how your service-learning experience relates to the class. Treat service-learning as a professional experience that allows you to network with other professionals and learn and practice new skills. Always keep in mind that community members depend on your efforts, so try your best at the site.

Recommendations For Community

We also have two recommendations for community organization leaders. The first recommendation is to provide students with opportunities for professional development. Many students lack extensive professional work experience, so they may feel intimidated at the community organization site. Guidance from organization leaders can help students gain experience, confidence, and skills. The second recommendation is to consider meeting with faculty members to identify which specific activities are most valuable for a particular course. Organization leaders may also consider discussing the course objectives with the faculty member, so that the organization leaders can identify ways to meet those goals through the service-learning experience.

Selected Resources

For more information on the Standardized Model at UTEP, please see the CCE website (utep.edu/cce). In particular, the service-learning webpage (http://academics.utep.edu/Default.aspx?tabid=36357) contains information on the specific community organizations, the number of participants and hours, important documents, frequently asked questions, and additional resources.

As aforementioned, the CUE (cue.utep.edu) is a website used by the CCE to collect and organize information related to the Standardized Model. The CUE also contains information on available volunteer opportunities for UTEP students and helps to connect UTEP students with community organizations. Organizations that are in need of volunteers may post a specific volunteer opportunity on the CUE, and UTEP students have the opportunity to view and respond to specific posts. After completing a volunteer opportunity, UTEP students can use the CUE to record the number of hours that they completed. In this way, the CUE keeps track of both service-learning hours and volunteer hours at UTEP.

Other Tools

In the following list, we include a set of questions that help students reflect on, and learn from in their service-learning experiences.

1. What did you enjoy most about your service-learning experience?
2. What did you least enjoy about your service-learning experience?
3. Did the experience teach you something new about yourself? If so, what?
4. Why do you think your instructor decided to include service-learning as a part of this course? Why do you think she/he decided to offer your specific service-learning program?
5. Which community need(s) is the community agency attempting to address? Is the agency successful?
6. Imagine that you are the community agency representative in charge of coordinating service-learners. What do you think are the main challenges of that job? What, if anything, would you do differently?
7. Is it worthwhile to spend time in the community as a part of a class? Can the community context and fellow community members teach us valuable lessons? Why or why not?

Conclusion

As a high-impact practice, service-learning contributes to several desirable outcomes for higher education students. The Standardized Model is one way that service-learning can be implemented in a community setting. A unique feature of the Standardized Model is that the academic center plays a prominent role in building partnerships with community agencies and coordinating the service-learning program. For this reason, the Standardized Model requires an institutionalized academic center with strong support from university administrators.

Through the Standardized Model, students have the opportunity to 1) learn about, and from, their community; 2) develop a deeper understanding of course content; 3) gain professional skills; and 4) address local community needs. While service-learning often requires students to leave their comfort zones, it represents a great opportunity to acquire new knowledge, skills, and contacts. It also allows students to share their talents and energy for the benefit of the community.

Even though service-learning is a high-impact practice, there is no guarantee that all service-learning experiences will boost student learning. To increase the likelihood of having a successful service-learning experience, we encourage faculty members, community organizations, and students to follow the recommendations identified in the previous paragraphs. With proper adaptations for specific community settings, the Standardized Model can help increase student learning and reduce community needs.

References

Bringle, R. G., & Hatcher, J. A. (1995). A service-learning curriculum for faculty. *Michigan Journal of Community Service Learning*, *2*(1), 112–122.

Kuh, G. D. (2008). *High-impact educational practices: What they are, who has access to them, and why they matter*. Washington, DC: Association of American Colleges and Universities.

Kuh, G. D., & O'Donnell, K. (2013). *Ensuring quality & taking high-impact practices to scale*. Washington, DC: Association of American Colleges and Universities.

Lipmanowicz, H., & McCandless, K. (2014). The surprising power of liberating structures: Simple rules to unleash a culture of innovation. Seattle, WA: Liberating Structures Press.

APPENDIX

The following is a listing of activities that were utilized during the in-class reflection session:

- Purpose of reflection session: To help students recognize that learning happens throughout their experience
  - Learning happens when think, write, talk about what they experienced
  - Learning can be relative and exploratory
    - When making comparisons
    - When ask questions

- **Activity 1:** Begin with personal reflection (think, pair, share activity)
  - What did you see
  - What did you hear
  - What did you feel
  - What did you discover
  - What surprised you
  - What disappointed you

- **Activity 2:** Share with group some of your answers from above
  - Introductions
  - Brief description of what you did
  - Share your responses to at least three of the personal reflections (in activity one)
  - Bonus: look for connections, comparisons, meaningful moments

- **Activity 3:** 9 Why's of a choice—Liberating Structures (http://www.liberatingstructures.com/3-nine-whys/)
  - Ask, "What do you do when working on . . . . . .?"
  - Make a short list of activities. Then ask, "Why is that important to **you**?"
  - Keep asking, **"Why? Why? Why?"** up to nine times or until participants can go no deeper because they have reached the fundamental purpose for this work.
  - May seem like a sibling's idea of annoying fun—channel your inner "toddler."
  - Reality: choices stem from values
  - Not always aware of them until we reflect

- **Activity 4:** Now what
  - Now that you have dug into
    - What you experienced
    - What you learned
    - Why you learned what you did
  - Answer: Now what?
    - Now plan and determine what you will do with what you learned
    - Where does it go from here? How will it go down in your history?

- **Activity 5:** Synthesize
  - What were the themes, values, experiences in your group?
    - Differences?
    - Commonalities?
  - What is a summary of what you discussed throughout?
    - In five sentences or less

- **Activity 6:** User Fishbowl Experience—Liberating Structures Activity (http://www.liberatingstructures .com/18-users-experience-fishbowl/)
  - ○ Sharing group summaries
  - ○ A small group is formed, one member from each group is selected to join small group
  - ○ Small group is invited to share what they experienced and relay information gathered from group discussions
  - ○ They are invited to have a conversation with each other as if they were in a smaller group and no one else was listening in
  - ○ The audience is invited to listen to the fishbowl but can choose to participate as well
    - □ Physically join in on the fishbowl
    - □ Ask a question from Audience
    - □ Or switch with their partners

Political Science

Chapter 16

Enhancing Democracy—Pathways to Citizenship and Political Participation

Irasema Coronado

SERVICE LEARNING,
COMMUNITY-BASED LEARNING

COLLABORATIVE
ASSIGNMENTS AND PROJECTS

DIVERSITY/GLOBAL LEARNING

Use these questions to guide your reflection prior to reading the chapter. Use the notes/follow-up section to write your thoughts after you have read the chapter. Your notes can include thoughts in reference to the reflection questions, or general observations about the chapter.

1) Have you ever attended a public meeting or community meeting where public comment was part of the process? What was it like? If you haven't, what do you imagine takes place in such a setting?

2) What elements of a higher education do you believe support a student's ability to develop as an engaged citizen in democracy?

3) What has informed your attitude towards civic engagement, voting or general participation as an active citizen? Is your participation and engagement at the level you wish it to be? Why or why not?

Notes/Follow-up:

_____

_____

_____

_____

_____

Introduction

In my American Government and Introduction to Politics classes, I incorporated three high-impact practices that have led students to improved learning outcomes and increased civic engagement: 1) students are required to attend two political events in the community, 2) students tutor senior citizens preparing for their citizenship exam, and 3) students develop a citizenship exam study guide in Spanish. While requiring considerable time and effort on behalf of the students outside of the classroom, these three high-impact practices provide students with opportunities for meaningful interactions with community leaders and engagement with people of diverse political ideas. Students reported that by participating in community meetings, they bridged theory and practice, and by tutoring elders preparing for their citizenship exam, they immersed themselves in the history, structure, and function of the U.S. political system. Additionally, by preparing didactic materials for the citizenship exam in Spanish, they increased their knowledge base in American Government, capitalizing on their bilingual and communication skills, as well. Students stated that by participating in these high-impact practices, they were inspired to participate in politics in the future, developed a deep appreciation for immigrants' contributions to American society and were motivated to help others become American citizens. Participation in high-impact practices are life changing (Kuh, 2008).

As a lifetime resident of the U.S.-Mexico border region, and as an academic activist, I have long seen the need for citizen participation and engagement in communities. In the early 1990s, as a PhD student in the Department of Political Science at the University of Arizona, I learned the importance of political participation in class, and simultaneously realized that there were many questions of political incorporation without easy answers. The main question I wanted to answer was: if, as the literature indicates, parents are important actors in the political socialization of children (Verba, Schlozman, & Brady, 1995), how then are children of immigrants socialized into the polity, especially if the parents are newly arrived, do not speak English, and are not knowledgeable about the United States political system? How do immigrants' children become socialized into politics in their new host country when their parents are not familiar with the government system and institutions? A related question is, whether immigrant children—by taking social studies and American History and government—in some way, facilitate the political incorporation of their family. Research indicates immigrant children do help their parents navigate social and economic institutions in the United States (Foner & Dreby, 2011).

I learned early on that one key aspect to promoting the political incorporation of immigrant families was through their obtaining U.S. citizenship. In 1993, I helped organize a citizenship drive in Nogales, Arizona. In collaboration with the City of Nogales Public Library, and armed with a citizenship drive guidebook provided by the National Association of Latino Elected and Appointed Officials, we launched a citizenship drive. Our first meeting led to an overwhelming response that led to a major traffic jam requiring the Nogales Police Department to send extra officers to monitor traffic, and later the Nogales Fire Marshall had to intervene because the library had reached capacity. Subsequently, the library staff and I worked together with community volunteers to host information sessions, limiting the number of attendees and assisting people with filling out their forms and conducting classes to prepare people to take the naturalization exam. Over 500 people became U.S. citizens through that effort, and, of course, they became future potential voters. That experience taught me that people really did want to become U.S. citizens, but they just did not know how to go about doing so; with a little help, they were able to achieve that goal. Hence, by encouraging and requiring students to participate in the aforementioned high-impact practices, participation in politics would increase and American democracy would be enhanced.

Case Study: High-Impact Practice—Civic Engagement Model

In my American Government class, I used three high-impact practices that have led to improved learning outcomes and increased civic engagement by the students: 1) students are required to attend two political events in the community; 2) students tutor senior citizens preparing for their citizenship exam; and 3) students developed a citizenship exam study guide in Spanish.

The State of Texas requires that all undergraduate students take American Government and Introduction to Politics as part of the core curriculum. At the University of Texas at El Paso (UTEP), these two classes are also taught in Spanish to better serve the needs of our students who are enrolled in English as a Second Language classes and simultaneously taking academic coursework to advance academically. Introduction to American History, Psychology, Sociology, and Biology are also taught in Spanish. Students enrolled in American Government in Spanish are mostly international students or newly arrived immigrants who are learning about the structure and function of government in the United States. In UTEP's American Government classes, students are U.S. citizens, legal permanent residents, international students, or have benefited from Deferred Action for Childhood Arrivals. Discussions surrounding "citizenship" are extremely interesting. We all learn from one another as students share their own "citizenship" experiences. Some students were born in the United States, but were raised in Mexico and were not socialized politically in the United States. Other students were born in Mexico, and grew up in the United States, and were thoroughly familiar with, and knowledgeable about, structure, and function of American Government; others were legal permanent residents and/or working on becoming United States citizens. Some students spoke of their experience with the naturalization process and how they ultimately became U.S. citizens. My goals for these classes are for students to learn the structure and function of government, and to become involved in politics in their community. Also, as is common for immigrant students, I wanted them to they take their newfound knowledge into their homes and share their learning experiences with their families.

When I started teaching American Government, I decided that I would teach the structure and function of American Government by engaging students in activities through which they became involved in the political process. My approach to teaching American Government has been to embrace a Civic Engagement model that combines civic responsibility with academic preparation. As part of their academic instruction, students engage in activities that teach them about citizenship in a democratic society (http://fod.msu.edu/oir/civic-engagement).

Students volunteered as instructors with a national service-learning initiative titled: Students Helping in Naturalization of Elders, known as Project SHINE, a national program that builds partnerships between community college, universities, and community-based organizations serving immigrant elders. (https://www.research.utep.edu/Default.aspx?tabid=30478). UTEP's Center for Civic Engagement (CCE), in collaboration with community-based organizations coordinated this effort. UTEP students volunteered throughout the community to tutor people preparing to take the U.S. citizenship exam.

By participating in Project SHINE, we learned that some immigrant elders who were eligible to take the U.S. citizenship exam in Spanish (people who are over 50 years of age and have 20 years of legal permanent residency) needed materials in their native language to be able to learn American History and government and to study for the citizenship exam. Students saw first-hand how difficult preparation for the examination was for the immigrant elders, especially those who were not fluent in English.

Students went online seeking materials regarding American Government and History in Spanish, only to learn that the materials available to tutor immigrant elders in Spanish were extremely limited. Students in my Introduction to Politics class (taught in Spanish) became very excited about the possibility of creating didactic materials and started to explore the citizenship process online (https://www.uscis .gov/citizenship/learners/apply-citizenship).

Students reviewed the 100 questions on the U.S. citizen exam and developed five PowerPoint presentations that included 20 questions each. Students also read articles on adult literacy and learning strategies that informed the development of the slides. They found photographs in the public domain that would help the elders make associations with the questions. A healthy competition ensued as students wanted to have more interesting, engaging, educational slides than their classmates. Developing these study tools led to excellent collaboration and team work. Additionally, students "piloted" the study guide in Spanish with their families/ friends and made changes based on their feedback in order to enhance the quality of the final product. At this juncture, students reported that several of their families and friends indicated an interest in becoming U.S. citizens and had asked them to find out more about the naturalization process.

Successful Implementation of the Study Guide in the Community

In the summer of 2012, the study guide was posted on the university website, with the expectation that this material would be used by schools, community centers, non-governmental organizations, advocacy groups, and educators. The study guide is at: (http://academics.utep.edu/Default.aspx?tabid=72472).

We organized a press conference and invited several media outlets and community-based organizations involved in citizenship drives to attend the launching of the Study Guide in Spanish. The Spanish language media—both television and newspaper—in the community covered the event, along with English language television and newspapers. Additionally, UTEP's website highlighted the event and the study guide.

The media exposure that the study guide received had an unintended and positive consequence—the Department of Political Science office fielded many phone calls asking for information on the naturalization process. Staff was instructed to give callers the website for The Department of Homeland Security and United States Citizenship and Immigration Services (https://www.uscis.gov/citizenship/learners/ apply-citizenship). However, several callers indicated that they wanted to speak to a person regarding the process. We contacted Diocesan Migrant and Refugee Services (DMRS) and met with the executive director, Iliana Holguin. We shared the study guide with her and asked if we could refer people calling our office to DMRS, and, of course, she agreed. DMRS offered citizenship classes as well as assistance with filling out the forms. She indicated that the study guide would be very useful not only for their classes with elderly immigrants, but also, with people who were learning English and American History and government; this study guide would facilitate aspiring U.S. citizens to learn the materials in Spanish and armed with this knowledge, they would more easily transpose the information into English. We also shared the study guide with La Fe and Las Americas, two community non-governmental organizations that also offer citizenship classes.

Since students had to learn the material thoroughly to be able to prepare the study guide, learning outcomes for this particular class were greatly enhanced. Students, who were U.S. citizens, at times, were surprised that they did not know the answers to some of the questions on the citizenship exam. During class discussions, we also evaluated the effectiveness of the citizenship exam in promoting civic engagement. The students concluded that the questions on the examination were rather factual in nature and that the materials available in English to prepare for the naturalization exam did not include information on how to participate in local school board or City Council elections, engage with other citizen groups, or give information on how and where to register to vote. Students were inspired to continue developing materials that promoted civic engagement and encouraged people to participate in politics at all levels of government.

What Made These High-Impact Practices Successful?

Attending Political Events

Students were provided a variety of options to fulfill this assignment: attending a City Council meeting; panel discussions with political leaders in the city, county, or state; a government official's town hall meeting; a school board meeting, or any community event or meeting that is political in nature. The goal of this assignment is for students to see "government in action" and to be inspired to get involved in civic and political affairs. Students submitted a reflective essay on what they learned and experienced at the event they attended. In those essays, students reported 1) "this is the first time ever that I attended a political event"; 2) "I had never talked to a public official until I attended this event"; 3) "I was surprised that people did not agree and that people were arguing publicly"; 4) "protesters were there with signs yelling at public officials—I had only seen this on television or read about it"; 5) "I am inspired and motivated to get involved." Several students attended Parent Teacher Association (PTA), School Board, and neighborhood association meetings for the first time ever when they were required to do this class assignment. Students shared their experiences at meetings, rallies or marches, with their classmates, encouraging them to get involved and complete the class assignment. Several students reported that if they had not been given the assignment to attend a community meeting, they would not have done so on their own volition.

Students that volunteered with Project SHINE reported that they enjoyed the experience for a variety of reasons: 1) Students learned more in depth information about the history, structure and function of U.S. government in order to be able to teach and tutor future citizens; 2) Students reported an appreciation and better understanding of the immigrant experience in this country, learning how immigrants integrate into society economically, socially, and politically; 3) Students developed a stronger work ethic and the importance of commitment, because the immigrant elders that they tutored were present every day, on time to learn; and 4) Students mentioned that this experience was life changing because they were inspired and encouraged by the immigrant elders to do well academically and complete their degrees; many elders reinforced the importance of education and many lamented that they had not had an opportunity to attend an institution of higher learning. Students reported that they continued to volunteer with Project SHINE, even after the semester ended because the experience was so rewarding and enriching.

Developing the citizenship exam study material in Spanish also reinforced learning as students were able to capitalize on their bilingual skills. Most importantly, the publicity surrounding the launching of the material on the UTEP website empowered students—they prepared for television and newspaper interviews, met with reporters, and appeared on several television channels; since the launch took place close to the 4th of July holiday, this was timely. We were able to raise awareness about the availability of the study guide in Spanish, thanks to the local media and press. Students also visited several community-based organizations to share the study guide. An added benefit is that this study guide is free and can be easily downloaded. We certainly wanted the study guide to be accessible to anyone who wanted to use it.

This practice of community engagement contributes to life-long learning and deepens and enhances political participation. In the final course evaluations, students noted that this high-impact practice of engaging with the community was one of the highlights of the class. Through the use of a civic engagement model of teaching in American Government courses, one can take positive steps to sustain a democratic society. Students need to know how government works in theory and in practice; they should learn how to work with others to solve community problems, how to build and sustain coalitions, and how to effectively communicate and lobby elected officials. This is an area where there is much room for improvement in American society. Political scientists have long noted that "citizens participate in public affairs less frequently, with less knowledge and enthusiasm, in fewer venues, and less equitably than is healthy for a vibrant democratic polity" (Macedo, 2005, p. 1). Low-income, less educated citizens, recent immigrants, and those less proficient in English are often underrepresented in the political process and have far less voice (Kahne & Sporte, 2008, p. 739). Hopefully, our efforts in developing a study guide and tutoring elders helps change these undemocratic trends.

Hence, this practice of teaching American Government through a civic engagement model, through student participation in political events, participation in Project SHINE, and development of a study guide to assist people with the naturalization process enhances the learning outcomes for students and provides ways to participate politically by taking this course. Engaging the community and helping future citizens in preparing to take the naturalization test was very important and meaningful for students.

What Were Some of the Challenges?

Challenges were few and we overcame them with increased communication and by allowing students to collaborate during class time to coordinate schedules. Many students who had never attended a political or community event, felt more comfortable attending as part of a group; hence, 3–4 students would agree to attend a certain event, together. Dispersing information on upcoming community events was challenging for me. A few students with extremely limited time (working full-time, supporting families) found it difficult to carve time to attend a meeting. To address this challenge, they were encouraged to attend events such as community clean-ups sponsored by environmental organizations and to take their children along. Students whose children were in school attended school board or PTA meetings; afterward, some of them reported they continued their involvement after the course. Some students had no transportation, so we encouraged carpooling to events; this had the added advantage that students conducted debriefing sessions on the ride home. Students were also advised of public hearings on campus or in their neighborhood community centers or libraries.

I encourage other political science professors to use the civic engagement model in their classrooms by combining theory and practice. Students benefit tremendously from cooperative learning and by interacting with community members. They become motivated to get involved in their communities and make a difference. My experiences have taught me that when students engage with their community they have life-changing experiences that inspire them to become community leaders and activists.

Tutoring senior citizens led to a very special bonding experience between elders and students in addition to creating a mutually beneficial learning. Developing the study guide in Spanish was very rewarding. Students felt that they were contributing to a greater good, and perhaps, in a small way enhancing democracy in the United States. During interviews by local media and press, students showed leadership, by speaking about their class experiences and study guide development. These class practices yielded high impacts, benefiting communities.

Replicating These High-Impact Practices

These three high-impact practices may be replicated in any university setting. Assigning students to attend two political or community events is relatively easy to do. Professors need to apprise themselves of community events through websites and local media and newspapers and share them with students. Students can also find and share these events. Students turn in a one-page reflection essay stating what event they attended, what they learned and how they benefited from the experience.

Participating in citizenship education programs requires coordinating with community-based organizations that sponsor the programs. In some cases, training is provided to better prepare students to engage with future citizens. Numerous opportunities exist to work with community-based organizations (CBOs) preparing people for citizenship exams, though there should be an agreement between the university and the CBO to formalize arrangements and establish lines of communication just in case there are concerns to address. Establishing the number of hours that students will volunteer each week and the location's safety is also important.

Recommendations For Faculty

If this is the first time that you include community engagement as part of your course, you might require that students only attend one political community meeting instead of two. Be prepared to make accommodations for a student whose time is limited for outside engagement or for whom transportation is a problem; such students might participate in a webinar, webcasts, or a live stream event on Facebook. When assigning the reflective essay, I ask students to describe why they selected that specific event, the essence of the activity, the audience, what they learned, and how they felt afterwards. These are usually one-page reflections, which sometimes are very emotional and heartfelt. Students reported feeling angry and upset when speakers at public events were told they had only 2 minutes to address the City Council or other elected officials. Other students were inspired to look up Robert's Rules of Order and to understand policies and procedures outlining how meetings were conducted; they wanted to understand procedural issues utilized in certain meetings. Students reported being inspired, angry, motivated, shocked, or surprised at what they witnessed at community meetings.

Should you want to branch out into a Project SHINE service-learning project, coordinate with the respective office at your university to ensure that there are formal arrangements with the sponsoring CBO. At UTEP, connecting with CBOs is relatively easy because the CCE facilitates arrangements and follows through with the details; this includes ensuring that students are actively participating in tutoring sessions and documenting their attendance. If your institution does not have a similar center, I suggest reaching out to a CBO and working closely with them to determine policies and procedures beforehand and perhaps, start with a handful of students to pilot the service-learning project.

In summary, be prepared:

1. Share with students many notices informing them of upcoming community events.
2. Establish a formal agreement between a CBO and your institution if engaging service-learning projects to ensure compliance at all levels and successful outcomes for all.

When collaborating with a community partner, it is very important to set forth a list of objectives that will be achieved with specific actions and requirements for all participants. Be as specific as possible: how many students will tutor people to take the citizenship exam? What hours will they be required to be present at the CBO? Provide an orientation and training session for students so that they are aware of expectations. Schedule weekly phone calls so that you can discuss how things are going and to determine adjustments needed on either end–students arriving late, leaving early, limited staff supervision provided by CBO, etc. It is important to have a clear channel of communication so the project and learning objectives are not compromised. Consider having the students sign a contract agreeing to certain behavior and complying with expectations of the program. In summary,

1. Set forth a clear plan of action with specific details between faculty and CBO.
2. Ensure students understand level of commitment and requirements beforehand.

Recommendations For Students

Be open to attending community meetings—they will challenge you and help you develop your networking skill set. Be prepared to introduce yourself and state why you are attending that particular meeting. Do homework before the meeting: is there an agenda posted online? Do speakers need to sign up beforehand to speak at the meeting? During the meeting, listen to everyone's point of view and try to understand their perspectives. Try to analyze the decision-making process and how the public and decision-makers interact. If you are signing up for a service-learning project such as Project SHINE, be sure you have time to fulfill the commitment. Keep in mind that you represent your university and your behavior and comportment sets the tone for continuing (or not) the program. List service-learning opportunities on your resume; they provide useful experiences in leveraging scholarships or future employment. In summary,

1. Be an active participant when attending community events, and take notes of the interactions you witness so you can write your reflection essay in a substantive manner.
2. If you commit to participate in a service-learning assignment be sure that you have the time and energy to dedicate to the project and to see it to completion.

Recommendations For Community

Students are future leaders and it is important to help cultivate their skills in engaging with community organizations. You can play an important role by partnering with universities and with faculty to achieve your goals. Students can assist CBOs in a variety of ways—helping with social media campaigns, assisting with technology, and providing new ideas and energy.

There are several ways to strengthen university/community relations: 1) create a university/community lecture series on campus where CBOs can talk about their organization; 2) CBO staff members should attend recruitment fairs on campus to interview potential interns; 3) partner with faculty members to work on research projects that are mutually beneficial to community organizations and enhance student learning outcomes; 4) CBOs can invite professors to give talks to their respective organizations; and 5) organizations can invite professors and classes to meet and tour their facilities, or host an open house, so as to further engage students academically and in the community, 6) collaborate with university professors on mutually agreed upon service-learning projects.

When working with a university professor and committing to the success of a service-learning project, keep in mind that students need mentorship and guidance; dedicated staff time ensures that students have successful experiences at your CBO. In summary,

1. Reach out to universities and faculty for mutually beneficial service-learning projects.
2. Students involved in service-learning projects require mentorship and staff dedication.
3. Opening doors to students cultivates future employees, board volunteers and donors.

Selected Readings and Resources

See Bibliography

Conclusion

The benefits of using the civic engagement model in teaching American Government yields positive results for democracy. Requiring that students attend community events where they witness people expressing different points of view and participating in the democratic process serves to socialize students into participation in the political process. Assisting others in the naturalization process reinforces student's basic knowledge of politics promotes participatory democracy. The incorporation of immigrants into the American polity is crucial for American democracy, and taking the first step towards the naturalization process is only a beginning. The development of didactic materials in Spanish to assist with passing the naturalization exam, is a useful tool that you can download and share with others. Community collaboration provides leadership opportunities for students, inspiring them to be active, engaged citizens in the future.

Bibliography

Civic Engagement. Retrieved from http://fod.msu.edu/oir/civic-engagement

Community Service. Retrieved from https://www.research.utep.edu/Default.aspx?tabid=30478

Diocesan Migrant and Refugee Services. Retrieved from http://dmrs-ep.org/

Foner, N., & Dreby, J. (2011). Relations between the generations in immigrant families. *Annual Review of Sociology, 37*, 545–564.

Kahne, J., & Sporte, S. (2008). Developing Citizens: The Impact of Civic Learning Opportunities on Students' Commitment to Civic Participation. *American Educational Research Journal, 45*(3), 738-766. Retrieved from http://0-www.jstor.org.lib.utep.edu/stable/27667149

Kuh, G. D. (2008). *High-impact educational practices: What they are, who has access to them, and they matter.* Washington, DC: Association of American Colleges and Universities.

Macedo, S. (2005). *Democracy at risk: How political choices undermine citizen participation and what we can do about it*. Washington, DC: Brookings Institution Press.

Study Guide in Spanish. Retrieved from http://academics.utep.edu/Default.aspx?tabid=72472

Verba, S., Schlozman, K. L., & Brady, H. E. (1995). *Voice and equality: Civic voluntarism in American politics*. Cambridge, MA: Harvard University Press.

Additional Resources

Application for Citizenship. Retrieved from https://www.uscis.gov/citizenship/learners/apply-citizenship

Citizenship Study Guide in Spanish. Retrieved from http://academics.utep.edu/Default.aspx?tabid=72472

Gonzalez-Barrera, A., Hugo Lopez, M., Passel, J. S., & Taylor, P. (2013). *The path not taken: Two-thirds of legal Mexican immigrants are not U.S. citizens*. Washington, DC: Pew Hispanic Center. Retrieved from http://www.pewhispanic.org/files/2013/02/Naturalizations_Jan_2013_FINAL.pdf

Humphries, M., Muller, C., & Schiller, K. S. (2013). The political socialization of adolescent children of immigrants. *Social Science Quarterly, 94*(5), 1261–1282. doi:10.1111/ssqu.12025

Krogstad, J. M. (September 2016). *Immigrant naturalization applications climb, but not as much as past years*. Pew Research Center. Retrieved from http://www.pewresearch.org/fact-tank/2016/09/15/immigrant-naturalization-applications-up-since-october-but-past-years-saw-larger-increases/

Rytina, N. (2013). Estimates of the Legal Permanent Resident Population in 2012. Office of Immigration Statistics, Policy Directorate, U.S. Department of Homeland Security. Retrieved from https://www.dhs.gov/sites/default/files/publications/ois_lpr_pe_2012.pdf

Terriquez, V., & Kwon, H. (2015). Intergenerational family relations, civic organisations, and the political socialisation of second-generation immigrant youth. *Journal of Ethnic & Migration Studies, 41*(3), 425–447. doi:10.1080/1369183X.2014.921567

Torres, M. A., & Paral, R. (2006). The naturalization trail: Mexican Nationality and US citizenship. *Latino Research@ND, 3*(2), 1–7.

Environmental Science

Chapter 17

Community-Based Research Pedagogy for Ecological Change

Amy Wagler, Janae' Renaud Field, and Karla Martinez

SERVICE LEARNING,
COMMUNITY-BASED LEARNING

UNDERGRADUATE RESEARCH

Use these questions to guide your reflection prior to reading the chapter. Use the notes/follow-up section to write your thoughts after you have read the chapter. Your notes can include thoughts in reference to the reflection questions, or general observations about the chapter.

1) What has been your experience with the use of statistics or statistical methods in society? What applications or use of statistics come to mind in your everyday life?

2) Assume you are a researcher. How would you go about establishing and developing a research question along with a community partner? Would you anticipate this process to be simple or complex? Explain your answer.

3) What does it mean to "translate research for the community"? Have you ever found yourself in a position to "translate" communication between two or more different types of groups? If so, what was that like?

Notes/Follow-up:

_____

_____

_____

_____

_____

Introduction

Since the advent of modern statistics as an academic subject in the late 19th century, there has been a growing appreciation for how data can provide insight into societal issues and also help communities make data-informed decisions. While the role of statistics and the statistician has arguably never been more apparent, there is a rising culture of mistrust of data and data-based reasoning. Perhaps negative perceptions about the role of statistics in society are formed when large segments of society feel unconnected to those who produce and use these tools. Those who teach statistics should be considering this as we design courses and pedagogy for both producers and consumers of statistical knowledge. Creating competency in both applied statistical practice and engagement in community could alleviate some of this disconnection. This was the objective of integrating community-based issues into applied statistics research projects at The University of Texas at El Paso (UTEP). This chapter describes and assesses a community-based research (CBR) project designed for an undergraduate applied statistics course with dual learning objectives: to apply statistical reasoning in a real-world context and to learn more about the impact of statistical reasoning for a problem affecting the students' everyday life. The community component of the project was familiar to students in the outset, however, in the process of the project, the students learned more about their region and some grew in appreciation of their community.

The high-impact practice (HIP) utilized is an undergraduate CBR project. CBR is a collaborative research project between a community partner(s) and researchers (Strand, Marullo, Cutforth, Stoecker, & Donohue, 2003). A CBR project builds on the strengths of both parties to address a community need identified by the partner. In CBR projects, students work in collaboration with, rather than on behalf of, the community partner. In contrast, traditional research projects may take place in a community setting, but does not work with the community partner to devise and direct the research focus. The collaborative element is what makes CBR projects distinct from traditional research projects and important in addressing a community partner's needs. In the CBR model, the community partner can tailor the project to suit their needs as an organization and the researchers regard the community partner as an equal partner in the research process. Some may view CBR projects as incorporating a service-learning project, which is a valid perspective. Though communication with community partners is essential and frequent, most of the research activities take place in either class or, most often, on the students' own time. This makes the CBR project somewhat distinct from traditional service-learning activities, which typically solely occur in community settings. The CBR model is also distinct from community-based participatory research models where the research process is more iterative actively involving the community partner and researchers throughout (Hacker, 2013). Students, faculty, or community partners could use a CBR project framework in other settings: whether differing content settings (not a statistics class) or other community settings. The framework is adaptable to almost any community need or academic focus.

Contributed by Amy Wagler, Janae Renaud Field, and Karla Martinez. © Kendall Hunt Publishing Company.

Use of CBR Pedagogy in Statistics

Inclusion of CBR into a statistics pedagogy is consistent with the nature of the discipline of statistics as a whole. Cobb and Moore (1997) stated that "data is not just numbers, they are numbers with a context." This context can be very impactful on how students perceive and understand statistics and the role of statistical reasoning in modern society. That impact can be positive or negative depending on the context and is a vital consideration for statistics instructors. To a student already unfamiliar with statistics, an unconnected context can present additional learning struggle since students must not only focus on understanding the statistical concepts but also decode the contextual meaning. Additionally, a context that students do not find compelling or meaningful belittles the impact of statistical reasoning in the students' perspective and doesn't provide an opportunity for them to apply and appreciate their newfound skills in statistical reasoning in a manner that is personally impactful. Having the context connected to culture is important (Lesser & Wagler, 2016), but it is also important to have the statistical process applied for meaningful purposes. These two criteria for context, cultural relevance and meaning, guided my decision to choose a community-based context for the student-directed research projects.

A best practice in teaching statistical reasoning is to make use of student-directed research projects that require application of the entire process of statistical analysis (GAISE, 2016). Finding an appropriate research study for undergraduate students is not always a straightforward task. In the past, Dr. Amy Wagler used project-based learning activities that centered on student-generated research questions. This approach is strong in many respects, but students were often frustrated by not having resources available for conducting the type of research study they desired, and Wagler was unable to fully anticipate their needs with project on 30+ different topics. Furthermore, students often had interest in certain subjects, but due to time and money constraints, were unable to pursue their interests and chose a simple "cookie cutter" experiment for ease.

There are several reasons to use a CBR framework for project-based learning in an applied statistics course. First, most students enrolled in data science or statistics courses don't take them voluntarily but to satisfy degree requirements. Moreover, statistics courses are consistently not highly regarded courses at the university level (Feldman, 1978). Perhaps one of the reasons that students do not look forward to or enjoy taking statistics courses is due to the traditional focus on the mathematical basis of statistical analysis with little attention to the practical impact of the analysis (Gal, Ginsberg, & Schau, 1997). However, researchers found that student attitudes towards statistics involve components of anxiety, cynicism, fear, and contempt (Hopkins, Hopkins, & Glass, 1996). Even when context is employed, usually the hard sciences, engineering, and Euro-centric real-world settings are emphasized. These factors create a disconnect for students that make the course not only unenjoyable to most but also not impactful. In contrast, a CBR approach to teaching may improve the connection to the course content by allowing the students to apply statistics in a familiar context. In other words, the CBR approach makes the "numbers with context" aspect of statistical analysis even more impactful and meaningful. Secondly, CBR projects can teach an important philosophical lesson about how statistical knowledge, when best practiced, informs without intentional bias. The CBR project provides a meaningful context, whether individual students agree or do not agree with the community partner perspective on the issue being explored. The CBR project is an effective way to engage students with philosophical differences between knowledge and opinion, statement of fact, and viewpoint. It helps students, in a very personal manner, understand how statistical analysis is ideally objective, even in the face of strongly held personal beliefs.

The case study that follows depicts a CBR partnership between a college-level statistics class and a land trust organization with the objective of assessing the value of open space (undeveloped land kept in a natural state) on home valuations in El Paso, Texas. After the case study is a discussion about the relative advantages and disadvantages of CBR as a HIP and including community partner and student perspectives. The chapter conclusion includes additional resources, tips and questions for implementing a similar project in other settings.

Case Study: Assessing the Value of Open Space in the El Paso Region

The Frontera Land Alliance (TFLA) is a land trust group in the El Paso region that actively works with government and business leaders to promote conservation of land and water resources. The TFLA worked with Wagler and her Applied Regression Analysis class to investigate how open space affect house valuations in the region. Other land trust groups have conducted similar studies for other regions and found that proximity to open space increased home prices. This was a timely choice since there was increased attention on the organization thanks to a regional push to conserve natural spaces and the visibility of the TFLA was on the rise. The executive director of TFLA (Fields) encouraged the collaboration due to her desire to increase the organization's ability to argue for the conservation of natural space in the region. TFLA had been working increasingly with local governmental and business agencies and needed information from the government and business perspective in order to make an effective case for conservation.

Step One: Define Research Topic/Question

Wagler and Fields collaboratively worked out a research question with the class: "Does proximity to open space affect house valuations in the El Paso border region?" If properly understood, this relationship between house valuations and open space would motivate regional developers and planners to allocate open spaces in proximity to residential areas.

Step Two: Do Research into Issue

Following formulation of the research question, the next task was to introduce students to the issue. For this, Executive Director of TFLA met with the students to discuss the organization's mission and role in El Paso. Ms. Fields handed out information about land conservation and a current initiative to make one particular area a national monument. Throughout the semester, students spent time each week talking about and planning components of the project and TFLA. In particular, students first spent time learning more about land conservation and became more familiar with the concept of open space while class activities were centered around the theory of regression analysis.

Step Three: The Research Process

The data collection occurred in two parts: first, students were provided with Multiple Listing Services (MLS) data obtained from a local realtor. This contained basic home specifications, listing and selling prices of homes purchased in the region in the past 3 months. In order to make the project manageable to first year statistics students, the data was limited to homes in particular region of El Paso. MLS data does not contain information about open space. Thus, in collaboration with Ms. Field, we formulated a strategy for measuring the response variable: proximity to open space.

This was a lengthy process that first required our community partner and the students to describe explicitly what is considered true "open space." After deciding on the definition of open space, students used Google Earth (2017) to map each property and use the ruler tool (an integrated tool in the software) to measure the "as the bird flies" distance to Franklin Mountain State Park. See Figure 1 for a screen shot.

Each student group was responsible for validating their data and preparing it for analysis. This was performed with varying levels of rigor and was reflected upon at the conclusion of the project since some students saw differing results depending on how well their data was cleaned and validated. However, the screening and validation taught a practical skill and lesson that data is almost always "messy." Moreover, it also taught students to think carefully about the levels of measurement (nominal, ordinal, ratio, and interval) of data.

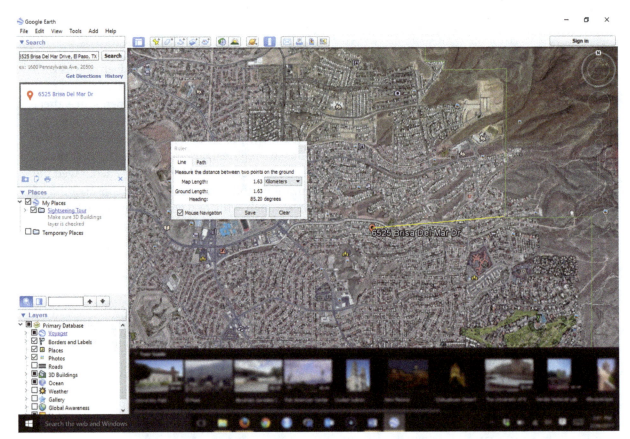

Figure 1 Illustration of How Students can Utilize Google Earth to Find Distances to Open Space

Step Four: Translate Research for the Community and Community Partner

As the class progressed through the course, they completed the three parts of the project: 1) Exploratory Data Analysis, 2) Statistical Modeling, and 3) Final results and discussion. Students were given due dates for each component and were responsible for the content of the reports. Students were also told to make parts 1 and 2 technical and appropriate for a statistics practitioner but make part 3 for a more general audience where they translate their statistical results into plain language results. Sections 1 and 2 were graded for rigor and accuracy of the analysis. These were the technical sections where most of the points were assigned to correct statistical methodology and reasoning. In contrast, section 3 was graded on the basis of how well students translated the results of their technical statistical analysis for the community partner. Section 3 was limited to one page plus figures in order to encourage students to write up their results without relying on formulas and statistical jargon. The students were instructed to write the results so that someone who does not understand regression analysis can understand the answer to the research question: Does proximity to open space affect house valuations in the El Paso del Norte region?

Step Five: Dissemination to Community

Following completion of the projects, students presented it to the TFLA Executive Director. The students and Ms. Field discussed the meaning and impact of the results. The instructor combined the results into a summary report and it was provided to TFLA Board of Directors and gave them release to use the analysis results for promotion and marketing.

For a senior class project, one of the students (Ms. Martinez) plans to expand the analysis to other parts of El Paso and write a formal report that she will make available to the TFLA and El Paso community leaders.

What Made This HIP Successful?

Starting in Fall 2015, Wagler started providing students with CBR opportunities, proposed by a community partners in the El Paso region. Since a majority of our students grew up in the surrounding region, the community issues addressed were familiar to them and, at times, personally significant. In the past, I'd worked with Kids Excel El Paso and area hospitals (Wagler, Field, & Baray, 2017) and found that a CBR projects had more benefits than drawbacks. The benefits include enhanced cultural relevance, meaningful context, impactful results, and a creating a feeling of "doing good" among the students. Many past students reported feeling a personal sense of satisfaction by knowing that their class work was helping an organization whose work they supported. With particular projects, the results of the students' analyses were used in future grant proposals by the community agency (Kids Excel El Paso) with success. In this case, the students felt personally invested and proud of the work they had done for arts education. Another value-added benefit of using a CBR project approach is that it places statistical reasoning in a context that is personally known to students. This is particularly true for students attending The UTEP since they predominantly come from the El Paso region. We personally believe this teaches about the impact of statistical reasoning more effectively than traditional academic research projects since they are focused on issues often affecting the students' everyday lives. These projects are objective but not alienated from their everyday experiences and can have a transformative impact on how they view the use of statistical reasoning.

In order to assess how well these objectives were met, a post-course survey was administered following the course and assignment of final grades. All responses were voluntary and feedback was provided without the instructor or community partner present. Figure 2 presents the results of the Likert-scale questions that were about the CBR project. Note that the label CBR was never used during the semester so the questions just use the term project. Due to space limitations, the descriptions in Figure 2 are shorted from what appeared in the scale but retains the core idea of each item.

The students were also asked to provide feedback for some open-ended questions. Wagler used open coding to summarize the 17 responses to the two questions regarding the CBR project. To the first question, "Have you learned anything through the project that you would not have learned otherwise in the class?", six students stated that it made them more aware of a local issue, four stated that it helped them understand how to apply statistics in the real world, four stated that it helped them better understand technical issues (statistical and coding), and three simply responded with a "Yes" but provided no explanation. To the question asking, "Have any of your views of perspectives on our community changed as a result of working on this project?", nine felt like it made them either more aware, appreciate or respect natural areas in El Paso, five did not feel like it changed their views (though two stated they already agreed that we should have more natural areas), two made a general statement that the project made them feel better, and one did not respond. This summary of the two open-ended questions make clear that students saw the value of the context for the project and appreciated the increased learning potential of the CBR project. Since most of the students in the class intend

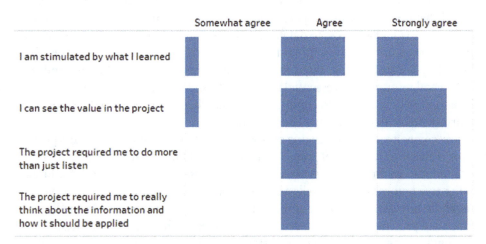

Figure 2 Student Responses to Applied Statistics CBR Assessment Questions

to stay in the area to teach secondary level mathematics, it is important that they understand these issues in a community context as future adult community members.

The use of CBR projects in an undergraduate statistics class had two primary objectives: 1) to provide a project-based learning experience for students to apply their skills in a culturally relevant setting; and 2) to provide a meaningful context that would also impact student knowledge and perceptions about their community. While these objectives were met with the CBR project survey results will assess whether these learning objectives were met and, following that, open-ended student feedback will be described to assess why the CBR project was successful.

What Were Some of the Challenges?

For the Students

The CBR approach is not without drawbacks. A CBR project approach is organized around a community partner's research question and does not provide the opportunity for students to generate an original research question. However, in some cases, the community partner has a vague sense of what research project they want done, but cannot define a research question that is relevant for a statistics research study. For example, if you want to know about open space, the question "How much open space is in El Paso county?" is too specific and not a statistics question. Similarly, the question, "What are the effects of having open space in El Paso county?" is too broad and not focused enough. Thus, students often work on helping the community partner take an everyday question and transform it into a statistics research question.

Another drawback of CBR projects is that not all students will agree with the work of the community partner. This has never dramatically affected any of my students since none have been outright opposed to a community partner's work. However, We could imagine a scenario where a student actively opposed the community partner's work. As with all community-based projects, Wagler provides an alternative project for students who do not care to work with a community partner. In most cases, this satisfies students who are in opposition to the project.

Students reported that their primary difficulty had to do with the technical and programming processes involved. This is a senior-level mathematics course designed for future teachers and requires more use of computing than almost any other mathematics course. As a whole, mathematics students are not comfortable with the programming aspects of the course and always find it difficult. However, no students expressed any difficulty involved with working with either Ms. Field or TFLA.

For the Instructor

Another drawback of CBR projects is that they require more work at the outset. For each class, a community partner is selected that needs to address a particular research question affecting their organization. Ideally, the community partner will have access to data and other research resources, such as some literature review and background information. However, this is not always the case (and was not for the CBR project being described in this chapter), and in these cases, it is up to the team (instructor, students and community partner) to obtain data and resources. It is essential that the data and research resources be ready for the onset of the project since there is limited time to complete the research and, in particular, lack of validated data can provide an insurmountable bottleneck in a 15-week course.

The community component was challenging only with regard to data collection. The type of data needed for the project is not available to the general public or members of TFLA, hence, Wagler sought other resources. Wagler contacted a local realtor who was sympathetic to the cause of land conservation and she provided data on a subset of the area homes where she sells and buys real estate. A more comprehensive set of data would complete the analysis, but was not available at the time. The next step was to use Google Earth (Google Earth, 2017) to approximate proximity to open space as is described in the case study. These two steps provided minor difficulty, but such is expected for data analysis projects. In contrast, the project proved time-consuming for TFLA as Field frequently came to class meetings and it is difficult to find parking for university visitors.

How to Create a CBR Project to Assess Open Space in Your Community

One of the strengths of this community-based undergraduate research project is that it can be easily replicated in many communities given the instructor or students have access to a realtor for data and a land trust or conservation group. Additionally, there is a dire need nationally for communities that border significant natural areas that need protection to make the case for land conservation with government and community groups. An argument based on economics and quality of life is able to bridge political divides on this issue and speaks to anyone in the community who wants to see their area grow and thrive. Doing analysis about property valuation and open space is a topic that is good for young adults to learn, especially at a time when they are developing to be civic-engaged adults. If more people understand the relationship between economic growth, quality of life, and open space, then more communities will have effective advocates to keep open space a priority for their region.

There is likely a regional effect to the relationship between open space and property valuations. This relationship depends on so many factors and even frequently changes over time. This is why each community needs to do this analysis and understand their unique regional situation. Additionally, a qualitative methods course could work on understanding better community perceptions of open space. This too is likely to vary based on region and would provide valuable insights to a land trust or conservation group.

Recommendations for Faculty: In the Voice of Faculty Amy Wagler

If a faculty member wishes to undertake this kind of project, I recommend the following. First, make sure that you are address a true community need by closely working with your local land trust or conservation group. Land trust or conservation groups may be identified by searching on the Land Trust Alliance website (https://www.landtrustalliance.org/topics/accreditation) or search for non-accredited land trust groups on the Conservation Registry website (http://conservationregistry.org/). If these do not lead to any regional land trust or conservation groups, then it may be necessary to simply "Google" for a regional group. Once a land trust or conservation group is identified, I recommend setting up a meeting with the Director or Board to understand their current focus and how you may contribute. They may have already conducted similar projects and prefer some other focus for the project. It is important that the faculty member work closely with the land trust or conservation group and regularly communicate updates and developments. There were issues that came up during our project that I ran by Ms. Field and cleared our proposed solution with her before proceeding. This is important in order to maintain mutual respect and cooperation in the long term.

For Students: In the Voice of Student Karla Martinez

In our research with TFLA, we discovered that the proximity to greenspace does affect the house closing price, or value in the North-west area of El Paso. It was interesting to see how the concepts of the Applied Regression Analysis could be used to further research issues that relate to the community. Both community-related examples and other examples were used throughout the course; however, this specific project resonated with us since it was more relatable and useful. I learned to work in groups to analyze data and to use RStudio, a programming tool, to model, plot data, and gain results. The project was both challenging and exciting.

Using RStudio was somewhat tedious at first. However, by the end of the project, we were writing codes and plotting different types of graphs. Students who are unfamiliar with RStudio's programming language might feel overwhelmed, but I would reassure future students to not feel overly stressed about it. I would tell others unfamiliar with programming language, not to panic. Throughout this project, we were not completely alone. There were plenty of materials and examples from class lectures in between the three stages of the project. As a group, we were encouraged to meet with our professor outside of the classroom whether it be during her office hours or via email. Also, after group presentations of our results, findings, and conclusions, my peers and I were able to share our experiences and subtle differences in our data. Upon the completion of this project, I was inspired to ask follow-up questions that would generate future research and discussions such as: 1) What further research and similar studies could be conducted in other parts of town, and what similarities or differences could exist? 2) While some parts of town could be considered as not being esthetically pleasing or a community is considered to be of a lower socioeconomic standing (less-affluent community) while others are thought to have more-affluent standing (more resources), would there be drastic differences? and 3) What effects would any of these factors have if they are incorporated or applied to different studies? Overall, this was a pleasant and helpful experience as it prepared us for future projects and research in the workplace as well as in academics. As our community grows, evolves and expands, so should our interest and involvement, especially in order to empower and protect both the community and the environment.

For Community Partners: In the voice of Community Partne Janae' Renaud Field

TFLA has enjoyed the partnerships that we have formed over the years with students and other organizations in the region and nationally. A benefit of students assisting us is that they may come in with a fresh way of looking at a situation versus our regular methods for completing a program or project. Through the years, we have learned that we need the student or volunteer to have a certain level of skill to have a successful program. Dr. Amy Wagler worked with TFLA to assist us in meeting a need: knowing what financial value home owners put on living next to or access to open space/trails. TFLA wanted to show that homes next to or with access to open space had higher valued homes. Dr. Amy Wagler's class at UTEP studied the value of homes next to open space with various covariates. The outcome was surprising. Initial research completed in the fall of 2016, concluded that open space only affected home valuations when central air was present in the homes. Overall, we learned that more research needs to be done with a larger dataset to see what other neighborhoods indicate regarding the value of open space/access when they look to purchase a home.

In conclusion, though a collaboration such as this open space project is a lot of extra work for any non-profit, in the end you will have a more invested volunteer/student and positive response from the public. We look forward to a stronger and more involved relationship with UTEP as we grow in the region to include science, research, education all which will benefit the conservation of water and natural open lands.

Selected Resources

If you wish to pursue a CBR project about open space valuation in your community, the resources listed in the following paragraph should be helpful with learning about land trusts and conservation, CBR pedagogy, and regression analysis. I recommend doing this with students who have taken at least one rigorous applied statistics course who have or are currently learning about Applied Regression Analysis. The guidance of an experienced instructor is also needed since "real-world" data analysis projects are always messy and an experienced applied statistician's perspective is needed when students encounter roadblocks in the modeling. Books about CBR projects in higher education settings:

- *CBR and higher education: Principles and practices.* Strand et al. (2003).
- *CBR: Teaching for Community Impact.* Eatman (2016).

Learn more about land trusts and land conservation groups by visiting the following websites:

- Land Trust Alliance: https://www.landtrustalliance.org/topics/accreditation
- The Conservation Registry: http://conservationregistry.org/

Other land valuation studies and descriptions that would be useful for the literature review:

- Walls, M., Kousky, C., & Chu, Z. (2013) Is What You See What You Get? The Value of Natural Landscape Views. Report. Retrieved from http://www.rff.org/files/sharepoint/WorkImages/Download/RFF-DP-13-25.pdf

- Land Trust Alliance Fact Sheet, Economic Benefits of Open Space. Retrieved from http://fronteralandalliance.org/site/wp-content/uploads/economic-benefits.pdf
- EcoNorthwest (2002) Economic Benefits of Protecting Natural Resources in the Sonoran Desert. . Retrieved from http://www.sonorandesert.org/uploads/files/economicreport.pdf

Resources for regression analysis and statistical programming:

- Faraway, J. *Linear models with R*. Boca Raton, FL: CRC Press.
- Faraway, J. Practical regression and ANOVA using R. Retrieved from http://www.ats.ucla.edu/stat/r/sk/books_pra.htm
- RStudio Team. (2015). RStudio: Integrated Development for R. Boston, MA: RStudio, Inc. Retrieved from http://www.rstudio.com/

Questions for Starting a New Project on Economic Impact of Open Spaces

In each region there are significantly different conditions and areas of impact for open space. Project organizers should begin by contacting a local land trust or conservation group and assessing their priorities. The following questions may also help guide the research process for both the university and community partners:

1. What economic impacts are most relevant for outcome measures? For example, in our project, per TFLA request, we analyzed house valuations since one focus is to conserve open space in neighborhood settings. Other measures such as assessing change in tax base, may be more applicable for other objectives.
2. For your outcome measure, what covariates are available that would typically be used for prediction? Consultation with a subject matter expert (such as our consultation with a realtor) may help.
3. How do you define open space in your community? This proved to be a difficult issue that was only provisionally resolved. We used a rigid and admittedly crude measure to define open space (space designated as a state park), but with more time to plan and consult with land trust groups, this could be improved.

Conclusion

This chapter described a case study of a CBR project in land ecology suitable for undergraduate regression analysis students. The project involved many components, but the most significant were the following: 1) university students worked to apply newly acquired skills in regression analysis to address a community need, 2) the instructor was a support via her connection to the community organization and by facilitating the partnership, and 3) the community partner was a co-researcher with the students and instructor. Students enjoyed applying regression analysis to a non-textbook problem and self-reported that they learned significant amounts about regression analysis as well as our local environment in the process. It is arguable that students also gain a more comprehensive and realistic view of the role of statistical reasoning in society when applying their skills to real-world problems that affect their daily life. This aspect cannot be replicated without involvement of a community partner willing to work with students and co-advise students in the project. Though the project presented some technical challenges, such as obtaining valid data, navigating the analysis and software, these challenges are common to any authentic statistics-based research project. Overall, students reported a greater appreciation of the natural world, a feeling of "doing good," and an enhanced appreciation of the application of statistical analysis to address community issues.

References

Cobb, G. W., & Moore, D. S. (1997). Mathematics, statistics, and teaching. *The American Mathematical Monthly, 104*(9), 801–823.

Eatman, T. K. (2016). *Community-based research: Teaching for community impact.* M. Beckman, & J. F. Long (Eds.). Sterling, VA: Stylus Publishing, LLC.

Feldman, K. A. (1978). Course characteristics and college students' ratings of their teachers: What we know and what we don't. *Research in Higher Education, 9*(3), 199–242.

GAISE College Report ASA Revision Committee. (2016). Guidelines for Assessment and Instruction in Statistics Education College Report 2016. Retrieved from http://www.amstat.org/education/gaise

Gal, I., Ginsburg, L., & Schau, C. (1997). Monitoring attitudes and beliefs in statistics education. In I. Gal & J.B. Garfield (Eds.), *The assessment challenge in statistics education* (pp. 37–51). Amsterdam: IOS Press.

Hacker, K. (2013). *Community-based participatory research.* Los Angeles, CA: Sage Publications.

Hopkins, K. D., Hopkins, B. R., & Glass, G. V. (1996). *Basic statistics for the behavioral sciences* (3rd Ed). Needham Heights, MA: Allyn and Bacon.

Lesser, L., & Wagler, A. (2016). Mathematics, statistics, and (Jewish) culture: Reflections on connections. *Journal of Mathematics and Culture, 10*(2), 127–156. Retrieved from https://journalofmathematicsand-culture.files.wordpress.com/2016/09/lesser-final-august.pdf

Strand, K. J., Cutforth, N., Stoecker, R., Marullo, S., & Donohue, P. (2003). *Community-based research and higher education: Principles and practices.* Hoboken, NJ: John Wiley & Sons.

Wagler, A., Field, C., & Baray, E. (2017). *Seeing community needs through a statistical lens: Undergraduate and graduate level consulting with community organizations in the El Paso border region.* Experiential Education published by Rowmann & Littlefield.

Environmental Science

Chapter 18

Buen Ambiente/Buena Salud: An Internship Program Aimed at Building Capacity to Address Environmental Issues on the US-Mexico Border

Wen-Whai Li, W.L. Hargrove, Manuel Piña Jr., Elaine Hampton, and Jennifer M. Lujan

INTERNSHIPS

SERVICE LEARNING,
COMMUNITY-BASED LEARNING

LEARNING COMMUNITIES

Use these questions to guide your reflection prior to reading the chapter. Use the notes/follow-up section to write your thoughts after you have read the chapter. Your notes can include thoughts in reference to the reflection questions, or general observations about the chapter.

1) The internships described in this chapter were funded to help students explore future careers in an "air quality" field, and were funded by the Environmental Protection Agency. Do you think this is a good funding strategy? Why or why not?

2) Supporting student education can sometimes be managed through as cohort models. Based on your understanding of cohorts, what are the pros and cons of these models?

3) What do you understand to be the difference between multidisciplinary and interdisciplinary approaches to social problems? What are the benefits of each?

Notes/Follow-up:

_____

_____

_____

_____

_____

Introduction

Internships provide students with a direct experience in a professional work setting, ideally related to their career interests and mentored by professionals in the field (Kuh, 2008). An internship is one of the ten high-impact educational practices identified by the Association of American Colleges and Universities because educational research has shown that they increase rates of student retention and student engagement (Kuh, 2008). Internships are a form of active learning, which is also one of the seven principles for good practice in higher education (Chickering & Gamson, 1987). Along with service-learning and community-based learning, internships can provide experiential learning built on local context and relevance for students that cannot be obtained through formal course work (Bass, 2012).

Most internship experiences for university undergraduate or graduate students have the following characteristics:

- They are most commonly one semester or a summer term in length.
- They can, but not always, result in course credit. If taken for credit, a project output or paper is required, subject to approval by a faculty member to obtain the credit.
- They may or may not include a stipend.
- The intern has an assigned mentor who supervises the activities of the intern and serves as a professional coach during the internship. The mentor may or may not receive a stipend.

Some of the practical benefits of an internship to a student include:

- Hands-on experience in their field of interest.
- Immersion in a professional culture/work setting in their field of interest.
- The ability to "try out" a field of interest as a potential career if they are uncertain about their career goals.
- Enhanced "soft skills" such as communications, leadership, negotiation, conflict resolution, and teamwork.
- Improved competitiveness in the job market after graduation, or perhaps a job offer resulting from the internship upon graduation.

Furthermore, educational research has shown that internships promote greater student engagement, a key predictor of educational success and lifelong learning (Kilgo, Sheets, & Pascarella, 2015; Kuh, Pace, & Vesper, 1997). Key factors contributing to enhanced student engagement resulting from internships are the perceived career relevance of the experience, the level of faculty/student collaboration, and the focus and intensity of the learning experience (Kuh et al., 1997; Miller, Rysen, & Fritson, et al., 2011). An internship experience

Contributed by Wen-Whai Li, W.L. Hargrove, Manuel Piña Jr., Elaine Hampton, and Jennifer Lujan. © Kendall Hunt Publishing Company.

has a particularly big advantage for high impact if it is perceived by the student to be directly relevant to the student's long-term career plans (Miller et al., 2011). Through an internship experience, students gain personal competence in their field of interest, verbal and quantitative skills, and cognitive complexity that will lead to success in not only their professional life, but also their personal and social life (Kuh, 1995).

Our Air Quality Internship Program

In 2011, the U.S. Environmental Protection Agency (EPA) funded an educational project aimed at improving air quality on the US–Mexico border, including sources, abatement, and control; impacts on public health; environmental and social justice issues associated with poor air quality, especially for vulnerable populations (children and the elderly); and sustainability. The University of Texas at El Paso's (UTEP) Center for Environmental Resource Management (CERM) led a team to address this challenge that included two major components: 1) development and implementation of an inquiry-based curriculum for grades 3–12 in public schools and 2) an internship program for UTEP students.
Our team consisted of:

- W.L. Hargrove, Director of CERM and Environmental Scientist
- E. Hampton, Professor of Science Teacher Education in the College of Education
- W.W. Li, Professor of Civil Engineering and Air Quality Engineer
- M. Piña, Associate Professor and Evaluator
- A. Gonzalez and Jennifer M. Lujan, Center for Civic Engagement

Our team had considerable experience in developing curriculum (Hampton); managing internships (Li and Hargrove); program evaluation, especially educational programs (Piña); and service-learning, community engagement, and community-based learning (Gonzalez, Lujan, and Hargrove). We functioned as an interdisciplinary team, each individual contributing to all parts of the program, and committed to the principles of inquiry-based curriculum, experiential learning, and community-based learning.

The focus of this chapter is on the internship program that we successfully designed and implemented. It is an example of a high-impact practice that also incorporated community-based learning. EPA's long-term goal for this program was to train professionals who would be prepared to address air quality issues and their impacts and to better communicate environmental risks to vulnerable populations in the US–Mexico border region. To meet this goal, we recognized that we had to increase the quality, number, and diversity of air quality and pollution control professionals in the region. Furthermore, we recognized that internships are an effective way of combining learning and real-world experience at a local level, resulting in increased student retention and success (Kuh, 2008; O'Neill, 2010).

Our project goals were specifically related to the US–Mexico border and its air quality challenges, and in building capacity at a local level to address those challenges, including health impacts and social justice issues. We recognized that combining internship experiences with community engagement and community-based learning would be a fruitful approach for achieving our goals in this project. Placing the focus of our internship experiences and training on the air quality, health, and social justice challenges in a local community setting provided opportunities for the students to apply knowledge and skills to "real-life" problems and to engage with local professionals and local communities in identifying and solving local issues. Thus, we designed the internship program based on common elements of many internship programs as described by O'Neill (2010), but also we incorporated principles of service-learning and community-based learning. We utilized many well-known "best practices" such as those identified in True (2002). In addition, we included a significant training component in technical aspects of air quality and in development of "soft skills."

The title of our project was *Buen Ambiente/Buena Salud* ("Good Environment/Good Health"), to connect environment with health impacts, and in Spanish, to place the project in an appropriate cultural context. Experiential learning, combined with community engagement and community-based learning, is especially applicable and appropriate for environmental science related disciplines since environmental challenges are very place-based. We describe our program in detail in the following case study with the intention of sharing the elements that made it successful and the challenges that we overcame, and most importantly, offering our approach as a reproducible one for others who have similar needs and goals. This project exemplifies three of the high-impact practices, as described by Kuh (2008): undergraduate research, service-learning/community learning, and internships. These high-impact practices have been shown to be very effective for college student success. The evaluation of this project also showed several levels of success for the students and the community involved in the activities of the *Buen Ambiente–Buena Salud* Internship Program.

Case Study: The *Buen Ambiente–Buena Salud* Internship Program

Context

The Paso del Norte region, located on the US–Mexico border, includes the metropolitan areas of El Paso, Texas, and Ciudad Juárez, Mexico, plus several smaller towns and communities in an approximate 50-mile radius of El Paso. Air pollution in the region is considered the worst along the U.S.-Mexico border, with arid weather, occasional high winds, frequent air stagnations, shallow nighttime and morning mixing depths, complex topography, high percentage of unpaved roads, and uncontrolled waste burning. When these conditions are coupled with a depressed economy, poor sanitation, an underserved population with respect to health care , and a complex system of international, national, and local government jurisdictions, residents in the region are affected by poor air quality with high risks of environmental health consequences (Li et al., 2001). These factors plus a poverty rate that is considerably higher than the national average, make this a vulnerable community with respect to health risks associated with air pollution, especially for children and the elderly.

The Internship Program: Basic Elements

A schematic of our entire internship process is presented in Fig. 1. Students were admitted into the program through a competitive screening process. Successful completion of our internship program required six tasks that the students had to accomplish in a twelve-month period. The six tasks were the following:

- Complete a one-credit hour workshop course in air quality;
- Complete an eight-week full-time summer internship on air quality, health science, or environmental justice;
- Complete one graduate course in air quality related to their field of study (for graduate students);
- Make a final presentation describing the internship experience;
- Attend a number of public meetings that related to air quality issues; and
- Participate in at least one community service project.

Through these tasks, students acquired basic science and engineering knowledge in air quality and related health science and received pedagogical training in preparation for the internship. To reinforce their knowledge, students also participated in community environmental activities aimed at air quality improvement, related environmental health, and/or environmental justice. Students attended monthly meetings where UTEP faculty presented science-based information and methods relevant to air quality. A number of field trips were conducted, for example visiting local facilities that implemented environmental air quality controls.

(Continued)

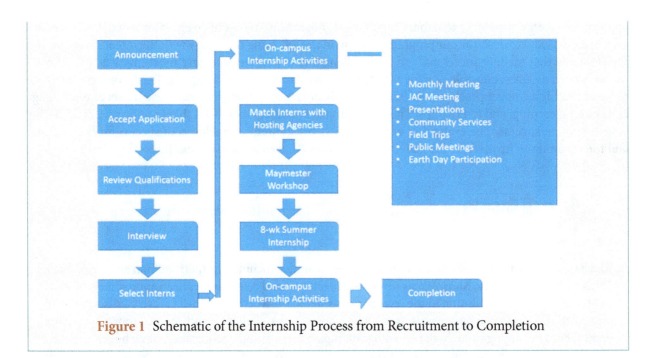

Figure 1 Schematic of the Internship Process from Recruitment to Completion

We incorporated a formal evaluation process into the project, led by an external evaluator (Piña). A mixed method, including quantitative and qualitative data, was used. It was a *formative* process that provided timely feedback to project leaders via milestone reports based on successes and concerns expressed by stakeholders involved in the effort. It was a *summative* process that provided feedback to project leaders via milestone reports based on assessment of progress being made toward reaching the objectives set for the project. At the onset of the project, a table to monitor progress was developed. The table included outputs, outcomes, baselines, performance measures, method, status, and next steps. With respect to the internship program, the evaluation consisted primarily of a *preflection* survey by the students when they began the program and a *reflection* survey when they completed the program. The evaluation outputs were not only reported to the funder, USEPA, but also, and perhaps more important so the project leaders, so that they could be used to make adjustments or improvements to the project in a timely manner. Some of the results from the evaluation are discussed under the **Evidence of Success** section.

The major costs of the internship program included the following:

- Faculty time to organize, manage, and deliver the program; this might vary from year to year but averaged about 2.0 months per year total.
- Consulting time for external evaluation, about 0.5 month of professional time per year.
- Tuition payments of about $500/yr/student for the one-credit hour Maymester course (varied according to the student's degree level).
- Stipends of $3200/yr/student on the average, depending on the degree program of the student.

In our case, the grant from USEPA provided the financial resources to cover these costs.

Who Were the Interns?

Our program was aimed at students in the colleges of science, engineering, health sciences, and related fields. UTEP students were recruited through intensive web announcements, postings on college list serves, and posting of recruitment flyers across the campus. Students were invited to an information session with refreshments each year before the application deadline to provide interested students information, answer questions, and receive comments.

Acceptance into the program was competitive based on an open solicitation and selection by a faculty review committee. During the 5 years of the project, a total number of 216 students applied. Of these, 55 students were selected and successfully completed the program. All 55 participants expressed an interest in pursuing advanced degrees in engineering or science at the completion of their program. The vast majority of students who completed the program were Hispanic (52 out of 55 or 95%).

Preparation for the Internship and Supporting Activities

The internship program required a 1-year residence in which students were asked to participate in monthly program meetings, field trips to one or more industrial and/or research facilities, a graduate course in an air quality-related subject (graduate students only), at least one community activity, and one or more public meetings on issues related to air quality, public health, and/or environmental justice. Students were required to complete their internship of at least 8 weeks in the summer. The host organizations and mentors were arranged by the director of the program (Dr. Li), based on the interests of the students and the hosts. Student participation and performance were monitored throughout the year by program leaders.

Students were expected to acquire basic science and engineering knowledge in air quality and related health science in preparation for the internship. Their technical knowledge and understanding were reinforced by the internship and by participating in community environmental activities aimed at air quality improvement, related environmental health, and/or environmental justice. Some of the required activities that were designed to reinforce learning are described in the following paragraphs.

Monthly Meetings and Presentations: Interns met regularly every month with the program leaders during the academic year. Speakers, including potential internship hosting agencies, UTEP faculty members, and interns from previous years, were invited to make presentations and conduct open forum discussions with the students.

Site Visits: Site visits to industrial facilities and state agencies were made during the academic year to give students information on current practices in air pollution control and monitoring. Through these visits, students were better informed about how regulatory agencies and industrial partners work together to control air pollution. Examples of site visits include El Paso Electric Company, Western Refining Inc., Texas Commission on Environmental Quality Region 6, and the remediation site for a local copper smelter, the former American Smelting and Refining Company (ASARCO).

Special Activities for Students from Public Schools: An example of an activity that we organized to engage the interns with younger students was an Earth Day event for approximately 200 students from 11th and 12th grades. Interns presented to students in three separate sessions plus a laboratory visit. The event lasted for four hours and provided active learning for both our interns and the high school students.

Participation in Community Environmental Affairs and the Community Service Activities: This component was designed to increase students' awareness, interest, and involvement in emerging air quality problems, related environmental issues, and environmental justice in the local community. Students were required to participate in a variety of local public meetings on air quality, environmental justice, and/or public health, and to participate in a short-term service-learning experience, requiring a few hours of volunteer service, which was organized by UTEP's Center for Civic Engagement. This is where our program integrated the internship experience with community-based learning. These specific activities are identified and described in more detail in the following paragraphs.

- The Joint Advisory Committee (JAC) for the Improvement of Air Quality in the Ciudad Juárez, Chihuahua; El Paso, Texas; Doña Ana County, New Mexico air basin. The JAC is the only body of its kind along the entire US–Mexico border and is considered a model for binational cooperation at the regional level. It is sponsored by USEPA and the Mexican environmental agency, SEMARNAT, with participation from local, state, and federal government officials, as well as representatives of non-governmental organizations and the public. These meetings are a local forum for discussion of air quality problems and/or community actions related to air quality on the border. The UTEP interns attended these meetings to observe and then reflect upon and discuss the content of the JAC meetings at the subsequent monthly meeting. The JAC meetings are often characterized by "heated" discussions on subjects associated with environmental justice and pollution prevention.

- Beyond Border 2012: Improving Border Environmental Quality, chaired by U.S. Sen. Tom Udall (NM), was a panel discussion including the EPA Region 6 Administrator, General Manager for the Border Environmental Cooperation Commission, Deputy Executive Director for the North American Development Bank, Secretary of the New Mexico Environment Department, and Executive Director of the Southwest New Mexico Council of Governments.
- Public meeting in El Paso to discuss the demolition of the ASARCO stacks and their environmental implications.
- A roundtable discussion with USEPA Administrator Gina McCarthy during her visit to El Paso.
- Chamizal Neighborhood Toxic Tour in downtown El Paso, including stops to observe and discuss hazardous materials and toxins that surround several schools and environmental injustice issues, hosted by *Las Familias Unidas,* a local community action group, and *La Mujer Obrera,* a local community-based NGO.
- A workshop on an Integrated Heat-Health Information System for Long-Term Resilience to Climate and Weather Extremes in the El Paso-Juárez-Las Cruces Region, hosted by the National Oceanic and Atmospheric Association and the University of Arizona.
- Environmental Education Community Service Activities. UTEP's Center for Civic Engagement facilitated a community service project for the student interns during the last 2 years of the project. The service project entailed teaching an air quality lesson at one of the El Paso Young Women's Christian Association's afterschool programs. The community service project began with a two-hour training course for the interns in which they were taught about each of the learning activities they were to utilize. The lessons were age appropriate and could be completed in about one hour; examples of topics include "How is Electricity Generated" and "The Creation of a Windmill." This activity provided interns with an opportunity to interact with grade school students on the importance of air quality in the border region and how it affects them. It also promoted professional growth for the interns as they gained important leadership and communication skills.

Field Trips: Interns attended two field trips to nationally-recognized laboratories where students met with experts in air quality research. These trips provided important opportunities to learn about state-of-the-art facilities and the importance of air quality monitoring and research. The first trip was to EPA Region 6 Laboratory and other facilities in Houston, Texas. The tour included: 1) the EPA air quality analytical laboratory; 2) the Houston Ship Channel industrial corridor to observe the joint efforts made by federal, state, and local regulatory agencies and industrial partners to improve air quality in the region; 3) the Clean Harbor Waste Recycling facilities to witness how wastes are being minimized to protect the environment; and 4) the City of Houston Air Monitoring Laboratory where engineers briefed them about air monitoring operations and analyses. The second field trip included visits to: 1) the University of California—Davis Crocker Nuclear Laboratory, an EPA-designated laboratory that analyzes particulate matter air pollutants; 2) the California Air Resource Board Air Quality Analytical Laboratory; and 3) the California Resource Board Air Monitoring Network.

Maymester Course. Interns were required to take a preparatory Maymester course prior to their internships. UTEP's Maymester is a two-week period of intensive coursework between the spring semester and the first summer term. In our case, the course provided intensive training in air quality measurement methods, air quality principles and processes, as well as hands-on experience in air quality monitoring and modeling. Students also received soft skills training such as communicating with the public, leadership, and professionalism in the workplace. Students participated in a role play in which they had to explain an air quality issue and introduce a technology to address it in a mock public meeting. Finally, students were required to develop their own learning objectives for their internship, and each student kept a personal journal to record their activities, reflections, and progress toward their educational objectives.

At the end of the course, students completed an EPA online training course, SI 460: Introduction to Permitting, and received a certification of completion. Students also completed two sessions of training from the Online School for Weather and received certificates on Jet Stream's Remote Sensing Topic and Jet

Stream's Global Weather Topic. Students attended class for a full day for two weeks to complete this course for the one hour of credit.

The Internship Hosts and Locations

In determining the host and mentor for each student, it was important to match the students' interests to those of the potential host. The program solicited numerous federal, state, and local regulatory agencies and research institutes as well as industrial partners and nonprofit organizations to serve as hosts. Twenty organizations hosted at least one intern and several of them multiple interns. The majority of hosts were local (within the El Paso/Las Cruces area) but a number were either out-of-state or in central Texas. Because of the high-quality performance of each intern, the program established a good reputation with all hosts. The result was that our interns were highly sought after by many hosting agencies.

What Made This Internship Program Successful

The Elements Of Success

We identify in the following paragraphs the critical elements that made our program successful.

1. **The competitive selection process**—We used an open solicitation followed by a screening and selection process that was competitive based on written application materials and a personal interview. This allowed us to select students with strong academic credentials who were motivated to participate in the program.
2. **Treating each group of students as a cohort**—We treated each group of interns, who were from different academic disciplines, as a cohort. This enabled them to learn from each other as an interdisciplinary team and built a process of co-learning among the students and project leaders. The monthly meetings as a group reinforced the cohort structure.
3. **The preparatory course**—The required Maymester course provided excellent preparation for the students before their internship. Not only did the course provide a foundation of technical information and knowledge but also some preparation for the professional "workplace" and soft skills training to support their experience.
4. **Supporting activities**—The supporting active learning activities that we provided, such as field trips, site visits, community activities, and others, provided context, and additional technical information that deepened the interns' learning and increased their preparation for the internship experience.
5. **UTEP/Community relationships**—UTEP's existing community relationships and collaboration provided a foundation for the student internships. Both CERM's and Dr. Li's years of interactions with the border environmental community provided a set of organizations who welcomed UTEP students as interns at their facilities.
6. **Context and content**—Connecting with relevant and complex content surrounding important environmental issues in the community enhanced the learning experience for the interns. As evident in the previous list of events that the students attended, they experienced the complexities of social, political, and scientific interactions to address serious environmental justice issues at a local level.
7. **Community service activities**—The community service activities not only provided context for the overall training program but also provided an opportunity for the students to "give back" to their community. Giving back to the community is a strong cultural value in the El Paso region, held by many of the students at UTEP, who generally come from less affluent backgrounds.
8. **The external evaluation**—The external evaluation activities allowed us to get regular feedback over the course of the project (5 years) and to make adjustments to the program to improve the outcomes.

9. **The final presentation**—Each student was required to make an oral presentation of the activities of their internship and its learning outcomes. This forced the students to reflect upon their experiences and communicate them to their peers and mentors.

10. **The project team**—The five-member project team met regularly (monthly in the beginning, and every 2 months later in the project) in order to discuss progress, plans, and areas for improvement. This established and maintained a strong interdisciplinary team approach to the project with everyone contributing and taking responsibility for outcomes.

Evidence Of Success

The program had some noteworthy short-term outcomes: 1) all 55 interns in the program continued their studies at UTEP, that is, none dropped out of the university; 2) 52 of these were from STEM disciplines and three were from non-STEM disciplines; 3) 10 of the undergraduate interns continued to pursue M.S. or Ph.D. studies at UTEP or other universities; and 4) most of the interns were Hispanic (95%).

The design of this internship met several important objectives of particular interest to our students and to our region.

- The program provided training and experience for UTEP students that facilitated them to become professionals able to address air quality, environmental health, and environmental justice issues of the region.
- The program provided financial assistance, especially important for students to complete their education.
- The majority of the students were Hispanic. The program trained them to become professionals and leaders in the "21st Century Demographic," one in which Hispanics are projected to be the majority ethnic group in the United States before mid-century.

Additional evidence of success collected through the evaluation process is manifested by the fact that this program attracted students that not only wanted to know more about air quality issues, environmental health, and environmental justice, but also expressed strong emotions about links between human health and air quality in the border region. In the preflection surveys, many students expressed a lack of awareness about air quality and its impact on low income populations, and they wanted more information and research about these issues. They felt that they could make positive changes through research and education and indicated a desire to do outreach and have community level impact. They wanted to network, have hands-on experiences, and conduct research. Data from reflection surveys provided evidence that the program met all the interns' expectations. They reported having very responsible assignments in their internships, and they experienced a wide range of science and real-world activities related to air quality. Because of their quality performance, half of the students received offers to extend or participate in another internship. Some even received job offers from their hosts. The students reported on their experiences positively, highlighting that they liked the learning and research experience in a real-world context, while being supported and mentored by people who made them feel like members of a team.

Feedback from the internship supervisors was consistent with responses from the interns, reflecting success. The tone and content of responses from mentors were extremely positive and complimentary. It was clear that the selection and preparation of the students for the internships was effective and successful. The interns gained real-life experiences and developed contacts for future employment to address air quality in the region.

When asked whether the community participation aspect of the internship helped them to see how the subject matter they learned could be used in everyday life, 70 percent of interns agreed and 30 percent strongly agreed. Fifty percent of students agreed that the community work involved in this course helped them to become more aware of the needs in their community, while 50 percent of the student interns who were surveyed, strongly agreed.

Challenges

The greatest challenge that we faced, and that is faced by all training/educational projects, is documenting the impacts of the project in the medium to long-term. We were successful in documenting short-term impacts, but medium (3–5 years) to long-term (>5 years) impacts are much more difficult to document due to the duration of the grant and the difficulty of contacting and tracking students after they left school or the university.

We also had a few students who were accepted to the program but then dropped out either early on or just before doing their internship (about one per year, out of 10–12 accepted to the program), primarily because they discovered that it was too time consuming for them or that they needed to work to earn money. The additional active learning activities, like field trips and site visits, added to the students' learning but also required a time commitment.

Lessons Learned About Implementing Effective University Internships: Making It Work in Other Settings and Circumstances

Several important lessons learned in implementing our internship program include:

1. The student preparation and orientation through regular cohort meetings over a semester and the one-week intensive Maymester course were instrumental in preparing the student interns for a successful internship experience. The students generally knew what to expect and had a common foundation in terms of air quality knowledge. The soft skills training that they received improved their ability to practice leadership, communications, and scientific presentation skills.
2. The field trips and other experiential learning opportunities reinforced both the classroom learning and the internship experience.
3. The participation in public meetings and in community service activities provided opportunities for them to observe and practice community engagement and to better understand and appreciate its value.
4. For our project implementing team, regular face-to-face meetings, conference calls, and email communications resulted in positive communications and good working relationships among the key participants. Project meetings were approached as opportunities to brainstorm and strategize through constructive criticism and suggestions for improvement. This resulted in an interdisciplinary working environment where all contributed to identifying problems and solutions, rather than multidisciplinary where each participant just "did their part." Shared accountability with clear roles and responsibilities resulted in effective and efficient performance of the tasks.
5. The community partners who hosted our interns had a very positive experience and were even asked for additional opportunities to host student interns at the end of the project. They characterized our students as technically well-prepared, possessing a strong work ethic, polite and well-mannered, and eager to learn. They generally recognized and relished their contribution to preparing professionals who will be prepared to enter careers that deal with air quality, environmental health, and social justice issues in the US–Mexico border region. This positive experience of the mentors and hosts of our interns resulted in an unexpected outcome of our program in that it strengthened UTEP's relationship with many community partners.
6. Offering students a stipend with the internship was important, especially in a community where students are financially "strapped" to support their education. More than half of UTEP students are first in their family to attend college and come from working class families. Many students would not have been able to afford an internship if they had to give up their summer work income.

Moving Forward

What made our internship program "high impact" was the preparation and additional experiential learning activities that we provided to the cohort of students in addition to the internship experience itself. These preparatory and additional activities enhanced and deepened the learning experience of the internship. This also sets our program apart from many internship programs where students are just sent to a mentor/host with an expectation that the student will write a paper or make a presentation about their experience. The experience that we afforded our students was enriched by supplementary experiential learning activities, plus our evaluation process required our students to reflect more deeply on what they learned. Feedback that we received from the students revealed that the additional field trips and their experiences in community service were highly valued. In fact, from our evaluation data, 42% of the graduates of our program asked for even more field trips, hands-on experiences, and group activities than what we provided. Clearly it is not enough just to provide the internship experience.

Thus, a paramount consideration in designing future internship programs is how the experience can be enriched through preparatory activities and additional experiential learning activities that will supplement and support the learning experience of the internship. The challenge of meeting this goal is the time and resources required to do so.

Additional Resources

A detailed description of our program can be found in Hargrove, Hampton, and Li (2017). Listed next are some web-based resources for how to design internship programs. Some are more oriented toward the private sector as hosts to student interns, but some are oriented to university managed internship programs. None are oriented to maximizing the learning experience for the student nor do they include the kind of comprehensive program that we designed and implemented.

http://www.virginia.edu/career/intern/startinganinternship.PDF
http://www.internships.com/employer/resources/setup/12steps
http://career.bryant.edu/resources/files/RI%20Employer%20Guide%20Good%20Internships%20are%20Good%20Business2%20(3).pdf
http://www.naceweb.org/talent-acquisition/internships/15-best-practices-for-internship-programs/
http://www.stevenson.edu/career-success/choosing-your-direction/employers/documents/developing-an-internship-program.pdf
https://www.dol.gov/odep/pdf/InclusiveInternshipPrograms.pdf

Conclusions

We developed and implemented an internship program based on principles of service-learning (including student preparation and a mentoring program) and experiential training that augmented the actual internship experience. Successful completion of the internship program required six tasks that the students had to accomplish in a 12-month period. The six tasks were:

a. Complete a one-credit hour workshop course in air quality;
b. Complete an eight-week full-time summer internship on air quality, health science, or environmental justice;
c. Complete one graduate course in air quality related to their field of study (for graduate students only);
d. Make a final presentation describing the internship experience;
e. Attend a number of public meetings that related to air quality issues in general;
f. Participate in at least one community service project.

Students in the program received financial incentives through a stipend during their internship and tuition reimbursement for completing the one-credit hour course.

Students were admitted into the program through a competitive screening process. They acquired basic science and engineering knowledge in air quality and related health science and pedagogical training in preparation for the internship. They re-enforced their knowledge and understanding by completing a paid internship and by participating in community environmental activities aimed at air quality improvement, related environmental health, and/or environmental justice. The cohort of interns participated in a number of activities both on and off campus including:

- Monthly meetings and technical presentations
- Site visits during the semester
- Earth Day activities
- Community environmental affairs
- Field trips
- At least one community service project

In addition to these activities, the students enrolled in a Maymester course before their internship to receive intensive training, including air quality measurement methods, air quality principles and processes, and soft skills such as communicating to the public, leadership, and professionalism in the workplace. Each student did an eight-week internship during the summer with a host that met their educational and training objectives.

A total of 55 students (our original goal was 50) successfully completed our internship program; 95% (52) were Hispanic. The following outcomes were realized from the internship program.

1. **100% Retention Rate**—All participants in the air quality internship program continued their study at UTEP. None have dropped out of the university.
2. **Produced more than 50 graduates**—The program has produced 55 graduates which exceeded the goal of 50 graduates over 5 years.
3. **High percentage in STEM disciplines**—Out of the 55 graduates, only three were non-STEM majors and all have expressed interest in pursuing advance degrees in engineering or science.
4. **High percentage of minority student participation**—96% of the program graduates were either Hispanic or African American. Thus, the program produced professionals and leaders for the "21st Century Demographic," one in which Hispanics are projected to be the majority ethnic group in the U.S. by mid-century.
5. **Pursuing Advanced Degrees**—Ten undergraduate students who participated in the program have since entered M.S. or Ph.D. programs at UTEP or other universities.

If the educational goal is "high impact," internship programs should be enriched with preparatory training, additional experiential learning activities, and community engagement.

References

Bass, R. (2012). Disrupting ourselves: The problem of learning in higher education. *Educause Review, 47*, 1–14.

Chickering, A. W., & Zelda, F. Gamson. 1987. Seven principles for good practice in undergraduate education. *AAHE Bulletin*, March Issue, 3–7.

Hargrove, W. L., Hampton, E., Li, W.-W. (2017). *Buen Ambiente-Buena Salud:* Educational Strategies for Addressing Air Quality on the Border. 2017. Grant #IT-83509301 Project Final Report submitted to the U.S. EPA Office of Air and Radiation. December, 2016, 72.

Kilgo, C. A., Sheets, J. K. E., & Pascarella, E. T. (2015). The link between high-impact practices and student learning: Some longitudinal evidence. *Higher Education, 69*, 509–525.

Kuh, G. D. (1995). The Other Curriculum: Out-of-Class Experiences Associated with Student Learning and Personal Development. *Journal of Higher Education, 66*, 123–155.

Kuh, G. D. (2008). *High-impact educational practices: What they are, who has access to them, and why they matter*. Washington, DC: Association of American Colleges and Universities.

Kuh, G. D., Pace, C. R., & Vesper, N. (1997). The development of process indicators to estimate student gains associated with good practices in undergraduate education. *Research in Higher Education, 38*(4), 435–454.

Li, W.-W., Orquiz, R., Pingitore, N. E. Jr, Garcia, J. H., Espino, T. T., Gardea-Torresdey, J., Chow, J., Watson, J. W. (2001). Analysis of temporal and spatial dichotomous PM air samples in the El Paso-Cd. Juarez air quality basin. *Journal of Air & Waste Management Association, 51,* 1511-1560.

Miller, R. L., Rycek, R. F., & Fritson, K. (2011). The effects of high impact learning experiences on student engagement. *Procedia – Social and Behavioral Sciences, 15,* 53–59.

O'Neill, N. (2010). Internships as a high-impact practice: Some reflections on quality. *Peer Review, 12*(4). Assoc. American College & Universities. Retrieved from https://www.aacu.org/publications-research/periodicals/internships-high-impact-practice-some-reflections-quality

True, M. (2002). *Starting and Maintaining a Quality Internship Program. Pittsburgh Technology Council and Messiah College.* 2nd Edition. Retrieved from http://www.virginia.edu/career/intern/startinganinternship.PDF

Social Work

Chapter 19

Community-Based Learning Practices with Persons Experiencing Homelessness

Eva M. Moya, Guillermina Solis, Silvia Maria Chávez-Baray, Jacen Maire-Moore, Carla Ellis, Elizabeth Camacho, Sarah M. Norman, and Ray Tullius

SERVICE LEARNING,
COMMUNITY-BASED LEARNING

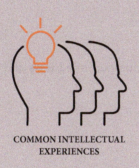

COMMON INTELLECTUAL
EXPERIENCES

DIVERSITY/GLOBAL LEARNING

COLLABORATIVE
ASSIGNMENTS AND PROJECTS

Use these questions to guide your reflection prior to reading the chapter. Use the notes/follow-up section to write your thoughts after you have read the chapter. Your notes can include thoughts in reference to the reflection questions, or general observations about the chapter.

1) What is your understanding of homelessness? What has shaped your knowledge and understanding of homelessness?

2) Will your profession ever have a connection or role to play to address homelessness in your community?

3) What disciplines do you believe are most likely equipped to address and connect with the homeless population? Explain your answer.

Notes/Follow-up:

_____

_____

_____

_____

_____

Introduction

Community-based learning and service initiatives are essential to integrate clinical and community health practices to address health inequalities. This chapter describes a collaborative project between graduate, undergraduate university programs, and community partners grounded on experiential-based learning and problem-solving practice to serve persons experiencing homelessness. We describe the **H**ealth **O**pportunity **P**revention and **E**ducation Project (HOPE), a health fair model led by community organizations, faculty, and students. HOPE is an amalgam of high-impact practices to address homeless populations.

Faculty and students from nursing, pharmacy, and health science programs in social work and clinical laboratory science from the University of Texas at El Paso (UTEP) created a successful partnership with the Opportunity Center for the Homeless (OCH), a grassroots community-based organization, and other local partners to serve persons experiencing homelessness. We describe how students effectively translated cognitive skills and theoretical knowledge into an experiential learning environment while providing assistance to the OCH. Challenges, opportunities, and recommendations for faculty, students, and community partners are presented.

Case Study

HOPE Background

Ray Tullius, founder and executive director of the OCH (co-author), did a lecture to graduate social work students for the policy and macro practice courses regarding the mission of his organization. His described personal journey of homelessness and resilience inspired students to contextualize homelessness, and provided a glimpse into the challenges associated with homelessness and inequalities. The presentation offered the students real-life examples of grassroots community organizing. From this experience, a partnership between UTEP and the OCH developed into a hands-on social work course on homelessness, and with the support of the university administration, the macropractice course was moved from the traditional academic setting to the modest conference room of the OCH in 2014 (Moya, Chavez, Adcox, & Martinez, 2017).

One of the class assignments was to develop group intervention projects focused on homelessness. Two of the projects stood out, one focused on the delivery of health and human services for the residents of the OCH and the other on integrating rehabilitation counseling and social work to assist the residents with employment, vocational guidance, and disability services.

Subsequently, the Provost's Office and the University Center for Civic Engagement hosted a series of faculty-oriented tours of community organizations which included the OCH. One month after visiting the agency, scholars from social work, nursing, clinical laboratory science, and pharmacy, along with a cadre of students, came together to grow the existing partnership and to pioneer what became known as HOPE.

Contributed by Eva M. Moya, Guillermina Solis, Silvia Maria Chávez-Baray, Jacen Maire-Moore, Carla Ellis, Elizabeth Camacho, Sarah M. Norman, and Ray Tullius. © Kendall Hunt Publishing Company.

The project was designed on the features of a traditional health fair model (Castañeda, Islam, Stetten, Black, & Blue, 2017) grounded in community-engagement values (Pascual y Cabo, Prada, & Lowther Pereira, 2017) and service-learning practices (Young, McCorriston, & Ritchie, 2017). Basic health screenings and connection to human services for 190 homeless individuals, under the direction of 10 faculty members representing social work, nursing, clinical laboratory science, and pharmacy were provided. This collaborative partnership engaged the efforts of 62 students and 24 volunteers from community agencies including the Department of Public Health, local pharmacies, a private hospital, a philanthropy club, and a community health center.

A second HOPE was organized by the university rehabilitation counseling program. The focus was employment and rehabilitation. Over 100 persons experiencing homelessness were coached in mock interviews, enhanced their resumes, connected with rehabilitation and vocational services, and some accepted employment (Kosyluk, 2016). A protocol for the project, including data collection instruments, was established.

In the fall of that year a research protocol was approved by the University Institutional Review Board. HOPE brought together 130 students to conduct service-based learning activities and began to have a direct impact on the lives of individuals experiencing homelessness. Nearly 141 residents received screening for tuberculosis, sexually-transmitted infections, vision, hearing, and foot care, and were provided with clinical laboratory services, vouchers for mammograms, and flu vaccinations. A medical follow-up care has been established by the on-site community health center to ensure appropriate care for those with more complex medical needs. HOPE inspired students to apply knowledge and serve outside of the traditional classroom setting.

Successful High-Impact Practices

We followed a person-centered service model. In the preplanning stages, faculty, community partners, and center managers (former members of the homeless population) identified the needs and essential resources to deliver services for residents. The center's managers provided a unique perspective, which increased the likelihood of success.

The project was built on community-engagement principles that revolved around, co-shared leadership, humility, integrity, and mutual respect. Students learned from each other, the population served, and the community organizations. Faculty members were role models for students and personified the application of scholarship, and community partners showcased their practices. Planning meetings were held at the OCH, and students observed the challenges faced by a grass-root organization that may not have had the same resources available as a traditional classroom or simulation venues. HOPE became a community of practice for both the agency and the university.

Challenges Encountered

Effective and meaningful learning must be bi-directional. A challenge was the unification of teaching and community practices outside of the traditional classroom setting. We initially experienced difficulties in garnering administrative support for off-campus service experiences for students, due to concerns over logistics such as transportation to and from the venue and over liability including faculty and student safety. Some students expressed general discomfort regarding the potential stigma of being seen entering a homeless shelter and working in a socioeconomically distressed neighborhood. Since some of the students, faculty members, and community partners had not worked with homeless populations, concerns were expressed about contracting communicable diseases through direct interactions with the residents. Students received orientation on universal health precautions and safety practices to address these concerns.

Historically, health fairs for persons experiencing homelessness have been operated as individual silos of service with each university department functioning independently. HOPE created an environment of collaborative practice among university programs, students, and community agencies.

Other challenges encountered included, stretching clinical laboratory reagents and supplies donated by local partners, limited health literacy, and fear by frail and mentally distressed residents to socialize with strangers. Faculty mentored students, modeled and practiced critical, creative thinking, and used problem-solving skills to address these challenges.

HOPE Intervention Process

High-impact practices create an environment of learning and share common intellectual experiences both inside and outside of the classroom (Bechtold, 2017). Faculty mentors observed the students throughout the processes for effective functioning and provided feedback as needed to optimize proficiency and to help prepare students for transitioning to the workforce with a sense of service. During the planning, the team was courageous and bold in teaching and leading. We used role playing and simulated on-site tours for each service station. Students were instructed to use simple language or terminology to avoid isolating or distancing the residents. Faculty encouraged the students to reflect after the event using tools such as essays or exemplary case studies. Social work faculty also utilized learning environments including OCH programs, course curricula, teaching practices, and facilities as part of the educational goals, creating a social agency climate that lead to improved educational outcomes (Hatch, Crisp & Wesley, 2016).

In order to focus on individual needs that would have a direct impact upon the residents, the students engaged in face-to-face interactions with the residents to assess perceived barriers to care and provide resources and services. Students interacted with participating agencies and organizations to understand how policies impact services. These activities allowed students to apply their practical skills while feeling valued and recognized for their service. It is known that students who complete courses with service-learning components develop a wide range of practice skills, exhibit greater self-efficacy in group and organizational skills, develop more favorable attitudes toward community practice, gain confidence and competencies as practitioners, and are more likely to engage in advocacy after graduation (Steen, Mann, Restivo, Mazany, & Chapple, 2017).

Moving Forward

HOPE is well-suited for adaptation in other communities where institutions of higher learning in partnership with organizations can positively impact student training and community engagement, as well as serve populations in need. Connecting theory with practice continues to be a challenge for some disciplines. Integrating service-learning with community practice not only enhances educational preparation but also makes teaching more dynamic, effective, and meaningful, by putting into practice what we teach (Fogel & Ersing, 2016).

Recommendations for Faculty

Faculty members had the opportunity to value their own and others' contributions to education and service outcomes. Through HOPE, faculty practiced and improved multidisciplinary communication, used problem-solving skills, and validated respect of the unique attributes of each discipline, including the variations in professional orientations and personal values. Empathy and compassion are critical for student development (Bajracharya, 2006).

Addressing safety, mitigating stigma, and increasing confidence through dialogue helped overcome challenges and perceived barriers. Faculty engaged students in discussions about the OCH mission and the population's vulnerabilities for becoming homeless to help mitigate stigmas toward the residents. Students transitioned from fear and skepticism to comfort and empathy.

Recommendations for Students

Students became comfortable in engaging with, delivering information to, and empathizing with residents both intellectually and emotionally by observing the impact of putting their education into action. Face-to-face interactions with residents allowed them to be aware of from someone else's point of view, and understand the impact of a person's difficulties living and experiencing health inequalities. The residents reported feeling treated with dignity and respect by students.

A student described *"I enjoyed being at the OCH knowing that the services we provided actually mattered. In most places we do health screenings, we see a more well-off population. Seeing the people that we helped and hearing their stories really enlightened me to their hardships."* Another student described the importance of working across disciplines in the community: *"I was happy to see that social work, nursing, clinical laboratory and everyone else there came together for a great cause and helped people in our community."* The importance of serving the OCH inspired students to view their profession as more than just a job. *"It is a humbling experience to see how bad things can get for the less fortunate. It was an inspiration to live a life that shows consideration for others. I would be happy to volunteer there again and use my developing professional skills to help the people with the most need."*

Community-based activities like HOPE allowed students to polish their skills and see first-hand how the work they perform has a direct impact on the lives and health of individuals and communities. Through community-engagement, students' identified real world opportunities to be creative. Community partners identified opportunities for co-leading and mentoring the scholarship of students and faculty (Brown, Shephard, Warren, Hesson, & Fleming, 2016). It took team building, patience, understanding, and perseverance to launch the community of practice.

Recommendations for Community

HOPE is inspired on the principle of working 'in' rather than on working 'with' communities (Militello, Ringler, Hodgkins, & Hester, 2017). This transition involves honoring the wisdom of those who reside in the communities one wishes to serve and focuses on the 'gifts' community members hold. In turn, the organizations (like the OCH) served are impacted, and ultimately the larger communities become an authentic partner, the gap between the 'expert' at the university and the 'expert' in the community are bridged (Young, McCorriston, & Ritchie, 2017).

Integration and interconnectedness between universities and communities are gaining significance in response to social and civic engagement. Community-engaged scholarship has emerged as a reciprocal learning response to address inequalities in power relations between higher education institutions and collaborators. As practitioners and scholars, community-engaged learning opportunities and experiences like HOPE can leave a profound and meaningful impression on teaching, learning, and leading.

Selected Resources and Tools

- Principles of Community Engagement. Second Edition. https://www.atsdr.cdc.gov/communityengagement/pdf/PCE_Report_508_FINAL.pdf
- Community Tool Box. http://ctb.ku.edu/en
- Engagement Scholarship Consortium. https://engagementscholarship.org/awards/wkkf-award/2013

Guiding Questions

The following questions are useful at the beginning of new collaborative community projects:

- What does community-based learning look like for your discipline? For the community?
- What are the challenges that you anticipate in launching community-learning efforts?
- How will the community benefit from high-impact practices?

Conclusion

Student success is achieved by setting high expectations for commitment of time and effort, mitigating attrition, and addressing individual factors to ensure that education thrives in the 21st century (Murphy & Murphy, 2017). Community-learning initiatives like HOPE need to be expanded so the community becomes the classroom. Research suggests that engagement in community scholarship under the guidance of faculty mentors has a substantial impact on student retention and graduation rates (Young, Uy, & Bell, 2017). Communities of practice like HOPE can play a role in transforming inequalities into practice opportunities by preparing the workforce to be aware of and confront head on the changing times where service-learning practices can have a positive impact in student learning outcomes (Reisch, 2014). Far too often, we pretend to be the experts—not realizing that no one person is the expert, but that collectively we are the expert. In working together—this builds compassion, recognition, and empathy.

References and Other Resources

Bajracharya, S. M. (2006). Community-based health education intervention: A service-learning approach. *Forum on Public Policy*, 1–11.

Bechtold, J. I. (2017). The idea of calling presented in light of high-impact practices in a general education course and beyond. *Christian Higher Education*, *16*(1-2), 79–91.

Brown, K., Shephard, K., Warren, D., Hesson, G., & Fleming, J. (2016). Using phenomenography to build an understanding of how university people conceptualize their community-engaged activities. *Higher Education Research & Development*, *35*(4), 643–657.

Castañeda, G., Islam, S., Stetten, N., Black, E., & Blue, A. (2017). What's in it for me? Perspectives from community participants in an interprofessional service learning program. *Journal of Interprofessional Education & Practice, 6,* 15–21.

Fogel, S. J., & Ersing, R. (2016). Macro-focused social work dissertations: A preliminary look at the numbers. *Journal of Social Work Education*, *52*(2), 170–177.

Hatch, D. K., Crisp, G., & Wesley, K. (2016). What's in a Name? The challenge and utility of defining promising and high-impact practices. *New Directions for Community Colleges*, 2016 (175), 9–17.

Kosyluk, K. (2016). 2nd Health Opportunity Prevention and Education (HOPE) Report: An Interdisciplinary community-engaged intervention for home-free communities in El Paso, Texas.

Militello, M., Ringler, M. C., Hodgkins, L., & Hester, D. M. (2017). I am, I am becoming: how community engagement changed our learning, teaching, and leadership. *International Journal of Qualitative Studies in Education*, *30*(1), 58–73.

Moya, E. M., Chavez-Baray, S., M., Adcox, C., Martinez, O. (2017). Community-engaged scholarship outside of the classroom with the homeless. SAGE Research Methods Cases. SAGE Publications Ltd. London. Online ISBN: 9781526419170

Murphy, J. P., & Murphy, S. A. (2017). Get ready, get in, get through: Factors that influence Latino college student success. *Journal of Latinos and Education*, 1–15.

Pascual y Cabo, D., Prada, J., & Lowther Pereira, K. (2017). Effects of community service-learning on heritage language learners' attitudes toward their language and culture. Foreign Language Annals.

Reisch, M. (2014). What is the future of social work? *Critical and Radical Social Work*, *1*(1), 67–85.

Steen, J. A., Mann, M., Restivo, N., Mazany, S., & Chapple, R. (2017). Human rights: Its meaning and practice in social work field settings. *Social Work*, *62*(1), 9–17.

Young, G., McCorriston, J., & Ritchie, K. L. (2017). A model to incorporate meaningful community engaged learning opportunities into medium. In Discussions on University Science Teaching: Proceedings of the Western Conference on Science Education (1, 1, p. 10).

Young, S., Uy, A., & Bell, J. (2017). Student engagement in research, scholarship, and creative activity (SERSCA) program: Sharing a program model from design and development through evaluation. *Innovative Higher Education*, *42*(1), 65–76.

Social Work

Chapter 20

Service-Learning with Refugees as a High-Impact Educational Practice

Mark Lusk and Linda Rivas

SERVICE LEARNING,
COMMUNITY-BASED LEARNING

DIVERSITY/GLOBAL LEARNING

Use these questions to guide your reflection prior to reading the chapter. Use the notes/follow-up section to write your thoughts after you have read the chapter. Your notes can include thoughts in reference to the reflection questions, or general observations about the chapter.

1) What do you understand or would like to know about the term "vulnerable populations?" What does it mean to you?

2) Do you think there is a certain personality type, set of skills or background necessary to be an effective volunteer or professional working with vulnerable populations? If so, please explain.

3) This chapter speaks about potential personal judgment that may be held by students serving vulnerable populations. How would you go about remaining objective or not judging people who have had different experiences from your own? Do you believe one may be objective? Why or why not?

Notes/Follow-up:

_____

_____

_____

_____

_____

Introduction

Service-learning with refugees can be an excellent way of learning about social justice, human rights, civic responsibility, and community engagement, and it can provide a global experience without travelling abroad.

At a time in which seemingly the values of self over service and profit over country are ascendant, engagement with migrants and refugees may serve as an antidote and balance by providing students with a perspective that sees merit in accompanying and learning about people whose experiences have pushed to them to the margins. Refugees are forced migrants whose experiences in their home countries have been perilous and even life threatening. Moreover, their journey to new lands have been fraught with hazards. Upon reaching their destination, many face harassment, detention, incarceration, and expulsion—particularly in the United States. Few other groups offer the student such challenges to their training, ethical formation, and personal growth and development.

Service-learning and community engagement are educational practices that enhance student learning by mobilizing the student as an active learner in a community setting (Lemieux & Allen, 2013). Social work majors and students in related disciplines such as sociology, anthropology, and political science are often trained in off-campus settings with clients and communities that are confronting considerable challenges. Service-learning with refugees takes community-based study to a more intense level by virtue of the social justice, ethical, legal, and moral questions that surround immigrants in a country that has conflicting attitudes and policies on immigration.

At the University of Texas at El Paso, a variety of service-learning opportunities are available for students to work with migrants, refugees, and displaced persons. In this particular case study, we summarize the opportunities and challenges working with refugees and two agencies that provide them with respite care and legal assistance.

Social Justice Work with Refugees: A Case Study

According to the United Nations High Commission on Refugees, there are over 21 million refugees worldwide. By definition, "a refugee is someone who has been forced to flee his or her country because of persecution, war, or violence. A refugee has a well-founded fear of persecution for reasons of race, religion, nationality, political opinion, or membership in a particular social group" (UNHCR, 2017). Under international law, refugees are afforded protection by virtue of their persecution or risk associated with their return to their home country.

People are largely aware of the huge migrations from war-torn countries such as Syria, Yemen, Lebanon, Afghanistan, Sudan, and Somalia. In these countries, the principal cause of displacement has been armed conflict and civil war. Syria alone is the source of almost 5 million refugees who have fled that country in the wake of a decade of civil war. Less well-known is the migration of refugees and displaced persons fleeing drug-related violence in Latin America. The past decade has seen significant increases in emigration from Central America's Northern Triangle nations of Guatemala, El Salvador, and Honduras. Migration from these nations has been primarily through the US–Mexico border. Consequently, the border region has become increasingly militarized and one of significant political interest as elected officials have sought to create greater barriers to human migration from the region.

At the University of Texas at El Paso (UTEP), located directly adjacent to the border and overlooking Ciudad Juárez, migration and refugees are not an abstract issue for classroom debate, but a tangible issue that shapes the fabric the city, region and university. It is not uncommon for student families to be of mixed immigration status nor is it unusual for students to cross from Mexico to attend classes. Many students know people who have fled violence, persecution, extortion, and organized crime. While strong anti-immigrant attitudes may prevail in other locales, in El Paso a more nuanced understanding exists in a community that is comprised of over 80% Latino population.

Because El Paso has been the transit point for thousands of refugees and forced migrants over the past decade, it is a perfect setting for a case study on service-learning with this population. In El Paso, numerous refugees have been released into the community after having been processed by federal border officials. Local non-governmental organizations (NGOs) and churches have provided respite care, hospitality, travel support, and legal assistance to these individuals and families. This has presented an outstanding opportunity for students to learn about social justice work with a vulnerable populations. Few groups have undergone greater adversity or overcome such enormous challenges as those who have left their country under duress to travel great distances with few resources than refugees from Latin America.

The Challenges of Working with Refugees

A decade ago, the flow of migrants to the United States from Mexico and Central America began to increase significantly as a result of drug violence in the region. As people in the region were increasingly caught in the crossfire of turf wars between cartels, many innocent civilians were forced to flee as they became victims of crime. Beginning in 2007, large numbers of business owners became the targets of extortion and kidnapping by organized crime. Throughout the past decade, the authors (Mark Lusk and Linda Rivas) have worked with hundreds of refugees from Mexico, Colombia, Guatemala, El Salvador, Honduras, and other countries that have been adversely affected by civil disorder and a vacuum of law-enforcement.

From the moment that asylum seekers step foot in the United States, they are confronted with harsh policies that immediately and arbitrarily detain them. Often people that present themselves to seek asylum at ports of entry are held for days or weeks in processing facilities that are not designed to house them. This means that after weeks and even months of struggling to make it to the border, refugees will be held without a shower or a proper bed for an undetermined amount of time. While policy dictates that Customs and Border Enforcement cannot hold a person for more than 72 hours, our interviews with refugees indicate that often people are held for much longer. Although the detention of asylum seekers goes against United Nations conventions, asylum seekers are regularly detained. A recent report, *Discretion to Deny*, based on detention practices in El Paso, reveals how asylum seekers are being systematically deterred from seeking asylum by abusive treatment while in detention, prolonged detention, and widespread denials of parole.

Detention issues are only part of the problem of systematic deterrence of asylum seekers. Families with children who seek refuge are often separated when seeking asyum at the border. These families are habitually separated when they request asylum at the border. It is also common for adult males, such as fathers and brothers, to be separated from mothers and minor children. Mothers and children may be released to family members that reside in the United States or shelters, or may be arbitrarily placed in secure family detention centers. While mothers and children may be released or detained, it is common practice for fathers to be separated from their families.

For example, a young couple from Michoacán, Mexico fled to the United States after their children were threatened by organized crime cartels. They were immediately separated after presenting themselves to U.S. border officials. The mother and her two young sons were released to a family friend while the father was locked up. Both received denials of credible fear by officials and were readied for deportation. Fortunately, because of a previous crime that had been committed against them in the United States, our team recognized that the entire family could be eligible for immigration relief. We filed a stay of removal to effectively stop their deportation as we explored legal relief based on the crime. The mother's stay of removal was granted; this stay included her two children. The father's stay was denied over a long holiday weekend and he was deported in the middle of the night before we were properly notified of the denial. After a difficult time raising two children without a work permit, the mother abandoned her pending relief and chose to be deported to join her husband abroad. This is not an uncommon story. Often wives that have been separated from their husbands suffer trying to raise their children alone while their partner is locked up with little chance of being released. The government is essentially separating families.

This past summer our concerns over family separation grew more urgent. We learned that mothers were being separated from their young children. It became clear immigration authorities would not necessarily keep mothers and children together. Instead, the government is essentially creating unaccompanied minors. Children who are U.S. citizens were deported or placed in the custody of state Child Protective Services

When asylum seekers are treated in ways that contribute to traumatization, it is difficult for them to continue their cases. Abuse in detention is prevalent, and the use of solitary confinement for an asylum seeker can have devastating effects. While there are some refugees who say they would rather be detained than be back in their home countries, many detainees get to a point where they state that they would rather go back to certain death than continue to be robbed of their liberty and dignity.

Social Work Refugee Project

Several nonprofit agencies in El Paso serve migrants and refugees. Since immigrants do not qualify for state or federal benefits, NGOs, and church-affiliated organizations have extended services such as respite care, hospitality, legal advocacy, travel assistance, and shelter. UTEP partners with several such organizations as part of its work in community-engaged scholarship and service-learning. Among the agencies with which we have worked are Las Americas Immigrant Advocacy Center, Paso del Norte Civil Rights Project, Diocesan Migrant and Refugee Services, Annunciation House, and Centro Sin Fronteras Farm Workers Project. Over the past decade, we have placed dozens of graduate and undergraduate students as interns, volunteers, and service learners in these settings. While each student's tasks and duties may vary considerably per angecy placement, one thing the students' experinces have in common is that in each setting, students are within close proximity with refugees and migrants. These experiences afford them the opportunity to "accompany the migrant" and to be fully present with each individual throughout their respective journey. Students who engage with the migrant report that they are enriched by the stories and narratives of people who are still on their journey toward safety and family. They recount how they were moved and changed by witnessing these testimonies.

In our project, we place students in service-learning settings to work directly with migrants and refugees over the course of one semester. They carry out supportive functions at shelters and direct service agencies that work with migrants and asylum seekers. While they may perform basic functions in the placement such as making beds, preparing food, and connecting guest to relatives by telephone, they are instructed to "accompany the refugee" by engaging them directly in open-ended conversations that use appreciative listening. In one class, their assignment has been:

> "The student will engage clients as a community-engaged volunteer providing service to
> and "accompanying" the client, migrant, and worker. This engagement includes focused
> conversations with clients to more fully understand their trajectories in the context of

their identity, culture, class, oppression and other elements of intersectional experience. Students will know the guests with an eye to deepening their understanding of people in the context of place in their life journey as framed in that person's narrative. Students will engage the client as meaningfully and deeply as time permits so that while proving the services that are offered by each agency, students are also encountering clients in an authentic way that is informed by their individual stories and aspirations within an overarching system of exclusion."

Students are fully present as resources, witnesses and temporary companions. In this way, they go beyond the utilitarian functions of a volunteer caseworker. Students come away from this experience with an expanded view of their place in the world and how they can make a difference. It connects them with a part of their community that heretofore had been known only at a distance and too often through the background narratives of exclusion and xenophobia.

What Were the Impacts of This Community Engagement?

Students

Engaging in service-learning with migrants has a high impact on student learning because it places students in a setting that is completely alien to them prior to this opportunity. For most Americans, refugees are people seen on television living in desolate camps in Turkey, Jordan, Greece, or Afghanistan. They are a distant problem that seemingly does not affect them unless a politician attempts to demonize the migrant by associating them with terrorism or some scheme in which they are a threat to national security. In those places where pockets of refugees have relocated, too often that have been comparatively isolated from the mainstream and shunned by nationalists and xenophobes. In contrast, a service-learning project that entails a sustained commitment through a semester to work alongside refugee migrants presents an unparalleled opportunity to know "the other"—put a human face in place of a stereotype or caricature and to hear a genuine testimony of the migrant as opposed to a manufactured political myth. The best antidote to prejudice and misunderstanding is cultural exposure and friendship. As much as racism is contagious, so is acceptance. To become a companion and act as a witness for the refugee is to grow closer to others, to experience their lives, to expand one's world, and to close the divides and break down walls between people. Such experiences can be transformative and life changing. Much like study abroad, service-learning with refugees and migrants exposes students to completely different human experiences than their own, and challenges their assumptions to the core.

Feliza Galindo, a service-learning student who worked with refugees said:

"My experience as a student doing research with and accompanying the migrant refugee has taught me that some of people that I had the opportunity to interview had been the victims of inconceivable violence. Still they remained hopeful of a better future and made the dangerous journey north to start over. There are certainly other factors contributing to the influx of desperate human beings who are risking their lives, and even the lives of their beloved children, to cross the border into the US. This experience changed me. I learned about how all of us can be vulnerable at any point in our life as a result of working with migrants and refugees."

I think service-learning i s an important part a college education because service-learning projects can be life changing for students. They learn empathy for others, and may even get the real life experience they need which will inspire them to find a career. Reflective practice makes the experience much richer because it means that the students and teachers have to think about the larger world outside of the classroom. It also offers the opportunity to learn how to make the next service-learning experience better."

Students in these settings said that they learned new skills and acquired new perspectives. A number commented on how their listening skills have improved as they learn to focus intently as people unveiled the narrative of their journey - in other words they learned appreciative listening in which they affirmed and reflected on the stories that they witnessed. Students also expressed that they were humbled by the strength, resiliency, and resolve of the people and families with whom they spoke. They learned the value of *cultural humility*. Others recounted how their need to "fix things" and "problem solve" got in the way of simply being available to someone and yet they learned the skill of empowering the refugee simply by accepting and validating their presence. Several students observed that their preconceived ideas about migrants dissolved in the face of the reality they witnessed in shelters and agencies.

Students also have commented on the value of service-learning and of getting off-campus to engage the community. Students have also commented on the value of service-learning and getting off campus to engage the community

> "(Service-learning) . . . is a teaching and learning strategy that integrates meaningful community service with reflection to enrich the learning experience and to strengthen communities."

> "(Service-learning) . . . makes me want to open myself up to other experiences outside of my current spheres of knowledge. It has struck a desire in me to want to seek ways to help others more freely and in a giving way."

> "(Service-learning) . . . is important because it allows students to have a longer-term involvement in the community as opposed to a one time volunteer opportunity, and an opportunity to learn from people with stories and histories that are unlike their own."

Community

Nonprofits and NGOs in the greater El Paso region tend to be overloaded with responsibilities and are under-resourced. The presence of a major state university with more than 23,000 students is a resource to them in many ways. Agencies that serve migrants in the US–Mexico border region are particularly challenged and poorly funded as the city is in a comparatively low-income region and migrants, documented or not, do not qualify for federal or state support. In weeks when federal officials released as many as 500 refugees and asylum applicants a week into El Paso, local organizations such as the Annunciation House had to find temporary shelter and travel assistance for them as they prepared to journey onward to meet up with family or friends in the nation's interior. For the past three decades, the Annunciation House, Las Americas Immigrant Advocacy Services, and related agencies have served this population with no government funding by relying on private donations of time and resources. This effort requires an extensive network of trained volunteers at a number of parishes and congregations throughout the city who are willing to host migrant guests for a few days or longer. University students are a major source of support as they are placed in these agencies as volunteers and service learners.

Most importantly, the community is providing a service to the migrants, who without respite and assistance would be released into the streets and bus stations to navigate a foreign country unsupported and without money, guidance, food, housing, or social assistance. Refugees who have been at great risk on their journeys arrive at these shelters and smile with relief at the warm reception they receive at churches and parish halls. Many weep with joy and relief.

What Were Some of the Challenges?

Sustainable community partnerships must be able to build relationships of trust as their clients are vulnerable, at serious risk, and have had traumatic or adverse experiences. There are an enormous privacy issues to be considered in service-learning and engagement in settings that serve refugees or other individuals who are at risk of official or unofficial retaliation. Community partners need to be reassured that faculty and students will be respectful of client privacy and observe safety rules, particularly with families and children. We found that agencies were more open to university partners when we approach them by considering their agencies needs above our own. Too often agencies in college towns have witnessed researchers and students who come into an agency to collect data or to complete a course assignment without considering the priorities and needs of the agency, particularly given that agencies must invest time and effort to orient and train students and faculty mentors upfront. We developed relationships with care and patience, cognizant that they must be mutually beneficial for them to be sustainable.

Moving Forward: Implications for Service-Learning

Recommendations for Faculty

The implication of service-learning with refugees as a high-impact educational practice is that much is to be learned from purposefully engaging with people whose experiences are distinctly different from their own with respect to privilege, exposure to hardship, trauma, adversity, discrimination, and exclusion. While many college students have struggled in their lives with economic, personal and familial challenges, there is benefit to be gained by engaging with individuals whose experiences make one's own pale by comparison. We can think of a number of examples of groups that students might engage to leave their comfort zone and plunge into other worlds of experience, such as with veterans who have experienced multiple deployments, survivors of intimate partner violence, hospice clients, persons in recovery, LGBT foster youth aging out of the system, migrant farm workers, and others whose coping skills are challenged by remarkable circumstances. What one learns in such setting can tell us much about the human capacity to overcome life challenges through resilience, accommodation, and cultural assets.

Recommendations for Students

Our experience indicates that if students are well prepared, working with vulnerable populations can be transformative and contribute to personal growth. This is particularly so for individuals who are preparing for careers in the helping professions such as psychology, social work, nursing, medicine, counseling, and related fields. Yet at the same time, working with these populations require seriousness and maturity so that one can use emotional regulation to maintain boundaries. By this we mean that vulnerable populations require delicate and careful interactions that always emphasize that well-being of the client over the provider.

It can be stressful and frustrating to work with vulnerable populations. Many refugees have said to us that when they arrived in the United States, they traded one hell for another. By this they mean that the circumstances they fled were singularly awful, but in many cases the way in which they have been received in this country by border enforcement officials and the general public has often been worse. Knowing that most refugees will be deported can be demoralizing for students and others who serve them. It requires some degree of fortitude and boundary maintenance to remain hopeful and generous. Similarly, students placed in agencies that serve survivors of intimate partner violence are often frustrated when victims remain with their abusive partner. Working in settings like this necessitates a nonjudgmental attitude and acceptance of client wishes. Yet, when placed on a balance, working with vulnerable populations can be a life-changing experience.

Recommendations for Community

University faculty who place students in social service and health settings can be frustrated when they learn that their students are often engaged in work that is seemingly unrelated to their curriculum or major. Students and faculty may fail to understand that the agency needs many types of work to be done to complete its mission, which may include routine and menial tasks. Yet community partners would do well to consider that each student has learning objectives associated with their service-learning project, which may require some accommodation by the agency for it to be mutually beneficial to both partners. There may be writing assignments, homework, or class presentations as part of the project. While the faculty member needs to explain these expectations in advance and assure that the needs of the agency are also being met, being cognizant of student learning objectives, work schedules, assignment due dates, and academic calendars is critical to the long-term viability of a continuing service-learning partnership.

Conclusion

If higher education has been pulled away from the traditions of civic engagement, public service and community service by careerism and a shift of universities toward research, countervailing forces such as service-learning and community-engaged scholarship are doing much to reverse this. Campus Compact, the Kellogg Foundation, and organizations like the Engagement Scholarship Consortium are working to restore the public mission of the university by advancing student and faculty community and civic engagement (Campus Compact 2017). Service-learning, particularly with vulnerable international groups, is one strategy in the toolbox of universities that seek to advance student engagement and social justice awareness in a diverse nation. This is particularly true when set against the current backdrop of nativism and xenophobia. At the UTEP, our service-learning project with Central American and Mexican refugees is one small effort to prepare students for democratic and global citizenship by working toward the public good through service to vulnerable migrants and refugees.

References

Campus Compact. (2017). Retrieved from www.compact.org

Lemieux, C. M. & Allen, P. D. (2013). Service learning in social work education: The state knowledge, pedagogical practicalities and practice conundrums. *Journal of Social Work Education*, 43(2), 309–326.

UNHCR (2017). Figures at a Glance. New York: United Nations High Commission on Refugees. Retrieved from http://www.unhcr.org/en-us/figures-at-a-glance.html

Selected Readings

Hope Border Institute. (2017). Discretion to deny. El Paso: Hope Border Institute. Retrieved from http://www.hopeborder.org/discretion-to-deny

Lusk, M. & Chavez, S. (2016). Mental health and the role of culture and resilience in refugees fleeing violence. *Environment and Social Psychology*, 2(1), 1–13.

Lusk, M., McCallister, J. & Villalobos, G. (2013), Mental health sequelae of migration among Mexican refugees. *Social Development Issues*. 35(3), 1–17.

Lusk, M. & Villalobos, G. (2012). Testimonio de Eva: A Mexican refugee in El Paso." *Journal of Borderland Studies*, 27(1), 17–25.

Quaye, S. J. & Harper, S. R. (2015). *Student Engagement in Higher Education: Theoretical Perspectives and Practical Approaches for Diverse Populations*. New York: Routledge.

Selected Resources

United Nations High Commission on Refugees

The largest and most comprehensive website of information, news and statistics on refugees worldwide. http://www.unhcr.org/

Center for Migration Studies

A website that includes a thorough array of research, news, publications and policy analyses of migration. http://cmsny.org/

Discussion Questions

1) The national narrative on immigration has become increasingly unwelcoming to immigrants in its tone. The rhetoric of elected officials is often xenophobic and nationalistic. Give the country's long and rich history of immigration, how does one account for the current tenor of national discourse on immigration?

2) How can the experience of working with vulnerable groups such as refugees, people in violent relationships, people who have survived serious crimes, individuals with mental disorders, or other at-risk populations be of benefit to the growth and development of students in the helping professions?

3) Are American universities too preoccupied with training people for the workforce? Do colleges have a public obligation to serve the greater good, to promote civic action, and to foster social justice? If so, how can this be incorporated into the university's mission and curriculum?

Women's Studies

Chapter 21

Project-Based Learning in an Introductory Course Setting

Naomi Fertman

COLLABORATIVE
ASSIGNMENTS AND PROJECTS

SERVICE LEARNING,
COMMUNITY-BASED LEARNING

LEARNING COMMUNITIES

Use these questions to guide your reflection prior to reading the chapter. Use the notes/follow-up section to write your thoughts after you have read the chapter. Your notes can include thoughts in reference to the reflection questions, or general observations about the chapter.

1) Think of a project that you either completed on your own or as a member of a team that you are most proud of. What ultimately made you proud of the project, whether it was the process, outcome or something else?

2) What kind of community engagement projects would you associate with a Women's Studies course? How would you go about establishing or designing such projects or activities?

3) Thinking about your own personal strengths. What kind of project would allow you to contribute your favorite or strongest skills and knowledge? What would it take to establish or implement this project?

Notes/Follow-up:

_____

_____

_____

_____

_____

Introduction

Project-based learning is a familiar method in upper level and more advanced courses; it is less often used in introductory courses. This high-impact practice has enormous value at every level and is worth incorporating in introductory classes in particular because of the remarkable impact and special opportunities to benefit students, faculty, and academic departments.

Students take introductory courses for a variety of reasons. Some students are taking necessary steps towards completing their majors or minors; some students are interested in a course subject but have no plans to major or minor in that field, some students have been guided into the class by a well-meaning advisor, and some students are simply trying to fill a hole in an already chaotic schedule.

Students in introductory courses are often early in their college careers and searching for an academic community as well as a potential social community that will support them. They are frequently looking for meaning and purpose in their academic field of choice, as well as searching out mentorship and relationships to help them build their professional skill sets.

Whatever brings students into an introductory classroom, from the professor's perspective, it's a chance to engage them in the topic and encourage them to take more courses within that discipline. From an academic program or department's perspective, it's a chance to bring more majors or minors into the field. Implementing a project-based learning method with a community-based component in an introductory course can achieve all of these goals—and add value to a class which may otherwise be forgotten.

My use of project-based learning has evolved from my personal experience with experiential and outdoor education, beginning with my undergraduate education. As a student I had the opportunity to minor in outdoor education as well as participate in two National Outdoor Leadership School courses. All of these experiences were essential to my belief in experiential learning and its academic power. Being fully engaged and actively interacting with the subject I was studying gave me more connection to the material. Experiential learning taught me to think critically, to push my own academic boundaries, and to want to connect beyond the classroom.

Following graduation, I worked as an outdoor educator off and on for 6 years working with students in an outdoor setting shaped my way of understanding how students learn. The outdoor education model allowed students to walk away with a host of skills far beyond what they—or I—had initially anticipated. This approach taught them to face adversity with strength, helped them to build community, gave them confidence, and instilled in them a sense of self-esteem that would be challenging to gain in any other setting. I loved seeing my students shine in this setting.

When I began as a full time lecturer at the university in Women's and Gender Studies (WGS) I noticed that students in the traditional classroom were not gaining the skill sets or the confidence that my outdoor education students developed. While some of this was to be expected (as the expectations for a college education are very different), I was continuously disappointed by what I saw as a lack of opportunity for my students to engage. Implementing high-impact project-based learning practices in community settings has been mine and my university students' bridge to the proverbial 'great out of doors'. This model allowed my university students to achieve successes in self-esteem, confidence, community building, critical thinking, and overcoming adversity in the same way that the outdoor education approach did for my previous students.

Case Study

Bella, Victor, Audrey, and Lia were students enrolled in an Introduction to Women's Studies (WS) course, they teamed up at the beginning of the semester to address the issue of sexual assault for high-school women. They decided that their response to the problem would be to teach a self-defense class to a group of women in this age range. They connected with an all-women's youth group that was looking for community-based education on a range of topics. Initially, the project group members, focused their energy on learning self-defense techniques. The more they researched sexual assault within the high-school population, the more they learned about the problem. At the outset, they had believed that rape by strangers and sexual assaults were the main concerns with this population. As they researched, students unearthed the more significant concerns: intimate partner violence, lack of knowledge about consent, and pressures to be involved in sexual relationships at an early age with little or no education about healthy sexuality. They shifted the focus from self-defense to education about consent and general self-esteem building as they planned what to teach the high-school students.

Near the end of the semester, WS students spent an evening with the youth group. They did teach them a few self-defense moves, but focused most of their energy on the bigger underlying issues facing women and girls in dating relationships. At the end of the evening the WS students provided high-school girls with follow up resources. The results were positive. The high-school students filled out a short survey that confirmed that they had understood what the group was sharing and that they felt empowered to speak up about these issues within their own relationships. The youth group leader was thrilled and gave the university students lots of positive feedback.

This group of WS students was proud of their work. As they shared their experiences and conclusions during the class presentation, it became clear that their learnings were on many levels. In exploring violence against high-school women, they came to recognize their own inaccurate, preconceived notions and understand more precisely the real issues and needs of this age group. In addition, and perhaps more importantly, they recognized, that they had chosen to talk to the women, the victims, rather than the men. The group established that in retrospect, they might have had more impact if they had directed their interventions to the young men, who are generally the perpetrators of said violence, instead of the women. They acknowledged that if their interest was in countering sexual assault in high-school-aged women, the best approach might have been to attempt to prevent the assault before it started.

History of the Practice

Project-based learning dates back to the 1920s. William Heard Kilpatrick (1921), the champion of the practice, supported the concept that experiences (unto themselves) are the heart of project-based and effective learning and teaching strategies. Adderly (1975) solidified the key components of Kirkpatrick's concept into a working definition of project-based learning to include the following:

> (1) [Projects] involve the solution of a problem; often, though not necessarily, set by the student himself [or herself]; (2) They involve initiative by the student or group of students, and necessitate a variety of educational activities; (3) They commonly result in an end product (e.g., thesis, report, design plans, computer program and model); (4) Work often goes on for a considerable length of time; (5) Teaching staff are involved in an advisory, rather than authoritarian, role at any or all of the stages - initiation, conduct and conclusion.

Project-based learning has evolved to incorporate a more Problem-based Learning Model, one which puts the problem being solved at the core of the project. More recently Laura, Päivi, and Erkki, (2006) have defined the combination of project and problem-based learning with more equal emphasis on the defining and understanding of the problem to be studied and working towards a completed finished product.

Project-based learning has been used in college classrooms as an effective model for promoting engagement, understanding and self-efficacy in students. A simple search through academic journals suggests that this model is used mostly in STEM field classrooms. The challenge in utilizing this model in a humanities course lies in understanding the strength of the model, the history of it's usage, and the ability to apply the concepts (albeit loosely at times) into projects that would engage, challenge and empower my students.

What Made This High-Impact Practice Successful?

Getting students to take what they learn in the classroom and transfer it into the community is challenging, but worth the work. There are a number of things that contribute to the success of the project:

- **Course set up.** Setting fixed due dates for critical components of the project throughout the semester allows students to see the project as a process and move through each section in a timely manner. Including the dates for group formation, proposal submission, service-learning engagement training, making contacts with your community partners and check ins with the instructor are all key for student success.
- **Immediate implementation.** Start on day one. It is easy to get waylaid by the fear that starting a project early in the semester will mean that the students are unprepared for the work. Much of the success of this project depends on students having the time to build student communities, connect to their passions, and develop and complete a project within the all-too-short semester. Trust that the students are ready to start working on day one of the semester.
- **Make passion the driver.** Encourage students to focus on project topics that they are connected to and passionate about. This allows them to build on their interests and areas of expertise, and increases likelihood of follow through and the level of commitment needed to complete their work.
- **Engage with all on campus resources.** Make efforts to connect to every resource available to faculty, staff, and students who are doing service-learning and project-based learning more specifically.
- **Give the students an opportunity to shine.** Bringing in other faculty or classmates at the culmination of the project showcases their hard work, reinforces their commitment and deepens their sense of pride and accomplishment. The majority of student projects will culminate in some type of a presentation or program, for example, teaching a self-defense class, providing information at a health fair, facilitating a class, etc. Showing up at these events helps with the project assessment as well as providing some extra support and encouragement to students in what may feel to them like a stressful moment.

What Were Some of the Challenges?

Anybody who attempts a project-based model with a community organization in an introductory course is going to face a host of challenges. Students' knowledge, potential lack of community and educational resources, and students' inability to commit to out of class work are just a few of the hurdles that any professor will face in the implementation of this type of project. The key to success is having confidence that the outcome is well worth the work—for both the student and the instructor- and the willingness to push forward in spite of the difficulties.

The initial and continued challenge with this population is out of class time commitments. Students are busy! A group project model has the double struggle of coordinating group members' schedules as well as coordinating time to be involved with an organization. As noted earlier, the best way to manage this is to get the students involved from the first day of class. If the students can understand the time commitment at the outset they can manage their schedules and set up the work around their other activities.

Managing student expectations and creating realistic projects can be another challenge. At the beginning of the semester students often set lofty project goals that are not realistic, although they may not be able to see this at the time. When students create unrealistic projects that involve community organizations, they not only let themselves down, they also let down their community contacts. A well thought out project proposal with substantial instructor input is the best way to manage these expectations. Quality over quantity has been an effective rallying cry with my students. Helping students understand that 2–3 hours of quality work with a group is more impactful than five missed attempts has been imperative.

The High Impact Practice Process

The project plays out in four steps: Project Development, Proposal, Implementation, and Evaluation/Presentation. The steps are outlined below and specific examples of materials given to students are included in the Appendix.

Step 1 Project Development

An integral part of the project is getting the students established in project groups during the initial weeks of the course. In an introductory course setting, many students are incoming first or second year students. In the state university where I teach, many of these students, at this early stage in their university careers, lack academic and social support from their college peers. A strong project group allows them to develop supportive bonds that will unite them throughout the project and that are likely to last beyond the classroom.

The initial 3 weeks of the introductory course are spent helping the students understand their own perspectives and historical connections to the issues. This is achieved through a written autobiographical essay assignment and subsequent in-class discussions and activities aimed at getting to know their peers and understand their shared interests and concerns. During this 3-week period the students work in constantly changing small groups as they complete in-class work. The combination of the personal writing exercises and the small group discussions allows the students time to connect to their peers and identify similar issues that they would like to focus on with their projects. At the completion of this phase, students have self-selected in small groups (3-5 students) and have decided on a problem that they are interested in responding too.

Step 2 Project Proposal

Students use weeks 3 through week 5 of the semester to complete their project proposals. The proposal assignment is included in the Appendix of this chapter. During the proposal period, students develop their core project ideas and identify the specific population that they will work with. For many students, identifying the target population is a major challenge. It is frequently hard for students to connect with a group of people in need of short term support. This is especially challenging when students identify a problem (such as lack of sex education to LGBTQI youth) that is not being responded to in any larger scale models.

To help the students with this step, I encourage them to look at the assets they have in their groups. To support them, I help them answer the following questions:

- Do they feel comfortable presenting to other college students?
- Do they have skills they believe they can teach other people?

I also ask the students to consider what kinds of community connections they each bring to the group project:

- Which of them goes to a church that has a youth group?
- Who is a member of a sorority or fraternity?

- What college resources are available to them to help them connect with the community?
- What projects are already being done that may benefit from collaboration?

The project proposal period is the most challenging phase of the project. It is during this period, that students need the most guidance and assistance. Class time must be reserved to address student concerns.

Step 3 Implementation

This phase lasts from week 6 through week 13 of the course and is the most exciting time. Students go out into their greater communities and complete their projects. There is frequently a lot of joy and energy during this phase. Students are connecting with other people, feeling empowered, and are proud of themselves. Of course, not all students are successful. This is when teammates not pulling their weight and busy schedules can disrupt a group's plan. I encourage my students to call on me as much as necessary during this phase. I can help them by doing a final edit on a handout they will be providing or by offering feedback on a presentation they are planning.

Step 4 Evaluation/Presentation

At the end of the course, students must complete two final steps to receive credit for their projects. The first is a presentation to their classmates during the final week of classes. The presentation outline is included in the Appendix. These presentations have proven to be inspirational, building pride in the work they have completed. Many are empowered by the experience and are eager to share it with others. The second and final step in the project is an individual essay (the essay assignment is included in the Appendix). The essay gives the instructor an opportunity to evaluate the way the student has connected the academic learning from the classroom with the practical application through the project.

Recommendation for Faculty

Implementing a project that incorporates community organizations and service-learning is a daunting task. Many campuses have programs that are set up to support service-learning and community engagement. Partnering with a support network of this nature can be hugely beneficial. Campus resources that work extensively with service-learning can offer support through tracking student service hours and helping to facilitate meaningful reflection at the close of the semester.

I use an additional assignment to assess my students' project learning at the end of the semester (rather than taking a final exam): the written essay. The written essay asks students to contextualize how the key concepts that were learned in the classroom played out in their projects. For example, in the case of Women's and Gender Studies, I review their essays looking at lenses of oppression and intersectionality of feminist perspectives specifically.

Recommendations for Students

Time management is key when working with project-based learning in community settings. With a long-term project of this nature, it is ideal to set up a timeline early in the semester. That should include what each member of the group will do and when each person will complete that work. I encourage my students to complete the project by the 12th week in a 16-week term. This gives them a few weeks of wiggle room if, and when, they fall behind.

In addition, it can be easy at the start of any project for students to dream big and set unrealistic expectations for themselves and their project mates. It is important to remind students to under promise and over deliver. They can almost always do more in the moment than they originally planned. They need to make sure they complete any project or commitment made to an organization. Big or small, other people are depending on them to follow through.

Recommendations for Community

Community organizations have a lot to gain from working with students. Students can bring energy, creative ideas, and other resources that organizations may benefit from. Community organizations that commit to taking on student collaboration should be open to the needs and challenges that the students bring and should be prepared to offer some support.

Community organizations can help facilitate a positive relationship with their students by being flexible and patient. While it is important to have high expectations for students, it is also important to be realistic. You can minimize struggles with student collaborators by making a mutually beneficial work plan at the onset of the project. Work with the students to set a realistic time line and let the students know when you will be available. It may also be helpful to set an expectation for how you will communicate, for example, if it usually takes you a week to return emails, be honest with students about that timeline.

Conclusion

Project-based learning can be applied in a multitude of course settings and across a multitude of disciplines. These types of projects seem especially relevant in the liberal arts and humanities fields. They are particularly effective in courses which may not have a lab type component and may subsequently lack some type of tangible practical application.

When using project-based learning in the community setting, it is easy to get caught up in the idea that the work that students do may have a serious impact on the community/organization/ group that they are working with. Making sure to keep the expectation of a modest impact for both the community group and the students is important. If all goes as planned, the students will offer something to the community that they may not have otherwise had access to. And of course, not everything will go as planned. There is an abundance of learning for the students and the community group in a noble failure. The students' ability to successfully complete a long-term project designed to respond to a problem that they feel passionate about, will ultimately benefit them in a multitude of ways. Students will make a practical connection to an academic concept and have contacts in the community that they may not have had previously.

Project-Based Learning and Service-Learning are both high impact practices. They have the potential to add value and depth to academic courses across disciplines. While previously only considered for upper division courses, there are many benefits to adding these learning models to your introductory courses. With planning and support, students have the ability to rise to the challenge. In the end, the connections students make with other students, faculty, and community organizations will have long-term effects that may benefit them throughout their academic careers and beyond.

References

Adderley, K. (1975) *Project Methods in Higher Education*. SRHE Working Party on Teaching Methods: Techniques Group. Guildford, Surrey: Society for Research Into Higher Education.

Kilpatrick, W. H. (1921). Dangers and difficulties of the project method and how to overcome them: Introductory statement and definition of terms. *Teachers College Record, 22*(4), 283–288.

Laura, H., Päivi, T., & Erkki, O. (2006). Project-Based Learning in Post-Secondary Education: Theory, Practice and Rubber Sling Shots. *Higher Education*, (2), 287.

APPENDIX

Project Proposal due Week 6

The proposal should be 2/3 pages. The explanation of the problem (listed below as number 2) and the explanation of how you will assess your project (number 5) need to be written in narrative form. Sections 3 and 4 can be charts, diagrams, or bullets as needed. You must include all sections to receive credit and to be granted permission to move forward with the project.

1. Project name and name of participants.
2. An explanation of what the problem your group is addressing. The more specific you can be in identifying the problem the better. An example of a problem that women might be facing is, sexual violence on college campuses. Please note how the problem includes a specific group and a specific geographic location. While this may not be relevant for all problems, please consider the ways that you can "narrow" your problem. If you are unsure of how to do this, please talk to me ASAP.
3. You can use the chart "Five Faces of Oppression" on page 53 of your text as another reference point for understanding the problem within a specific population.
4. A step-by-step layout of how you plan to address the problem through your group project. I want to know how you are planning to complete this project (you can include a chart/graph/diagram to illustrate your points). For example, If you are going to be giving a presentation to a group of high-school students you should think about all of the things that need to happen to be ready for the presentation and include these in the step-by-step plan.
5. A time line of when the work will be done and a description of what each member of the group will contribute to the project. I want to know how each person will be contributing to the success of this project. I do not expect you to do everything together (in fact that is generally inefficient and not helpful in the long run), but I do expect each person in the group to take an active role in the work, learning and eventual completion of the project. As you create your timeline remember that your group must present the project during week 14 of the class. That means that you need the project to be completely finished by that time.

An explanation of how you will assess your project and know whether or not you were successful. There are a number of things that you can consider when talking about project success. If you are hoping to raise awareness about an issue, then handing out a certain number of flyers, or talking to a certain number of people at a tabling session may be an effective measurement for gaging success. Please be aware that handing out a survey with questions like "were you a victim of sexual assault?" is not appropriate for this pro

End of Semester Essay

In addition to the work that you have completed with your activism project you will submit an individual essay that ties your out of class work to our in-class learning. This paper is a combination of analysis and reflection. Throughout the entire essay, you should be applying the ideas, terms, and theories that we have discussed throughout the semester.

You must use three sources in this essay. One of those sources must be our course text. There is no limit to the number of sources you may use for this assignment. Acceptable sources for this assignment are peer reviewed articles, textbooks, and academic/professional websites. You are also welcome to use one audio visual site (a podcast/documentary or news story). This audiovisual site can count as one of your three sources.

Your paper should be written in APA format. It needs to be double spaced and written in 12pt font. You must include a cover page and a reference page. You need to use in-text citations. The paper needs to be a minimum of four pages of text (this does not include your cover page and reference page).

Your paper should be broken into four sections:

Section 1: In the first section of the paper, you must identify the problem your project addressed and contextualize the issue in your community. You must cite at least two sources in this section of the paper that are not your textbook

Section 2: In the second section of the paper, you need to analyze the work you were attempting to complete using feminist perspectives on power and oppression. In this section you should consider who is affected by your identified problem and the way that group is affected by power and oppression issues. You must use your text as a source for this section. You are also welcome to bring in other sources but it is not mandatory.

Section 3: In the 3rd section of your paper, you need to assess your project as a form of social advocacy. In this section you need to think about the action piece your group worked on. Please consider how your project was empowering (to you, to your group members, to your target population and to the community at large). You must use your text as a source for this section. You are also welcome to bring in other sources but it is not mandatory.

Section 4: The final part of the paper is a reflection of your learning from the project. You do not need to include citations in this section. Please answer the following: What is one thing you learned from completing this project? In what ways were you challenged? In what ways did completing this project challenge any preconceived ideas you may have had about the problem your project was addressing and the women who may be experiencing that "problem".

Author Biographies

Isabel Baca

Isabel Baca, PhD, is an associate professor of rhetoric and writing studies in the Department of English at the University of Texas at El Paso. Her research focuses on service-learning in writing studies and across the curriculum and on community writing and bilingual professional communication. Baca has been a service-learning practitioner and advocate for over 20 years, and she directs the Department of English Community Writing Partners Program for which she recruited over 20 nonprofit organizations to work as agency mentors for students. Her major publication, *Service-learning and Writing: Paving the Way for Literacy(ies) through Community Engagement* (2012), contributes to the fields of rhetoric, writing studies, and education. Baca is a 2017 University of Texas System Board of Regents' Outstanding Teaching Award recipient.

Susan Brown

Susan W. Brown, PhD, is the interim associate dean of research for the New Mexico State University College of Education and the director of the STEM Outreach Center, which has provided support for K-12 STEM education for almost two decades. Her research focus is quality science education and the underrepresentation of minority students and women in the fields of science, math, technology, and engineering. She has received multiple and prestigious awards and millions in external funding to pursue this focus. Her efforts have provided understanding of and enjoyment with STEM education for tens of thousands of children in New Mexico through the after-school and summer active learning programs.

Amy Canales

Amy Canales is employed by STEMscopes providing STEM professional development in Texas and New Mexico. She has been a teacher, district science coordinator, a district early childhood facilitator, and was assistant director of curriculum and instruction for elementary science during this project where she oversaw curriculum, provided professional development, and directed STEM grant initiatives.

Elizabeth Camacho

Elizabeth Camacho is an assistant professor in the Clinical Laboratory Sciences Program at the University of Texas at El Paso (UTEP). She has a master of arts in teaching and is a medical technologist with a molecular certificate. She is responsible for coordinating clinical laboratory science student clinical preceptorship experiences with regional hospitals and engages in a number of service-based activities with the students to provide health screenings throughout the community. Through these experiences, the students are provided with mechanisms for practical application of their knowledge and leadership training while fostering empathy, compassion, and an understanding of the importance of service.

Silvia Chávez-Baray

Silvia M. Chávez-Baray, PhD, is a lecturer and a postdoctoral student in the Department of Social Work in the College of Health Sciences at the University of Texas at El Paso. Her research focuses on mental health, intimate partner violence, and sexual and reproductive health in Hispanic migrants. She utilizes service-learning practices with social work students, community partners, and community health workers to engage in community-engaged scholarship and psychoeducational programs.

Monica Galindo Chavez

Monica Galindo Chavez is an instructional coordinator for the El Paso Independent School District who ensured that middle school science teachers across the region were trained in the environmental curriculum and provided the resources to implement the lessons. She presented the culmination of this work at the 2014 NAAEE Conference. She has also served the El Paso District for 18 years as a biology teacher, a science coach, and science facilitator.

Jennifer Clifton

Jennifer Clifton, PhD, is an assistant professor of rhetoric and writing studies in the Department of English at The University of Texas at El Paso. She is the author of *Argument as Dialogue Across Difference: Engaging Youth in Public Literacies* and co-author of *Dialoguing Across Cultures, Identities, and Learning: Crosscurrents and Complexities in Literacy Classrooms.*

Irasema Coronado

Irasema Coronado, PhD, is a professor of political science at the University of Texas at El Paso, where she holds the Kruszewski Family Endowed Professorship. Coronado's binational research agenda focuses on the politics of the US–Mexico border with a focus on civil and human rights of immigrants and deportees. She has incorporated service-learning in her teaching as a way to engage students in community affairs and to enhance democracy; she has partnered with numerous civil and human rights organizations throughout the US–Mexico border region.

Sandor Dorgo

Sandor Dorgo, PhD, is an associate professor of kinesiology and graduate coordinator of health sciences and nursing at the University of Texas at El Paso. His research focus is on aging and physical activity, strength and conditioning, and physical training modalities. He has been teaching courses in higher education for about 20 years. He was in charge of designing, implementing, and teaching the undergraduate curriculum capstone course in kinesiology; he has taught this course for ten semesters. During this time, he established the capstone course fieldwork experience for students that he organizes and supervises along with the new course instructor, which is built on collaborative efforts with city departments and nonprofit organizations. He has received multiple recognitions for his work, including the Paso Del Norte Institute for Healthy Living 1st Annual Healthy Eating Active Living Hero Award, El Paso, Texas, in 2017; the President's Recognition of the Leadership of the Physical Fitness in the Golden Age Program in 2016; and the University of Texas System Regents' Outstanding Teaching Award (ROTA) in 2015.

Lucía Durá

Dr. Lucía Durá is program director and assistant professor of rhetoric and writing studies in the English department at The University of Texas at El Paso (UTEP). Her work on positive deviance, intercultural communication, and participatory methodologies focuses on understanding and leveraging the assets of vulnerable populations to solve complex problems. To do this work, she collaborates with local and global organizations including the Housing Authority of the City of El Paso, Creative Kids, the YWCA, Project Vida, Save the Children, and Minga Perú. She was a UTEP nominee for the UT System Regent's Outstanding Teaching Award in 2016 and is the author of numerous publications, including the following, which are relevant to high-impact practices.

Carla Ellis

Carla Ellis has a master's degree in nursing and is a registered nurse in the School of Nursing at the University of Texas at El Paso. She primarily teaches community and public health nursing and mentors students on successfully passing their board examinations after graduation. She uses the service-learning model as a project in class at various venues to promote strong positive nursing attitudes in the area of community service among the graduating seniors. Ellis was accepted as co-presenter on relevance and use of health fairs as a course project in the curriculum at the International Sigma Theta Tau Nursing Honors Society Conference in Dublin, Ireland.

Naomi Fertman

Naomi Fertman has a master's degree in public health and a master's degree in social work. She is a faculty lecturer with the Women's and Gender Studies Program at the University of Texas at El Paso. She works with first-year and upper-division students to engage them with the discipline and help them make connections between academia and advocacy. Her areas of interest include maternal health and issues surrounding access to health care with a focus on women and girls. She uses project-based and experiential learning concepts to help her students build networks and connections both in and out of the classroom. Students in her classes have worked with high school students, community organizations, and youth groups.

Eufemia Garcia

Eufemia (Pema) B. Garcia, MBA is regional director of Western Rio Grande Region, Colonias Program, College of Architecture at Texas A&M University, El Paso, Texas. She is a community leader and advocate who was born and raised in El Paso. She works with networks across colonias (unincorporated communities and neighborhoods) on the U.S.–Mexico border to enhance the quality of life through community education, advocacy, and infrastructure support. In the chapter on community and academic public health perspective, she shares her perspectives for students to consider as they begin to engage in the community. Insights in the chapter are based on her experiences working with and serving community residents and students of all ages.

Elaine Hampton

Elaine Hampton, PhD, is retired faculty in UTEP's College of Education and owner of STEM Education Associates, which provides program evaluation, curriculum writing, and research on border themes. She collaborates with Mexican Civic Association's education campaign to end sexual violence, and she is researching the impact of a large community collaborative in southern New Mexico to improve early childhood education. Her books include *Anay's Will to Learn: A Woman's Education in the Shadow of the Maquiladora* (2013) and *The Copper Stain: The Legacy of ASARCO in El Paso* (in press).

William Hargrove

William L. Hargrove, PhD, is director of the Center for Environmental Resource Management at the UTEP. He coordinates environmental research, education, and outreach activities, develops projects and proposals for funding, and serves as the point of contact for UTEP on environmental issues. His professional career of 35 years has focused on environmental issues and natural resources management, especially water resources management. Recent and current projects focus on air quality training, environmental health, health impact assessment, and sustainable water resources management. Almost all of this work has been conducted in a community-engaged context. His most recently published community-based project is "Transportation Matters: A Health Impact Assessment in Rural New Mexico" (Del Rio et al., 2017. *Int. J. Environ. Res. Public Health* 14, 629; http://doi:10.3390/ijerph14060629). In addition to his technical expertise in natural resources and environmental management, he has extensive experience in leading interdisciplinary teams and in developing and supporting interdisciplinary educational programs.

Wen-Whai Li

Wen-Whai Li, PhD, is professor of civil engineering at the UTEP. His research interests include air quality monitoring and modeling, risk assessment, accident analysis, and physical simulation of the atmospheric environment. He has completed more than 35 research projects as principal investigator or co-investigator and authored or coauthored over 200 articles in technical journals, conference proceedings and abstracts, and numerous technical reports. He serves as the U.S. academia delegate to the U.S.–Mexico Joint Advisory Committee for the Improvement of Air Quality in the Cd. Juarez, Chihuahua, El Paso, Texas, and Dona Ana County, New Mexico Air Basin, a binational committee organized under the La Paz agreement. He has worked closely with the border communities in the past 20 years to understand the characteristics of air pollution, evaluate mitigation strategies for air quality improvement, and develop associations between air pollution and health impacts on children. He and the coauthors of this chapter have designed this heavily mentored training program and collaborated with federal, state, local government agencies, nonprofit organizations, private industries, and community organizations to enhance the participation of future professionals of various disciplines in improving air quality in the border region. He received his BS degree from National Taiwan University, and MS and PhD degrees from Colorado State University. He is a licensed professional engineer in Texas and Illinois.

Josue David Lopez

Josue David Lopez has a BS in kinesiology from the University of Texas at El Paso. He works for the City of El Paso Park and Recreation Department, where he manages four senior divisions, eleven senior centers, youth program (after school and day care), special events, and parks and shelters permits. He has been working for the UTEP PE and PACE Continued Education program as contract lecturer and instructor. He has over 20 years of experience both in the academic and public recreation fields. He obtained multiple certifications to promote health, fitness, and corporate wellness. He is a member of UTEP Community Academic Partnerships Health Science Research (CAPHSR) Committee. His goal was to establish an Interagency Agreement between City of El Paso Parks and Recreation and the UTEP to work cooperatively in promoting health and wellness to overcome overweight and obesity in the city. The local Senior Games (Olympic-type sport events for 50-year-olds and over) played a key role in developing partnerships and strategies to develop healthy living habits and lifestyles, promote public health education, and encourage consistent exercise routines among young and older population.

Jennifer M. Lujan

Jennifer M. Lujan received both her BA and master's degree in education from the University of Texas at El Paso. She is currently assistant director at the Center for Civic Engagement at UTEP, where she is primarily responsible for managing the center's service-learning programs and other community engagement initiatives. In addition, she has experience in managing grant-funded projects and programs, developing and sustaining community partnerships, and developing and managing community-based student internships. She was also a co-instructor for a freshman University 1301 course titled "Leadership, Service, and Social Responsibility" at UTEP. She is the coauthor of various chapters in this book related to service-learning and community partnerships as high-impact practices in higher education.

Mark Lusk

Mark Lusk, PhD, is professor of social work and Provost's Faculty Fellow for Civic Engagement at the UTEP College of Health Sciences. His current research focuses on stress and resilience among migrants and refugees. As a community-engaged scholar, he partners with agencies that serve migrants in the El Paso and Cuidad Juarez, Mexico region where he also places his students in internships and service-learning projects. Among his recent publications is *Strength and Adversity: Testimonies of the Migration* with Feliza Galindo in social development issues.

Corina Marrufo

Corina Marrufo has a BA in psychology and is a graduate student pursuing her master of social work from the UTEP. During her undergraduate degree, she completed service-learning in a food pantry in a colonia community and participated in the City of El Paso's Senior Games while enrolled in an anthropology course. She has coauthored a chapter on food insecurity in colonias. In this book, she provides her insights as a student who has gained valuable insights and experiences working with older adults in a coauthored chapter with Dr. Nuñez-Mchiri and Mr. David Josue Lopez.

Karla Martinez

Karla Martinez is a student currently majoring in applied mathematics at the University of Texas at El Paso. She hopes to pursue a PhD in statistics in the future. When not studying mathematics or statistics, she enjoys gardening, cooking food, and listening to music in her free time.

Jacen Moore

Jacen Moore, PhD, is an assistant professor in the Clinical Laboratory Sciences Program at UTEP. His research focuses on autoimmune disease mechanisms in systemic lupus erythematosus and Sjögren's syndrome and the development of clinical laboratory instrumentation and methodologies for use in resource-limited areas. He actively engages students in his research projects and is very connected to advancing community and global health initiatives. He works to develop local and international interdisciplinary collaborations that will empower both individuals and communities and advance technological advancement and the continuum of care in resource-limited countries.

Irma Montelongo

Irma Victoria Montelongo received her MA and PhD in history from UTEP. Her fields of study include gender and sexuality, Latin American history, U.S. history with a subfield in immigration studies, and borderlands history with a subfield in race and ethnic studies. Her research and teaching interests focus on race, class, gender, sexuality, and criminology on the U.S.–Mexico border. She is a former fellow at the Center for Collaborative Online International Learning at the State University of New York Global Center. In addition, she developed and teaches two global learning communities linked with classes at Victoria University in Melbourne, Australia, and John Jay College of Criminal Justice in New York City. The courses focus on globalization and its impact on migration, race, ethnicity, gender, and sexuality.

Eva Moya

Eva M. Moya, PhD, licensed master social worker, is an associate professor and interim chair of the Department of Social Work at UTEP. Her research focuses on homelessness, tuberculosis, health inequalities, and intimate partner violence in the U.S.–Mexico border region. Her scholarly work is decidedly interdisciplinary, with a strong focus on community-engaged scholarship, service-learning practices, and student engagement. She involves diverse groups of students and community partners in her projects and research so they in turn are empowered with advanced knowledge, enhanced skills, and self-confidence. She has published research on tuberculosis, community-engaged scholarship outside of the social work classroom with homeless populations, and photovoice.

Sarah Norman

Sarah Norman has a doctorate degree in pharmacy and is assistant clinical professor in the Department of Pharmacy Practice and Clinical Sciences at the School of Pharmacy at UTEP. She has been engaged in mental health, pharmacist-led medication education, patient medication attitudes, and knowledge research since 2011.

She utilizes service-learning, specifically health screenings and medication reviews, as a way to integrate her teaching and research in various communities, most recently El Paso, Texas. She is currently involved in the El Paso community, providing health screenings and medication reviews as faculty and preceptor at UTEP School of Pharmacy. She has published research on blood pressure and heart rate changes during clozapine treatment and on patient attitudes and knowledge after attending pharmacist-led patient medication education.

Cynthia Ontiveros

Cynthia Ontiveros, PhD, is principal of the Young Women's STEAM Research & Preparatory Academy, El Paso Independent School District, which focuses on STEAM and service-learning. Ontiveros worked with UTEP in the EPA project to provided teachers and students valuable opportunities to connect curricula to real-world contexts. Her research examined the impact of the BAQ Ed curriculum on high school students' understanding of environmental justice. She is coauthor of *The Copper Stain: The Legacy of ASARCO in El Paso* (in press).

Manuel Piña

Manuel Piña, Jr., PhD, is associate professor, Department of Agricultural Leadership, Education, and Communications, Texas A&M University. His scholarship is in writing and evaluating proposals that concentrate on improving the number of minorities in education. Over a period of 10 years, he led an effort that sponsored 143 mostly minority graduate students at five universities in the U.S. southwest. Currently, he is co-principal investigator on a USDA-funded grant that focuses on improving higher education access to at-risk teens in two counties in Texas. His research and publications include "Children, Youth, and Families At-Risk Sustainable Community Projects," and "Developing Global-Ready Agriculturists through Experiential Learning Modules: Solving Problems of Food Insecurity & Human Suffering in Haiti."

Amy Reed-Sandoval

Amy Reed-Sandoval, PhD, is assistant professor in the Department of Philosophy at the UTEP, where she does research in social and political philosophy, feminist bioethics, Latin American Philosophy, and Philosophy for Children. She is the founding director of both the Oaxaca Philosophy for Children Initiative in Oaxaca City, Mexico, as well as the Philosophy for Children in the Borderlands program in El Paso, Texas and Ciudad Juarez, Mexico. She completed her PhD in philosophy at the University of Washington, where she worked as a Philosophy for Children facilitator for the University of Washington Center for Philosophy for Children.

Linda Y. Rivas

Linda Y. Rivas was born in Mexico and raised in El Paso. She attended the UTEP and received a bachelor or arts in psychology with a minor in legal reasoning. She received a juris doctor from Loyola College of Law in New Orleans. She tailored her experience to focus on immigration law from her coursework to a legal internship with the Department of Justice, Executive Office of Immigration Review under Judge Wayne Stogner. Her first job as an attorney was as the West Texas VAWA Legal Supervisor at the Paso del Norte Civil Rights Project where she worked in immigration law under the VAWA and U-VISA programs and engaged in domestic violence advocacy. She is currently the managing attorney at Las Americas Immigrant Advocacy Center where she is focused on serving detained asylum seekers.

Ivonne Santiago

Ivonne Santiago, Ph.D., is a clinical professor of the civil engineering (CE) department at the UTEP. As clinical professor, her main responsibility is to foster projects that connect education and research to engineering practice and real-world applications, a staple of which is the Coordination of the CE Senior Capstone design projects. Her research is focused on innovation and entrepreneurship for providing safe drinking water to underserved communities, water quality sensors, and engineering education in graduate and undergraduate students, with a focus on Hispanic and female students. She is dedicated to providing students with service-learning opportunities for underserved communities and uses team-based and project-based learning approaches and liberating structures for student engagement and sharing collective knowledge. She is currently part of UTEP's NSF-AGEP program focusing on fostering Hispanic doctoral students for academic careers and the Department of Education's (DoE) STEMGROW Program to encourage students to pursue STEM careers, is a faculty partner for the DoE's STEM Accelerator Program, and is fellow of UTEP's Center for Faculty Leadership and Development. Her commitment to connecting education to practice is demonstrated by the local and state teaching awards she has won: 2014 UTEP's CETaL Giraffe Award (for sticking her neck out); 2014 College of Engineering Instruction Award; 2014 The University of Texas System ROTA; and the 2012 NCEES Award for students' design of a fire station.

Gregory Schober

Gregory S. Schober, Ph.D., is a visiting professor in the Department of Political Science at The University of Texas at El Paso (UTEP). His research and teaching focuses on comparative politics, American politics, social policy, health politics, and political behavior. Schober regularly incorporates service-learning into his courses, and he is involved in multiple community-based research projects that address health and water inequalities in our region. His most recent work, listed below, was published in *Political Behavior* and *The American Journal of Kidney Diseases*.

Jeri Sias

Jeri J. Sias, PharmD, MPH, is a clinical professor at the UTEP School of Pharmacy, UTEP/UT Austin Cooperative Program in El Paso, Texas. Born and raised in the Midwest, she is a pharmacist educator who has been living and working in El Paso, Texas since 2000. Her areas of research include community-based participatory research approaches to smoking cessation, nutrition, and medication literacy. She enjoys engaging students and practitioners to actively learn about culture via community tours, census data exploration, engagement, and discussion. The reflections in the chapter on service-learning from community and academic public health perspectives highlight her approach, experiences, and lessons learned implementing service-learning and student research projects into doctor of pharmacy student education over the past 15 years.

Bora Simmons

Bora Simmons, PhD, serves as the founding director of the National Project for Excellence in Environmental Education, an initiative of the North American Association for Environmental Education. She has been actively involved in environmental education research, evaluation, and professional development for over 30 years. For her achievements, she received NAAEE's top awards, including Walter E. Jeske Award for Outstanding Contributions to Environmental Education (2000), the NAAEE Award for Outstanding Contributions to Research in Environmental Education (1996), Outstanding Service to Environmental Education at the Global Level (2009), and the NAAEE Executive Director's award (2013).

Guillermina Solis

Guillermina Solis, PhD, advanced practice registered nurse, family and geriatric nurse practitioner, is an assistant professor in the School of Nursing at the University of Texas at El Paso. Her research focus on chronic diseases affecting Hispanic adults and the end-of-life decision-making processes among older adults and their caregivers. She utilizes the service-learning experience for collaborating with other faculty and students for building a network that helps in understanding the needs of the community while mentoring nursing students and faculty. She has published her work on interdisciplinary research To Give & To Get: How Nurse Faculty Scholars Contribute and Benefit from Participating in Interdisciplinary Research Team in *Nursing Forum*.

Kathleen Staudt

Kathleen (Kathy) Staudt PhD, is a retired professor of political science and endowed professor of Western Hemisphere trade policy studies at the UTEP. She founded the Center for Civic Engagement and led it for 10 years. With a service-learning or internship component, she taught courses in border politics, public policy analysis, politics of developing countries, nonprofit management, democracy, and women, power and politics. In 2008, she received one of two statewide awards from the University of Texas Chancellor for innovations in teaching. She published 20 books (half focused on borderlands) and approximately 150 academic articles and chapters in books. She continues to be active in the community, particularly the Center Against Sexual and Family Violence, and to research and write articles (and blogs!).

Ray Tullius

Ray Tullius, with a master's degree in social work, is founder and executive director of the Opportunity Center for the Homeless in El Paso, Texas. As an Army veteran, the military helped him earn his bachelor's degree in social work. He received his master's degree in social work from the University of Texas at Austin. Since then, he has paid it forward by offering homeless people a warm meal, a place to sleep, and the support they need to get off the streets as the founder and executive director of the Opportunity Center for the Homeless in El Paso. Opened in 1994, the center is now the largest homeless shelter system in west Texas and southern New Mexico. He has been instrumental in developing a community-engaged partnership with academic and community-based organizations in support of the creation of the first community practice model between faculty, students, community partners and persons, experiencing homelessness in El Paso, Texas. In 2013, he was the recipient of the UTEP College of Health Sciences 2013 Gold Nugget Award.

Sarah De Los Santos Upton

Sarah De Los Santos Upton, PhD, is an Assistant Professor in the Department of Communication at the UTEP. Her research and teaching explore how communication can be used to create social change in the areas of community development, environmental conservation, and border activism. Her work also examines possibilities for greater civic engagement through service-learning on the Mexico/U.S. border where she lives and works. Her recent publications focus on Teaching Research for a Greater Purpose: Incorporating Community Engagement into a Graduate Qualitative Research Methods Course and The co-conspiring methodology: An invitational approach to action research appearing in *Action Research*.

DeAnna Kay Varela

DeAnna Kay Varela holds a BA in psychology and Spanish from the University of Texas at Austin and an MA in communication and graduate certificate in women and gender studies, both from the UTEP. She holds a full-time appointment as lecturer with the UTEP Entering Student Program. In 2012, she was awarded the University of Texas Regents Outstanding Teaching Award for her commitment to teaching and mentoring students. Her research interests include social justice movements and activism, cultural studies, and contemporary women and girls' issues.

Amy Wagler

Amy Wagler, PhD, is an associate chair and associate professor of mathematical sciences at The University of Texas at El Paso. She is currently serving as the Provost's Faculty Fellow-in-Residence for Civic Engagement. She is a winner of the University of Texas System Regents Outstanding Teaching Award. Her primary research interests are in multiplicity corrections and simultaneous inference in generalized model settings and studying how language and culture affect teaching and learning in statistics. She is involved in STEM-related education research and regularly works on projects with educators in the community. She is also a board member of the Frontera Land Alliance (a land trust organization) and does ecology–science education outreach to the community through this position. Her published works include *Seeing Community Needs through a Statistical Lens: Undergraduate- and Graduate-Level Consulting with Community Organizations in the El Paso Border Region* and *An Exploratory Analysis of the Usage by Spanish-Speaking English Language Learner Tertiary Students of a Bilingual Probability Applet.*

Ron Wagler

Ron Wagler, PhD, is an associate professor of science education and director of the Living Arthropod and Environmental Education Laboratory in the Department of Teacher Education: STEM Division. He has been recognized nationally and internationally for his research in the field of arthropod education. He is a winner of the University of Texas System Regents Outstanding Teaching Award. He pioneered the vast majority of the foundational research in arthropod education and is considered one of the foremost experts in his field. He has been conducting service-learning projects for the past decade that bring together his university students, the captive-bred living arthropods from his Living Arthropod and Environmental Education Laboratory and members of the community to teach others about the essential role arthropods play in maintaining the health of our global ecosystems. His published works include *Adventures with Arthropods: Eco-friendly Lessons for Middle School* and the 6th mass extinction.

CPSIA information can be obtained
at www.ICGtesting.com
Printed in the USA
LVHW061001191020
669154LV00012B/546